Creative Writing in the Community

The Creative Writing MFA Handbook, Revised and Updated Edition: A Guide for Prospective Graduate Students, by Tom Kealey

The Low-Residency MFA Handbook: A Guide for Prospective Creative Writing Students, by Lori A. May

Creative Writing in the Community

A GUIDE

TERRY ANN THAXTON

B L O O M S B U R Y
LONDON • NEW DELHI • NEW YORK • SYDNEY

Bloomsbury Academic

An imprint of Bloomsbury Publishing Plc

50 Bedford Square   1385 Broadway
London   New York
WC1B 3DP   NY 10018
UK   USA

www.bloomsbury.com

Bloomsbury is a registered trade mark of Bloomsbury Publishing Plc

First published 2014

British Library Cataloguing-in-Publication Data
A catalogue record for this book is available from the British Library.

ISBN: HB: 978-1-44112-776-1
PB: 978-1-44111-194-4
ePub: 978-1-44114-866-7
PDF: 978-1-44119-772-6

Library of Congress Cataloging in Publication Data
A catalog record for this book is available from the Library of Congress.

Typeset by Fakenham Prepress Solutions, Fakenham, Norfolk NR21 8NN
Printed and bound in India

To all of my students—past, present, future
—and in memory of my mother and her legacy of service

CONTENTS

Preface xi

Introduction 1

1 Storytelling is for Everyone 7
Why we tell stories 7
Community-based learning projects in creative writing 9
The first step 9
Structured reflection 11
Readings 12
"Landscape and Language," Lorraine Ferra 12
"Becoming an Ocean: Teaching Poetry in Nursing Homes," Silvi
Alcivar 18

2 Leaving Campus 29
Service-learning (and CBL) as citizenship 29
Key elements of service-learning 29
The next steps 32
Structured reflection 34
Readings 35
"What is an Author Off-Campus? The Writer in the Community
and the Corporate University," Julia Spicher Kasdorf 35
"Birth of an American Scholar," Heather Fiedler 43

3 Making a Plan 47
Envisioning your CBL project 47
Designing 10–12 weeks of session (lesson) plans 49
Preparing weekly lessons 50
Anticipations, hopes, challenges 51

Structured reflection 52
Readings 53
  "The Lawtey Workshop," Mark Powell 54
  "Linking the Creative Writing Program with the Community," Allen
    Gee 58

4 Taking the Leap 67
Creative writing and life experiences 67
Apprehension, resistance, fear 67
Service-learning vs. volunteering 69
Service-learning history 69
Service-learning in other disciplines 69
Service-learning in various creative writing classes and
  programs 70
Community partner staff as co-educators 70
Structured reflection 71
Reading 72
  "The Prayer Wheel," David Hassler 73

5 Writing and Being 85
Statistics and real life 85
Safety issues and boundaries 85
Writing and imagination 87
Checking in with self 88
Structured reflection 89
Readings 90
  "A Red Wheelbarrow, a Hammock, and a Pomegranate: Why So
    Much *Does* Depend Upon Poetry," Anita Skeen 90

6 Discovering the Pleasure of Poetry and Storytelling in the
   World 101
Building confidence as a teaching artist 101
Observing your surroundings 101
The immersed writer 103
Connecting your project with your own life experiences 104
Structured reflection 105
Readings 106

"*'The Sublime, the Unsettling, and the Exuberant'*: Changing Students' Attitudes Toward Aging through *TimeSlips* Creative Storytelling," Robin Mello and Anne Basting 106

"Teaching, or How to Fall in Love," Robin Reagler 116

7 Creative Writing as Social Activism 123

Art as resistance 123
Beyond your project 124
Structured reflection 126
Reading 127
"Activism in Academia: A Social Action Writing Program," Frances Payne Adler 127

8 Doing Creative Writing 141

Right to your life (and your voice) 141
Why *do* creative writing? 141
A very brief history of creative writing in the academy 142
Current issues in creative writing 143
Structured reflection 143
Reading 144
"The Assessment Wicket: How Can We Judge the Value of Writers Teaching in the Schools?," Terry Hermsen 145

9 Changing Them, Changing You, Changing the World 165

A deeper understanding 165
What you're getting: Transferrable skills 167
What they're getting 168
Structured reflection 168
Readings 169
"Citizens of Words: Service-Learning in Creative Writing Education," Nathaniel V. Mohatt 170
"Keeping it Real: Creative Writing Under the Shadow of Standardized Testing," Christopher McIlroy 177

10 Giving Community Members (a Loud) Voice 187

Turning words into voices 187
Celebrating 188

Publishing the work of participants 188
Structured reflection 191
Readings 191
  "The Children We Leave Behind," Lisa Chatterjee 192
  "Writing Out of Grief," Scott Parsons 195

11 Publishing Your CBL Project 203
Publication at your university 203
Publication beyond the university 205
Outreach and the university 206
Structured reflection 208
Readings 209
  "Poetry from the Inside Out," Terry Blackhawk 209
  "Who is the Self that Performs? Teaching and Learning Creative
  Identities and Creative Writing at a Youth Shelter," Sharlene
  Gilman 216

12 The Value of Creative Writing in the World 225
Civic responsibility 226
Imagine 227
Structured reflection 228
Readings 229
  "Poetry-in-the-World: Where Service-Learning Goes Beyond the
  Classroom," F. Daniel Rzicznek 229
  "How Service-Learning Cultivates Empathy and Social
  Responsibility," Carly Gates O'Neal 234

Appendix A: Resources for students 241
Appendix B: Resources for teachers 273
Appendix C: Additional Resources for teachers and students 289
Notes and Sources 293
Index 309

PREFACE

Creative Writing in the Community came about because when I first started sending my students into the community as teaching artists, I could find no guidebook for them. Without the help of my colleagues and a flashlight, I would not have found a way to make it work. I created a syllabus, which I pieced together using the fabulous resources from the National Campus Compact website. But I wanted my students to be part of a conversation with writers around the country who were involved in this kind of work. I wanted them to know the history of creative writers in the community. I wanted them to know how creative writing and community service could go hand-in-hand.

There are many great books about the work of teaching creative writing in the community, and there are many good books that provide writing teachers with ideas for lessons. The Teachers & Writers Collaborative and the National Council for Teachers of English (NCTE) have numerous resources for writers interested in this kind of work. And there are numerous books about the value of service.

This is a *guidebook*, an *anthology* (readings), and a *resource book* intended for creative writing students; however, writers outside the academy who wish to design their own community-based creative writing projects will find this book helpful as well. The guidebook provides weekly steps through a semester (or 10–14 weeks), from deciding where to conduct a creative writing workshop in the community, to preparing an overview of a semester-long project, to designing weekly lessons, to understanding the connections between creative writing in the academy and creative writing in the community. The readings include essays by writers who have been involved in this kind of work in various ways—some essays from former students, others from directors of nonprofit organizations, others from faculty members who have either integrated community-based learning (CBL) into their creative writing classes or designed courses solely for this purpose. The resources provide sample semester-long lesson plans, links to websites that provide lesson planning assistance, and links to websites of organizations that hire individual writers to do this work continuously.

I have always been involved with community service. As a child living in Florida, I rode with my mother from house to house, and then church to church to gather food and clothing for Cuban refugees throughout the 1960s. As a teenager, I designed my own service projects—taking food and talking to "shut-ins," organizing food drives at my high school, inviting and taking a young deaf boy to the Ringling Art Museum.

When I started teaching freshman composition in the mid–1990s at the University of Central Florida (UCF), I designed assignments that required experiential learning. Students selected a general diversity issue topic they would research for the entire semester. My "issues" list included poverty, gender, religion, age, sexual orientation, and disability. Once students chose a general topic, they were required to "experience" something within that topic that they'd never experienced before. For example, if a student chose religion, and he/she had always been a Catholic, that student attended a Hindu Temple or an evangelical church. If the student selected poverty, that student might visit a shelter for the homeless or free health clinic. The student then used these new experiences to compare with library research.

Then, in 2003, I met Joann Gardner, a professor at Florida State University who'd founded Runaway With Words (RWW), a creative writing community program that worked with youth in shelters. She wanted to offer an RWW workshop here in Orlando. Joann trained me and six students I'd asked to work with me. After our training, my students and I went once a week to the PACE Center for Girls to run poetry workshops. At the end of our 12 week session, we held a reading for them on-site. The girls at the school wanted a "boy band," and we recruited four young musicians from our university.

After that first semester-long workshop, my students suggested that I find a way to incorporate the type of work we did in creative writing workshops and classes.

Just about that time, Florida Campus Compact provided a grant to UCF to officially create a service-learning program. I began to require service-learning in my classes, sending students out into the community as writers of service. I then designed a course "Creative Writing in the Community," and taught it for the first time in 2005. Since then I've continued to develop guides and manuals for my students, presenting my syllabi and experience at conferences and with individual teachers across the country. I found other professors who were doing similar projects: some with institutional support; others without it.

I hunted for resources on how to integrate the type of project we'd done through RWW into a creative writing class. Michael Steinberg (co-author with Robert Root of *Those Who Do, Can: Teachers Writing, Writers Teaching*, 1996) suggested I contact David Cooper, who'd founded the Service-Learning Writing Program at Michigan State University. Cooper is the winner of the 1999 national Thomas Ehrlich Faculty Award for Service-Learning, awarded by the Campus Compact and the American Association of Higher Education. I am eternally grateful to him for his openness—sharing his writing class syllabi with me and encouraging me to tweak it to fit creative writing. When I asked David if he knew of a guidebook for creative writing students and their teachers who want to engage in this kind of work, he said he didn't know of any, and that perhaps I should write one.

Although I've never met or talked with Robert Coles, I would not have continued requiring service-learning in my courses without his books to push me forward. My copy of *The Call of Service* (1993) has a sticky note on every page.

I am grateful to all of my students—past, present, and future—who are most often excited about the possibilities, and to those students who sometimes resist the requirement of service-learning, yet trudge through—all of whom find the pleasure of giving others the opportunity to tell their stories.

Thank you to my first acquisitions editor at Bloomsbury, Colleen Coalter, for seeing the need for this book. Many thanks to all of the great editors at Bloomsbury, including Laura Murray and Mark Richardson. Special thanks to David Avital, Senior Commissioning Editor, for answering so many questions, and pushing the book forward. I am grateful to Dawn Booth for her good editing eyes, and to all the good people at Fakenham Prepress Solutions, especially Kim Storry.

My deepest admiration and gratitude to those teaching artists who allowed me to include their essays in this book. They persevered through several years from inception to production. Many thanks to everyone who expressed interest and excitement in a book like this: those who endlessly supported this process.

Eric Fershtman deserves more thanks than I can say for his editorial assistance and advice. I am grateful to all of the reviewers who gave their time and honest feedback, and whose suggestions made the final product better.

I owe a tremendous thank you to Don Stap who always believes in my projects and supports me through my days of doubt. I am grateful to my colleagues and writer friends who continuously encouraged me to get this book into the world.

I am deeply indebted to Amy Zeh, the Service-Learning Program Director at UCF, who is also my friend and colleague, whose support and encouragement have kept me moving forward when frustration or burn-out waited for me just around the corner. I would also like to thank Patrick Murphy, English Department Chair, for telling me in 2003 to keep the creative writing in the community projects going. Many thanks to the College of Arts & Humanities at the University of Central Florida for valuing service-learning and for providing me the time to write and work on this book.

Introduction

Creative writers have a long history of providing writing opportunities for people in their communities. During the 1960s and 1970s, Poets-in-the-Schools—an organization funded by the National Endowment for the Arts—paid poets and graduate students to teach in public schools on a weekly basis. Today, nonprofit organizations, colleges and universities, and individual writers around the country provide creative writing in community settings. Nonprofit organizations hire writers or enlist volunteer writers to provide free or low-cost creative writing workshops in public schools, community centers, assisted living facilities, shelters, prisons, etc. These organizations rely on external funding and/or volunteers. In colleges and universities, many writing teachers integrate community service into their course requirements.

Most of us initially think of "community service" as serving food at a soup kitchen or organizing a clothing drive. For writers, community service allows you to offer to your community what you already do well, what you feel passionate about: creative writing.

A degree in creative writing is not like a degree in accounting or business or nursing—there are no head-hunters looking for poets or fiction writers. The basic questions for writers often come down to why do I write? Why am I doing this? Who is going to read my story?

This is a book about expanding your own story by providing opportunities for others to tell theirs. The book is also a rich anthology, filled with essays from writers, students, and teachers who've been at this kind of work for a long time. And the book contains sample syllabi for teachers who wish to design courses that incorporate community work, as well as sample semester-long lesson plans for writers who lead creative writing workshops in the community. Community-based workshops are different from the types of workshops we usually run in academia. Community workshops focus on generating writing and helping participants revise as long as they are willing, but we don't generally run public critique workshops like you're used to in your college creative writing workshops.

Some teachers of creative writing have experimented with different types of community-based learning projects, but all of them find some way to use creative writing for the betterment of the community and to enhance academic learning in their creative writing courses.

While each project/program differs, there are some commonalities: each program views creative writing as an art; each program understands the value of creative writing as a way to build community; and each program places you, the writer, in settings where you have a great deal to offer.

Terminology

What is service-learning? Service-learning is defined by the National and Community Service Trust Act of 1993 as a method "under which students or participants learn and develop through active participation in thoughtfully organized service."[1]

The Office of Undergraduate Studies at the University of Central Florida defines service-learning "as a teaching method that uses community involvement to apply theories or skills taught in a course. Service-learning furthers the learning objectives of the academic course, addresses community needs, and requires students to reflect on their activity in order to gain an appreciation for the relationship between civics and academics. In other words, service-learning combines civic engagement with curriculum—students serve and learn. Each faculty member decides how to incorporate service-learning into his or her own curriculum: service-learning may be a requirement or not; it may be a single project or an ongoing placement."[2]

Generally, there are four to five components that make a particular project "service-learning" rather than volunteering (which will be discussed in more detail in Chapter 2):

1 Meets a real community need.
2 Integrates into and enhances the curriculum.
3 Coordinates with a community agency, another school, or the community at large.
4 Helps foster civic responsibility.
5 Provides structured time for reflection.[3]

In higher education, *service-learning* is sometimes referred to as *community-based learning* (CBL), *field work*, or *experiential learning*. Outside of the university, many of the nonprofit organizations and individual writers who direct community-based creative writing programs often refer to their committed service as a *Writing Residency*. I like the term "Writing

Residency" because it truly encompasses what a writer (whether a college student or professional writer) does for the *participants*. Writer-in-Residence suggests that you are entering into an agreement with a specific group of people for a specific amount of time, to lead them into their literary imaginations. However, in order to include all of the possible types of projects you might do as a writer in the community, I will forthwith refer to your work as your CBL project.

Throughout this book, you may encounter these different terms to refer to this same work. While there are distinctions between these terms—community-based learning, service-learning, field work, experiential learning—they all focus on taking the writer away from his/her writing desk and into the community, using the tools of craft in order to enhance the lives of others.

Community-based learning in creative writing classes can take many forms. I have a colleague who created a CBL project to gather oral histories from people in various groups, which they edited and gave to the local historical society. Another colleague takes her fiction writing students into different classrooms and has school children perform scenes from the stories the college students have written. In this way, the school children become active in literature, and the college students can see where their scenes lack detail and specificity.

For the purposes of a college classroom, a writing residency does not merely provide community agencies with student volunteers. The key for college teachers is to link the service directly to classroom learning. Some teachers have created new courses that focus exclusively on the writing residency, and others have integrated a writing residency into a workshop course.

In whatever way you're coming into a writing residency project, this book is about making your own writing residency a successful one. Once you've decided to conduct a writing residency, you must find a *community partner*. The community partner is the agency or school where you will work. More specifically, the community partner is your contact person at the *site* where you will conduct your writing residency. Your community partner may be the principal at a school, or a specific teacher. Your community partner might be the program director at a homeless shelter. The community partner may or may not be on site with you, but is your contact person(s) for the duration of your residency as you work with *participants* (the children, youth, or adults in your community workshop).

The book as a guide

The book has 12 chapters, coinciding more or less with the length of a typical college semester. Chapter by chapter, the book guides you through a semester-long writing residency (CBL project). The book is arranged with enough flexibility so that each teacher can use the book in ways appropriate to his/her own course design. Each chapter begins with a discussion of a topic appropriate for each week of the semester as you prepare and work through your CBL project. Chapters 1 and 2 focus on background information and getting things set up; Chapter 3 focuses on developing the overview of your residency; Chapters 4 and 5 focus on planning each site visit and coming to understand the people you work with; Chapters 6–9 delve into the purpose of this kind of work as well as guiding you through some of your possible reactions to working outside the classroom; Chapter 10–11 focus on preparing for publication and/or presentation of the work of your participants and your own work; Chapter 12 deals with concluding your residency and deciding what you might do next.

After the discussion and what-to-do sections are several *structured reflection* prompts: a vital component of service-learning. Structured reflection challenges us beyond superficial observations and assumptions. Structured reflection can lead to material for an article or a book, but, most importantly, it allows you, as a writer, to deeply reflect on the weekly work (satisfactions and challenges) of your CBL project. Community-based learning allows you to grow in three significant areas: personally, academically, and as a citizen of a democracy. The structured reflection prompts are designed to help you identify your growth in these areas.

More than simply a journal, structured reflection is best utilized if you design for yourself a question that you will seek to answer during the course of your residency. You might, for example, want to discover why people are interested in storytelling, or why there are children without books at home, or why creative writing matters in the first place. Your teacher might create additional prompts for you to respond to each week. At the beginning of a service project, we often feel idealistic. Robert Coles refers to this as "young idealism" (Coles, 1993, pp. 174–207). Later we might feel hopeless about poverty or homelessness. Later we might feel useful and more realistic about social issues, the value of writing, or what can actually be accomplished in twelve to fourteen weeks.

Finally, each chapter includes one or two essays by teaching artists, writers who have conducted writing residencies, and many who teach others to lead writing residencies. Robin Reagler (Executive Director of Writers in the Schools, Houston) and Terry Blackhawk (Founding Director of InsideOut, Detroit) each have an essay in the book about their work as directors of nonprofit organizations and their work as teaching artists. Lorraine Ferra, Silvi Alcivar, and Christopher McIlroy offer essays from the perspective of teaching artists who support themselves, either through grants or holding down other jobs while conducting residencies in their communities. Other writers direct literary arts outreach programs from within a university or college setting. Essays by David Hassler (Kent State University), Julia Kasdorf (Pennsylvania State University), Anita Skeen (Michigan State University), Terry Hermsen (Otterbein University), Allen

Gee (Georgia State College and University), Anne Basting and Robin Mello (University of Wisconsin), Mark Powell (Stetson University), and Frances Payne Adler (California State University) provide essays about these types of programs. Other essays include those by writers who served in these university programs when they were students, essays by school teachers who incorporate service-learning into their classroom or have writers work with their students. Heather Fiedler, Lisa Chatterjee, F. Daniel Rzicznek, Sharlene Gilman, Carly Gates, and Scott Parsons, and Nathaniel Mohatt address the impact this type of work on them personally, professionally, and on the community.

Beginning a writing residency is both exciting and daunting, especially if you've never done anything like this before, but I promise that it will affect your academic life, your personal life, and your sense of what it means to be a member of a community.

Many children, youth, and adults have no idea of the power of language until they encounter it in the way you can show them. Many do not know they have the capability to be creative, let alone write anything that anyone would want to read. Many do not know how to access their imaginations. They've never read poetry, or perhaps they've read poetry only for a school assignment, and have not experienced reading or writing as a pleasurable experience. There are adults in homeless shelters who want to tell their stories, but do not have paper or pencil or any idea how to begin. There are children in schools who have seen books only in their school libraries, who do not have books at home.

Creative writing students are often prodded by friends and family to explain how a degree in creative writing will prepare them for the "real world." Each semester numerous students change their majors from business or biology or even literature studies to creative writing. MFA programs across the country are full to the brim. What you already know is that creative writing—learning to hone the elements of craft—enlivens language, and draws readers into your understanding of the human experience. Writers are the ideal leaders for community-based creative writing workshops. Writers who are engaged in community activism— leading creative writing workshops for often-times marginalized community members—are reminded over and over again of the thrill of writing well.

You already know that your voice matters. You know the value of telling stories. You know the value of language and communication.

We need to experience the world in order to learn about it. Writers are in the world and, in order to do our job well, we need to know the world. What better way to learn about the world than to use our talent and knowledge to allow others to experience the profound excitement in words, in writing their own stories, their own essays, their own poems?

CHAPTER ONE

Storytelling is for Everyone

Why we tell stories

Whatever your reason for taking a creative writing course or your interest in creative writing in the community, you must be at least curious about why, in spite of knowing that you probably won't make millions of dollars for your writing, you still *want* to write. Imagine the people in your community with that same desire to tell stories, but with no understanding of how to begin, or no computer, or no pencil or paper. Imagine those who've never been encouraged to tell their stories. Imagine those who do not have the opportunity to write.

In his essay, "I Am Writing Blindly," Roger Rosenblatt, talks about how the "last occupants of the Warsaw Ghetto … took scraps of paper on which they wrote poems, thoughts, fragments of lives, rolled them into tight scrolls, and slipped them into the crevices of the ghetto walls." We want to tell our stories even if no one is there to listen. "We exist by storytelling" (2000, p. 142).

Why do we, upon seeing an acquaintance, or perhaps even a stranger, tell them what happened to us last week, yesterday, in our childhood? Why do we jot things down on napkins in restaurants? Why do we use technology to talk to friends several times a day? We write for many different reasons. We write to tell our stories.

Now, imagine the five year old who bounces into pre-kindergarten for the first day, and when her teacher asks her name, all she can do is shrug her shoulders and grunt. Or imagine a 70 year old man with Alzheimer's who's lost most of his memories, but when he sees a pot of chrysanthemums rises from his seat and dances. What is his story? Is there a way to help this five year old girl and this 70 year old man tell their stories?

Yes, there is. You possess skills that these folks don't have. What better way to learn the value of creative writing than to show a little girl or an elderly man (or a kid in foster care, or a family in a shelter for the homeless) how to use description or character development to tell the stories locked inside their imaginations?

Community-based learning (CBL) asks those with knowledge and skills to take their knowledge and those skills into their community. CBL, service-learning, field work, immersion, a writing residency, whatever you want to call it, simply asks that you use the elements of the craft of creative writing to the betterment of your community. Creative writing matters because using personal experience connects us.

William Wordsworth argued, in the "Preface to Lyrical Ballads," that the subjects of poetry should be chosen from 'incidents and situations from common life" (1965, p. 446) Wordsworth argued as well that the language should not be so formal as to exclude those who did not communicate in high English, but to use "Language really used by men, and, at the same time, to throw over them a certain colouring of imagination, whereby ordinary things should be presented to the mind in an unusual aspect." He explains that in his poems, unlike those of his predecessors,

> Humble and rustic life was generally chosen, because, in that condition, the essential passions of the heart find a better soil in which they can attain their maturity, are less under restraint, and speak a plainer and more emphatic language; because in that condition of life our elementary feelings coexist in a state of greater simplicity, and, consequently, may be more accurately contemplated, and more forcibly communicated; because the manners of rural life germinate from those elementary feelings, and, from the necessary character of rural occupations, are more easily comprehended, and are more durable; and, lastly, because in that condition the passions of men are incorporated with the beautiful and permanent forms of nature. The language, too, of these men has been adopted (purified indeed from what appear to be its real defects, from all lasting and rational causes of dislike or disgust) because such men hourly communicate with the best objects from which the best part of language is originally derived; and because, from their rank in society and the sameness and narrow circle of their intercourse, being less under the influence of social vanity, they convey their feelings and notions in simple and unelaborated expressions (Wordsworth, 1965, pp. 446–7).

Wordsworth valued the "simple and unelaborated expressions" not because he thought of them as "less than" or because they didn't have interesting stories, but because they were genuinely alive, living without the "social vanity" of the period, and without pretense. Authentic lives. Authentic voices.

Providing community members the opportunity to write creatively, to find their voices in their stories and poems, using words from their daily lives will bring you great satisfaction. There will be challenges along the way, but the satisfactions of watching a child in a shelter for the homeless describe in images what her life is will far outweigh the challenges.

Community-based learning projects in creative writing

Most CBL projects in creative writing are writing residencies where you, the writer, commit to going once a week to a designated site, and lead creative writing activities. Many writing residencies follow the academic calendar simply because many programs work with school children, and working with children during the school day is ideal. For example, in my classes, a writing residency is a 10–12 week commitment (the length of the university semesters), depending upon each community partner's needs and schedule. Professional writers who contract with a school or district might offer a residency for the entire school year. Others might contract with a shelter for the homeless for one calendar year.

The first step

The first step in creating a CBL project is to decide where you want to work, using your talent and knowledge. Heather Fiedler, a student in the very first service-learning course I taught, wanted to work at a shelter for the homeless with adults. Other students wanted to work with children at the shelter. Our university has had a long-standing relationship with the local shelter, so I spoke with the program coordinator immediately, and she was thrilled. Heather, and four other students in class, spent every Wednesday evening with a group of adults. Two weeks into the semester, when I asked them to reflect on why they chose the community partner site they had, I discovered that Heather had asked to work with homeless adults because her mother had been living homeless for most of Heather's life. Heather wanted to understand what her mother's life might be like. Other students who worked with Heather had different reasons for working there. Every reason, or even not really knowing why, was and is valid.

Students have decided to work at an assisted living facility either because they never knew their grandparents, they wanted to understand more about memory-loss, they felt uncomfortable around children, or this was the only site that fit their schedule.

I have spent a significant amount of time (years) cultivating relationships with a variety of organizations and schools. Additionally, because our university supports an Office of Experiential Learning, it is likely that students in my classes will have access to almost any type of organization, and be able to conduct their service-learning wherever they want to gain experience.

It might be that your teacher or the director or coordinator of the writing residency project you're involved in has done the initial planning. Perhaps you've been given a list of community partner sites from which you can choose where to conduct your residency. Perhaps you're starting from scratch.

Sometimes all students in a given class work with a specific community partner. This allows a small group of students to see the impact of four months of service at a specific site. Your teacher may have already committed you to a particular site. Or your teacher might have a list of possible sites that he has already contacted to make sure the clients at each organization have time and would benefit from creative writing. Or your teacher might ask you to find your own community partner. Whatever the case, there are many factors that play a role in your decision about where you will work.

1 Teacher's or organization's requirements: has a teacher or organization selected a site for you?

2 Schedule: will you be able to get to the community site each week at the designated time?

3 Location: can you reasonably and safely find and get to the site?

4 Emotional limitations: will you be emotionally able to see people week after week in this setting? One student writer wanted to work with children and youth, but knew that she could not work with homeless children. This, she said, would break her heart. Instead, she worked at a residential drug treatment facility for youth where she knew she could make a difference, and not feel hopeless from the beginning.

We will discuss the emotional process of this kind of work throughout this book, but at this point it's good to consider the challenges that might come from working with people in poverty, homeless children, angry teenagers, or lonely and dying elderly, and will bring you face-to-face with tragedies and social injustice.

You might feel overwhelmed, exhausted, frustrated, or upset. These emotions are common, and come with the territory of community service work of any kind. But if your work brings up emotional issues that require professional guidance, do let your teacher know. Remember, however, that your creative writing teacher is not a psychologist or therapist, and may refer you to a professional. At our university, students are able to see professional therapists free of charge.

Structured reflection

In the introduction, I mentioned structured reflection as a way to get beyond superficial observations and assumptions. Structured reflection can lead to material for an article or a book, but, most importantly, it allows you, as a writer, to deeply reflect on the weekly work (satisfactions and challenges) of your CBL project. The following set of questions is intended to get you thinking about where you will work and to examine your own approach, your own sense of community as you begin. I've separated the prompts based on its growth focus: your personal growth, academic growth, and/or growth as a citizen (a member of the community).

Personal

1   What are you most looking forward to during your semester of CBL?

Academic

2   Describe your understanding of what you're supposed to do at your community partner's location.

3   Consider the first time you realized the thrill of writing. Maybe it was a poem, a story, an essay, or a note to someone. Who was present? What did you write? How did this realization impact you? What was its value? What if you'd never had the opportunity to recognize this interest/talent?

4   What do you think is the value of community service to you as a writer?

Civic

5   What is your definition of "activism," "idealism," "civic engagement," and "education"? Avoid giving the dictionary definition. Instead, write a paragraph or two about what each of these means to you.

6   Where are you planning to conduct your CBL project? Why are you going to this location? Why did you choose this location? Rather than respond by saying something like "because I had to choose something," or "I want to go with my friend," or "my teacher selected my site for me," do a self-inventory—even if you had to choose something, even if your friend is going to

this site. You could have chosen to work at a different school, a different type of population. So why did you choose this site over the other choices? What do you think you will learn about yourself? What might you learn by observing something outside of your normal circumstances? What might you learn about the importance of real-life experience to writing poetry, essays, or stories?

Readings

Lorraine Ferra

Lorraine Ferra has taught extensively since 1980 as a poet-in-the-school in Washington, Utah, Delaware, Massachusetts, and Vermont. She has also taught in natural history museums, science centers, youth-in-custody programs, and senior citizens' centers. She is the author of two chapbook collections of poems: *Eating Bread* (1994) and *What the Silence Might Say* (2012). Her book on writing, *A Crow Doesn't Need a Shadow: A Guide to Writing Poetry From Nature* (Ferra and Boardman, 1994) has been endorsed by the National Council of Teachers of English. She lives in Port Townsend, Washington.

Landscape and Language

When the poet Rainer Maria Rilke admitted to his sculptor friend Rodin that he had come to a standstill in his writing, the artist suggested that Rilke leave his desk, visit the zoo, and look at an animal for a long time. On an almost daily basis, Rilke acted on the advice. He singled out a panther and watched it closely until he could *see* it. The outcome was his memorable poem ("The Panther," 1981), which reverberates with the monotony of the panther's pacing back and forth behind the bars of its cage.

As a sculptor, Rodin understood the necessity of keeping the senses alert, an ability considered basic to the visual arts but often neglected in language. Encouraging students to produce grammatically flawless compositions and stories, we often end up reading work devoid of visual and tactile imagery, music, and that aura of silence, which can draw us further into the depths of an experience.

I have been looking at the beginnings of two pieces by fifth graders encouraged by their teachers to write a story about floods coming down from the Utah canyons into the neighborhoods of Salt Lake City. The following was written by a student whose teacher simply announced the "assignment."

One year there was a great flood in Salt Lake City. Stores were closed, and homes were destroyed by the rough water ...

Well-written grammatically, but echoing in tone the nightly reports of newscasters on local, Utah TV stations.

Several students in another class mentioned that they were going to join their parents to help with sandbagging. Their teacher asked them to describe their experiences. She encouraged them to pay attention to the motion of the floodwaters, listen to neighbors' remarks, notice their facial expressions, and other surrounding activities. One of the students began her story this way:

Would you like to meet the father of a flood, stacking sandbags with tears in his eyes? His son ran away in the spring ...

What a magnetic invitation to enter the story. The imaginative intelligence and emotional engagement in these lines could have been generated only by attention and sensitivity to detail. Moreover, the fact that the student was present, looking and listening, enabled her to internalize the event, a necessary component of transforming the writing process into more than a mere exercise.

As a poet in education, I have been passing along Rodin-like advice to students: "This evening sit outside and watch the sunset. What does it remind you of? What does it smell, or sound, or taste like? Write a poem about your ideas while you watch the sun walk down the hills." As a result, I receive poems describing the sun on the horizon "quiet as a pumpkin sitting in my backyard" or "slipping away like someone turning off a lamp in the late evening." One student, whose attention had been diverted by a rainbow, handed me this short poem:

What is a rainbow? Sometimes
I think it is a beautiful bracelet
that turns on a girl's wrist.
Rick Lee Robins

The beauty of his image lies not only in the product, but also in the process; the student did not simply follow the idea of writing about a subject, but rather gave himself over to the few brief moments of the rainbow's sudden appearance. He was looking in the purest sense, without the self-consciousness that sees the object or occurrence as homework, without that myopic vision which blurs the possibilities awaiting the peripheral vision of the imagination.

Beyond encouraging students to observe and write outside the classroom, I have been taking them on what I call "poetry field trips" to such places as meadows and canyons, migratory bird sanctuaries, forests, beaches, wetlands, etc. The decision on a location could be connected to a current geography, science, or social studies unit, or, best, simply contingent and spontaneous. Regardless of the relationship to the curriculum, it is attention, perception, and the act of writing that are integral to the awakening of language.

Early one fall morning I arrived with a group of fifth graders at Utah's Bear River Bird Refuge, one of the country's largest sanctuaries on the Pacific Flyway. The sun was still low in the east as we began the 12-mile auto tour, and shadows began lengthening across the narrow road flanked by tall reeds. The students, having spent much of their travel time consulting various field guides and wagering over who could spot the most species of birds, suddenly quieted in the wild beauty of the place.

In preparation for the experience, I had suggested that they practice looking and wondering the way Walt Whitman did when a child brought him a clump of grass. I recited parts of Whitman's poem "Song of Myself" (1959):

> A child said *What is the grass?* fetching it to me with full hands,
> How could I answer the child? I do not know what it is any more than
>   he.
>
> I guess it must be the flag of my disposition, out of hopeful green stuff
>   woven.
>
> Or I guess it is the handkerchief of the Lord,
> A scented gift and remembrancer designedly dropt...
>
> Or I guess the grass is itself a child, the produced babe of the
>   vegetation...
> And now it seems to me the beautiful uncut hair of graves. (Section 6)

Although most students readily agreed that the last image was "weird," they were, nevertheless, enchanted by its haunting sense of wonder and open-endedness. They liked the way Whitman initially confessed his helplessness in satisfying the child's curiosity, and then enumerated the various "answers."

I suggested that they should not be concerned with rhyme when writing their poems, explaining that trying to find a rhyming word often cuts off the flow of their ideas and feelings. The Whitman poem was a good example of a poem that doesn't rhyme, filled as it is with its playful exploration, while moving with the natural rhythm of the human voice. It was also an inspiring model for a new way of looking and imagining. As we drove deeper into the refuge, the boy who had been reciting the old children's song about "The pelican—his beak holds more than his belly can," pulled his notebook out of his backpack after watching a flock of the magnificent birds descending about a hundred yards away. He began his poem with:

"Pelicans resting like huge white clouds on the blue river." I sensed we were on our way.

One girl, convinced that there were no birds more wonderful than the whistling swans, composed this gracefully tangled mixture of images:

WHISTLING SWANS

They float like leaves over the river,
like crowned kings, but different in ways—
their long necks resemble arches
that have been standing for thousands of years.
DeAnn Perkins

Besides capturing the majesty of swans in "crowned kings," she unconsciously unfolds her thinking process, which becomes part of the poem's movement as she pauses with "but different in ways—" and reveals the association of swans with arches. The association was real for her, since she had lived for several years near Arches National Park. The sight of swans had evoked her childhood world, which she transformed in her poem.

All the students were overwhelmed by the wide variety of birds, but one boy was particularly charmed by a snowy egret's alternating displays of what seemed to him as both stately and comic posturing.

THE QUESTION MARK

The snowy egret flaps his wings once
or twice, to show his pride. But
when a noise comes near, he pokes
his head up out of the water
like a question mark.
James Fairbanks

It was unmistakable that observing the birds intensified the students' pleasures in writing about them and wanting to share their poems as the day went on. Their poems were spontaneous celebrations of being in this landscape of birds, not written assignments based on looking up information with photos of birds.

Ultimately, what students discover through the experience of writing in the landscape of the natural world is an inner landscape: that realm of language in which they can wander about and conceptualize the world in its freshness and immediacy. Moreover, the accumulated experiences of observing and writing outside the classroom can encourage a habit of spontaneity among students. The next poem, in which the writer saved the breathtaking moments of watching a hawk devour its prey in her yard, is an example of this spontaneous writing:

THE HAWK IN MY YARD

The hawk comes in
on silent wings
and perches high atop
the old bare-branched tree.
His piercing beak pokes
his dead prey
and little sparrow feathers
fall to the ground.
He sits with his back to me
and, with a wary eye,
turns his head
to watch
over his shoulder,
then shifts his feet
and ruffles his feathers
as the cold night air draws near.
Allison Prescott

The writer just happened to be outside when the hawk came in "on silent wings." Her poem reads like a detailed account at the scene of a mysterious event, and her last line, "as the cold night air draws near," leaves her reader or listener shivering with her in the darkening yard filled with the hawk's presence. Also, this tactile ending of the poem points to the fact that once the practice of looking and seeing is encouraged, the other senses open naturally as we allow the daily events of our lives to penetrate the shell of routine.

With the same group of students I led another poetry field trip to a canyon just a few miles outside Salt Lake City. It was a weekday morning, and, as I had expected, we found ourselves alone on the canyon trail. Alone, that is, with aspens and pines, hawk's beard, lupine, and perhaps a dozen other newly opened, wild flowering plants. Each student had access to booklets on the regional wildflowers and had already thumbed through the pages filled with color photos of variegated flowers accompanied by their "wild" names: Rose Pussy Toes, Goatsbeard, Prairie Rocket, Yellow Monkey Flower, Creeping Barberry ... The names were enough to excite their imaginative instincts.

Before going off on the search, we gathered together, and I recited a poem for them by Denise Levertov in which she speaks of tulips "becoming wings / ears of the wind / jackrabbits rolling their eyes ..." (1961, p. 53).

Rarely do I ask students to write without first sharing a poem or two from selections of classical or contemporary poetry. I've found that this practice results in the stimulation of ideas and exposure to the various ways language can be explored. I ask them to recall favorite lines and to tell why they suppose the poet chose a particular word or phrase out of so many possibilities. This habit invokes a necessary attentiveness to language and, consequently, to more unpredictable writing.

The Levertov model was a good choice; its associations broadened the list of exotic names which the students had learned from the field guides. Its last stanza established the perfect mood: "… some petals fall / with that sound one / listens for" (Levertov, 1961, p. 53).

These last words drifted off in the cool mountain air, and so did the children, quietly, as if listening for the flowers. One student returned, after sitting for a while beside a wild rose, with his poem:

THE WILD ROSE

High in the silent forest
a wild rose sits. In its center
a harmless sun rests. Its petals
are wings of a baby chick.
Its leaves are hands waving
goodbye.
Adam Lewis

The delicacy of language and imagery parallels the fragility of the rose. "A harmless sun" is a wonderful metaphor for the flower's sun-like stamens, and the last image, in which leaves are seen as "hands waving / goodbye," suggests the transience of all living things, not only of the flower.

These kinds of insights come from the students when we gather again to share our poems. "It makes the flower seem like a person who's going somewhere. Maybe not coming back for a long time," one student remarked. Some students affirm the idea, while others volunteer other perspectives, and the writer listens, sometimes shyly, mostly pleased, and often happily surprised by his or her own poem.

Commenting on each other's work, especially outside the classroom environment, creates a unique communal experience and noncompetitive atmosphere in which students learn things about themselves and the world that they never considered before. And what better place to write and read about a wild rose than in the mountains on a spring morning while its fragrance mingles with the smells of pine and canyon life?

The following poem approaches that place in poetry where the barriers between thought and speech dissolve into simple acts of praise:

SHOWY GREEN GENTIAN

What are you,
a falling star,

or hidden fire growing
quietly by yourself?
Showy Green Gentian,
what a beautiful name!
Rosemary Fairbanks

The effortless conversational tone, so spontaneous and direct, reveals an intimacy with the subject which the young writer might not have achieved at her desk by simply looking at a wild-flower photo. It also accents the personal impact of the outdoor, observing/writing process that keeps students connected to what is most human in them and in their perceptual relationship with their environment.

The idea of "poetry field trips" does not imply that creative writing cannot happen in the classroom, for imagination can be stirred in any environment. But the imagination relies on senses not dulled by routine, by schedules, or by school bells moving us so quickly from one activity to another that we no longer hear them.

* * *

Silvi Alcivar

Silvi Alcivar, graduate of the Pennsylvania State University's MFA program, lives in San Francisco and teaches poetry workshops for nursing home residents with the IOA's Center for Elders Youth and the Arts program. One workshop includes sixth graders, another is taught entirely in Spanish. All her elder students are over the age of 60 and most have never written a poem before.

Becoming an Ocean: Teaching Poetry in Nursing Homes

In the marrow of my bones, I need poetry class for the forest of joy to
come into my heart, to live in my fantasy of riding a unicorn,
feeling as if I can fly with the expansion of my mind.
                                         The Marvel of Poetry
                                         by the CC Poets

I've always loved elders, and would like to teach them poetry, but I've never even been in a nursing home. What's it like?
That's a big question! It's hard to say. No two nursing homes are alike. You might find that your work with elders doesn't take you to a nursing home at all but a day-facility, an assisted living home, or a private residence.

One of the great things about teaching poetry is its mobility; you can teach wherever bodies gather and only need one student to have a class.

What do you remember from your first visit?

I remember wishing I'd toured the site beforehand. As a graduate student in a course called "Writer in the Community," I felt prepared to teach poetry but not for the hospital-like environment that surrounded me the moment I walked in. At 22, I had no previous contact with old, frail bodies, not to mention the smell of colostomy bags and government-issued lima beans, beeping machines, slurred speech, crippled hands, the reality of failing memories and bodies probably decades closer to death than mine.

A sign on my classroom door read, "Therapeutic Recreation Room." I realized then that recreation for elders—reading, watching TV, playing computer solitaire—was not just living life, but some kind of therapy. My goals for the class aimed to exercise our intellects, stretch our imaginations, and expand our understanding of what poetry is and what poetry can do for us. That seemed therapeutic enough.

This work is therapy?

In my eight years of teaching, I've found this work does have healing effects, but I'm not a therapist, nor do you have to be. While writing can facilitate healing, what we're doing isn't clinical. I don't plan classes aiming to heal so much as transform people's ideas about poetry and their relationship to writing, which sometimes also transforms people's relationship to themselves. If that's healing and therapeutic, great!

For instance, Lefty, an 86-year-old participant who referred to himself as "a hick from the sticks," wasn't ashamed of his career as a car mechanic, but was upfront in saying that someone who'd lived a life working with his hands didn't have much to offer a poetry class, especially because a stroke some years back made it difficult to hold a pencil. Much to everyone's surprise, I told Lefty that no one needed to actually hold a pencil to write a poem. If you could speak, we'd write your words down for you. Even if you couldn't speak, and could only gesture, we could ask yes or no questions and help you express your ideas. No matter how you showed up, I told the class, we'd work together and you'd surely be able to contribute. Within weeks Lefty was not only composing stunning remembrances of his time as a soldier and imaginative expressions of what kind of ocean he would be, he was also composing poems in his head, repeating them over and over, so we could write them down when he saw us. He even began writing them down himself, though it took minutes to write one word. "It's good for me," he said, "keeps my marbles moving." When we had a performance of the students' best poems, Lefty introduced himself with a pride in his voice that hadn't been there when we'd begun the class and announced, "I never done anything like this in my life."

Without a doubt, Lefty experienced a transformation of confidence and discovered a new skill, joy, and identity as writer. I don't know if that's "healing" but, as a teacher, I couldn't really ask for more.

Lefty: Guess you can teach an old dog new tricks.

Can you say more about how students write without holding a pencil?
In the vein of Kenneth Koch and Marc Kaminsky, poets who published books in the 1970s about teaching poetry to elders, our poetry comes from language spontaneously uttered that you don't necessarily need words to speak. Poems sometimes emerge from the movement of our hands, heads, or silence. Most often, we talk our poems into existence, editing as we go. I give prompts, ask questions, and write down what the students say on a whiteboard so everyone can see the poem emerging. Because not everyone can see the board—due to poor eyesight or blindness—I speak everything as I write, and repeat, repeat, repeat. Sometimes what I write down is a

```
I Remember
by Lefty

It reminds me of the song "My Clementine."
In it she stumbles and drowns in the crick.
It was 1942 and the situation was the same:
in the song she left, and I was going to leave.

I didn't know when I went into the service
if I would come back to my wife or not.
1 went to England for four years. I got to know
a Scottie girl. On leave we went up to Scotland.
We met her folks, but I had to part with her, too.

I went to France, then Belgium and Germany
before I came home. I saw many a German soldier.
Up north next to the Rheine River, we were on the edge
of the Battle of the Bulge--they were across the crick.
Several times I had a near-death deal but I got out of it.

Over there it's altogether different than here.
Even the fences are different. You laid behind that
and any Germans you would shoot. When you lay
there you didn't know if you'll be killed or not;
it's something I couldn't understand. You hear
about Vietnam now, but it's real quiet about WW II.
I came home in 1946.
```

FIGURE 1.1 *Written by Lefty when asked to finish the phrase "I remember ..."*

direct answer to what's asked. Sometimes it's whatever is being said at that moment. A lot of our poems include the words, "I don't know," or "I'm not sure," or "If I only knew," because that's how students respond. Little do they suspect they're uttering a perfectly legitimate addition to a poem!

One of my favorite spontaneous utterance moments occurred while discussing the idea of riches. I turned to Myrna, a quiet student with advancing dementia, and asked, "What do you think richness is?" She responded passionately, "MONEY? I don't have a million dollars!" The class burst into laughter. Because we'd just been studying the pithy, conversational poems of Richard Brautigan, the class agreed what Myrna said was a wonderfully complete little poem.

Is this how you expand students' understanding of what poetry is?

Exactly! So many students think poetry is an intimidating, esoteric, incomprehensible, overly intellectual, always rhyming entity. From day one I try to expand their definition. Harold, who came to class as the nursing home's resident poet, almost walked out saying, "Poetry rhymes. If it doesn't, it's a statement!" Luckily he stayed for years and eventually admitted, "I didn't think I would but I learned something."

This is why I love using spontaneous utterance. The method instantly debunks stereotypes and fears about what a poem is. It takes pressure off "being a poet" or "knowing" anything about poetry. In fact, I tell my

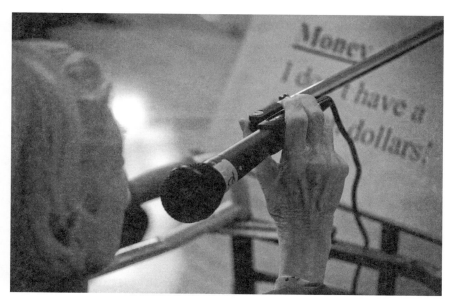

FIGURE 1.2 *A spontaneous utterance by Myrna when asked what she'd do with a million dollars.*

students they don't have to learn or remember any of the terms or concepts we discuss. If they do, fantastic! But if they don't, that's fine too. It's not important to me that a student can define metaphor, alliteration, meter, or any other poetic concept we cover. My job is to make sure my students understand the concept enough to employ it in a poem for a day. If they don't remember what the concept is called, it doesn't change the work we've done or the work we're now capable of doing. I'm not saying don't teach concepts, but I find taking away the pressure works well with the range of abilities my students have. Some hold degrees in law and philosophy. Others never reached high school. I aim for access and success for everyone. We learn a lot from each other this way.

> Wes: What in the heck is rheumatic fever?
> Emily: A disease I had as a child.
> Ronald: I believe it's an inflammation of the joints, sometimes your
>   heart. It's related to or caused by strep throat.
> Wes: What's strep mean?

Tell me more about who is in your class and how you write with them.
I've had students with difficulty remembering words or who couldn't speak and I found it helpful to ask them yes or no questions, then watch their eyes and body language for the answer. This technique works great when teaching people with Alzheimer's—there's no need to rely on their memories, not even to recall something said minutes ago. Relying on memory can lead to frustration, disappointment, even anger; so I invite students into their own success. Instead of asking, "What kind of ocean have you seen before?" or "What kind of ocean are you today?" I ask, "Are you an angry ocean, vulnerable, anxious?" And give space for the answer between options. The tactic may be leading, but it ensures participation and meets people where they are. This technique is not always necessary, especially if your students are highly cognitively functioning, but it helps and works for all cognitive levels.

```
Heartfelt Memory
by Emily

When I was 9 years old, I had romantic fever,
or maybe it was rheumatic fever.
I don't think I was in love yet.
```

FIGURE 1.3 *A spontaneous utterance by Emily when telling us what she thought about love*

Do you find your students often have a wide range of abilities?
Always. Doing this work will stretch your ideas about what aging is and what aging looks like. Try not to walk into the room with fixed expectations of who and what you'll meet. You'll meet 50-year-olds who could be in their nineties and 90-year-olds in their fifties. Some are able-bodied enough to do tai chi for an hour every morning, others need assistance getting in and out of a chair, others haven't walked in decades. Leave room to meet the individual bodies, personalities, histories, hearts, and desires in every room you teach—that's where all the poetry lives. You may even come to class one day and find that a student has died, so you throw your lesson plan out the window and spend the session writing remembrances, talking about grief, honoring your friend.

What's a typical class like?
My classes run 90 minutes and often look like this:

- For every class I make sure we sit in a circle. This helps us to see each other and talk to one another much more easily than sitting in rows. Sitting in a circle also helps us feel more like a cohesive group, which keeps the energy up.

- The beginning of class is spent building community and setting the tone for the day. We small talk. Make introductions. I often ask a get-to-know-you question that's linked to the day's activity.

- Once most students arrive, we play a 15–20 minute word game: take a long word, like *antidisestablishmentarianism*, and make new words using the letters of that word. Students love this! And love

```
I, the Ocean
by the VM poets

I, the ocean, look like emerald sky that never ends.
I have an unexplored deep full of catfish, humpback whales,
great whites, sunken ships, sea flowers, coral,
and a graveyard for anything living that has died.

I, the ocean, am soft orchestra strings--dun, dun, dun--
a banjo playing you're nothing but a hound dog,
and a bass deeply humming.

I, the ocean, sleep at high tide,
rising with rhythmic waves that say
I am the ocean.
```

FIGURE 1.4 *Written as a whole class, in about 30 minutes, with lots of furrowed brows*

FIGURE 1.5 *M. feeling proud of herself and her performance (as well she should).*

when I give clues, "This is a polite word for pimple." We always count the number of words found. Whether it's 20 or 120, we always cheer for ourselves.

- By this point, our energy is up, our minds and voices are activated. So, I introduce the day's lesson. Share an example. Discuss the task. Then we begin writing via spontaneous utterance. Depending on the activity and student energy, we may write several poems in a class.

- Students then read the finished poems aloud. We praise. Discuss.

- Last, I take questions. Then we applaud our job well done.

Following this structure for every class helps me plan and I've found that elders not only enjoy the routine but it also gives them agency. My students know when we'll shift activities and ask, "Silvi, you want me to read this poem now?" Once we've established a rhythm, participation becomes more volunteered. Having a structure also diminishes the anxiety that's often felt when tasked with writing a poem. Though I don't know if students with dementia and Alzheimer's remember there's a routine, I've found it creates a sense of comfort, more engagement and less "Are we done now? Can I go?"

I've stuck to this structure for years because it's open. People often come in and out of the room—insulin checks, phone calls, dentist appointments, the bathroom. You have to make sure the class isn't so tightly structured that your teaching and/or the student's ability to participate suffer from the interruptions.

How long does a class typically run?

This depends on your site and your commitment. I thought I would teach my first class for six weeks. I stayed for two years, and have continued to teach for almost eight years now. Whether I'm teaching weeks or years, I break the classes into 6–12 week themes. I plan mini-courses where each class builds off the previous, repeating the same concept, in nuanced ways, for weeks at a time. Repetition is the key to students' creative experience and learning.

A bonus to creating mini-courses: having lesson plans ready for use at a new site or to re-use but keep fresh by changing the example poems. Most students don't notice when we've done what we're doing before. And the poems they write always turn out to be different, even with the same prompts.

How do you typically begin the class sessions?

Before every first class I ask, "Will the poets in the room please raise their hands?" Few students ever claim the title. By the end of class, I aim to get everyone's hand in the air. When that happens, and it always does, you can feel the shift of people's understanding of poetry and themselves. Of course,

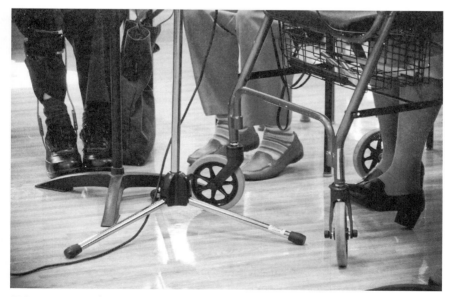

FIGURE 1.6 *Wheels and feet, practicing.*

FIGURE 1.7 *From a quiet man with resounding thoughts.*

some students remain utterly unconvinced, but I haven't met many. I think that's because I show up as my enthusiastic, poetry-loving self, who believes everyone is a poet. Even if I've had a hard day, I show up delighted to write poems because I know poetry class offers something most of my students don't get anywhere else: a room full of people willing to listen, engage their minds and imaginations, become friends, challenge ideas, laugh, and allow them to be who they are—happy, sad indifferent, alone, silly, whatever. It's all welcome. And it all shows up!

I also show up with unending amounts of praise, congratulations, pride, and applause. Nothing is too small to congratulate. When Paula tells a story about her time as a teacher, I thank her for the beautiful memory. When Bill suggests we use the word "dodecahedron" for our game, we applaud. When Grace cries so hard she can't finish reading her poem about her husband, I thank her for being so brave. When Robert suggests we write about bison burgers, I encourage everyone to have equally absurd ideas.

I encourage my students to stretch their limits, to speak up, to feel accomplishment in themselves and each other. I never leave a class without pointing out their growth. When we have enough poems to pull together an in-house performance, we showcase our work to family, residents, and friends. In rehearsal, we treat each other and our work as professional. In performance, we take our poems and our confidence to levels of expression we didn't think we had.

When you talk about engagement, what do you mean?
I'm talking about paying attention and participating, in big or small ways—showing up is really enough. I make sure each student feels invited into the community of writers, into the poem, and into the conversation with the work and each other. Every class period, each student gets asked at least one question, if not two or three. Some students always reply, "I don't know." It's okay that they don't know, especially because every once in a while, they'll give a shining answer.

Take James, a sort of statue of a man who seldom gives us the pleasure of his deep, quiet voice. He diligently comes to class and mostly snoozes. One day, while writing autobiographical poems, I noticed James writing something down. I asked if he'd like to share and his voice filled the room—"I'm a man, not a woman. Being alone is all I know. Life without the sun." There was a moment of beautiful silence before everyone cheered. He smiled shyly while we praised the depth of his words. He was sleeping again minutes later, but no one minded.

It sounds like joy, play, pride, and confidence, are among the benefits of this work. What else?
Although this may seem a strange thing to say, I now find the poetry is almost incidental to the real work of the class. Although my students are lured in by the promise of writing a poem, they come back for the community, friendship, and self-confidence that they find. They come because in writing poems we are finding and using our voices, being creative, stretching imaginations. We are expanding our knowledge of what poetry is, redefining the limits of what we believe we can accomplish, believing we can accomplish new things, and accomplishing new things. We are challenging each other and ourselves. We are caring about one another, noticing when someone's not in the room, welcoming each other and ourselves every time we meet. We are writing beautiful lines, having surprising and hilarious ideas. Laughing. Crying. Laughing some more. We are giving ourselves an hour and a half a week to leave everything behind and become an ocean of life so unlike all the other hours in our days.

You encourage imagination and play rather than memory. Why is that?
One of poetry's gifts, especially as it relates to elders/seniors, is its potential disregard for memory. It's entirely possible to write poems based solely on imagination. It's like I tell my students—memory sucks! Everyone roars in agreement. I've sat through too many minutes of the pained silence that comes from being unable to remember and I don't ever want someone to feel bad or uncomfortable about not remembering anything. Students, especially those with dementia and Alzheimer's, may get visibly and inconsolably upset. It's frustrating not to remember things you think you should know. Imagine if that feeling was the general state of your life.

Although it sometimes does, our poetry doesn't need to rely on memory. Our imagination is so vast, so accessible. If my students don't feel like they can make something up, we simply talk about what they see in the room, how they feel, or want to feel. I welcome imagination, especially its absurdity, because so many of my students' lives are too full of serious things—cataracts, deafness, arthritis, ill-fitting dentures, surgeries, dead friends, far away families, and sometimes a strong wish for, as one of my participants says, "the good lord to just take me away from these golden years." We're just human beings, aging ones at that, but through poetry we become oceans, mountains, fireworks, lovers, taxi cab chairs, famous dancers, the space between stars, silence, a mother's hands, transfixed and transformed. I see the happiness on my students' faces; I hear the confidence of their ideas, the encouragement of their peers, their commitment to not miss class, and their eventual ownership of the title "poet." It's a profound and deep honor to see this happen. And all of it happens just because we get together and write poems.

Bruce: I'm sorry I wanted to quit. I'll be back. I had fun.
Carlos: Thank you, teacher, for showing us how to write our words.
Emily: I think I feel a little better now.
Martha: See you next week! I'll have my bells on!

```
Poetry Is...
by the VM poets

        The beginning, it begins the begin.
        Something that rhymes in Grandma's day.
        The feeling of going into space.
        Not knowing, feeling in limbo.
        Nietzsche saying art makes life possible.
        Audible fingers that touch the strings of your soul.
        Love conquering itself.
        Your speech, the clothes you wear, the chair you sit in.
        The silence in the room, the stillness.
        Unknown to anyone but yourself.
```

FIGURE 1.8 *When asked to think about poetry as anything other than rhyme, they said this.*

CHAPTER TWO

Leaving Campus

Service-learning (and CBL) as citizenship

"The purpose of service-learning is not charity, but citizenship," notes Margaret Himley, in her syllabus for a course at Syracuse University: "Citizenship, the Narrative Imagination, and Good Writing." Like Himley, teachers who integrate CBL into courses know that CBL "is about learning the skills and knowledge important for all of us in our collective struggle for a more functional democracy and a more just society." CBL, or service-learning, provides real-life "situations in which to practice and to learn writing skills important for producing clear, effective, and responsible texts."[1]

Key elements of service-learning

"Learn and Serve," a program of the Corporation for National and Community Service, defines service-learning for all levels of education:

> Service-learning offers a unique opportunity for America's young people—from kindergarten to college students—to get involved with their communities in a tangible way by integrating service projects with classroom learning. Service-learning engages students in the educational process, using what they learn in the classroom to solve real-life problems. Students not only learn about democracy and citizenship, they become actively contributing citizens and community members through the service they perform.

Learn and Serve provides details on eight key elements to a successful service-learning project. The service must

1   be meaningful,

2   be linked to curriculum,

3   involve structured reflection,

4   promote diversity and mutual respect,

5   provide youth/students with a voice in project design,

6   involve partnerships that are collaborative, mutually beneficial, and address community needs,

7   engage participants in an ongoing process to assess the quality of implementation and progress toward meeting specified goals, and uses results for improvement and sustainability,

8   have sufficient duration and intensity to address community.[2]

Many schools, colleges, and universities compress these eight into four or five major elements, depending upon the needs and desires of administration, faculty, and community members. For our purposes, I'm going discuss five of these:

1   Meets a real community need.

2   Integrates into and enhances the curriculum.

3   Coordinates with a community agency, another school, or the community at large.

4   Helps foster civic responsibility.

5   Provides structured time for reflection.

1. Meets a real community need

It's exciting to use your knowledge of creative writing (good writing) to provide children, youth, and adults with techniques, insights, and skills in order to write descriptive and clear stories and poems. But is creative writing a community need?

Although it's not soup you're serving at the local shelter for the homeless, creative writing does meet several needs of the community and community members. Creative writing provides powerful tools that develop literacy skills and enhance self-confidence that lead to a stronger citizenry. Creative writing requires the use of strong writing skills and imagination.

In many public schools these skills are broken down into "core" requirements and expected to be taught to every child. Christopher McIlroy's essay in this book examines the skills students learn by engaging in poetry writing and storytelling against the backdrop of standardized test in his home state, Arizona. Terry Hermsen's essay describes ways to use various assessment tools to how learning outcomes and skills learned. Nathaniel Mohatt's essay discusses his research of the impact of creative writing on community members.

Creative writing uses imagination, of course, and develops writing skills. Literacy is a real need in the community. As writers, we would argue that imagination, storytelling, communication, and all of the skills that we develop when we write using elements of craft are greatly needed in our communities.

Community opportunities for creative writing provide children, youth, and adults the tools to communicate and tell stories and read them to each other, and to receive feedback on their writing.

Perhaps, as you conduct your CBL project, you can ask yourself to make some casual observations about the link between creative writing, literacy, poverty, self-confidence, and belonging.

2. Integrates into and enhances the curriculum

An effective service-learning project not only meets a need in the community, but is directly linked to your course objectives and learning goals. We've already discussed this a bit, but what does it mean to be an author off-campus? How does a writing residency increase your own knowledge of creative writing? Appendix B of this book has several syllabi that provide ways to integrate this into different creative writing courses. I'll assume, since you're already reading this book, that your teacher has created objectives for you that connect your writing residency with the course goals. Some of these objectives might include:

- To understand the elements of poetry, fiction, and/or nonfiction.

- To develop writing prompts that integrate the elements of poetry and storytelling.

- To articulate the difference between academic creative writing and community-based creative writing.

- To discuss the value of art in community.

3. Coordinates with a community agency, another school, or the community at large

Obviously, in order to conduct a writing residency, you need a community partner. This might be a school, a nursing home, a foster-care facility, a nonprofit agency that trains and supports writing residencies, or any other place where creative writing is needed and wanted.

4. Helps foster civic responsibility

The very act of leaving the college campus and visiting your site puts you in touch with your community in a way that staying on campus cannot. While you leave campus many times—to go to movies, visit friends, out to eat, etc.—leaving campus with the intention of using your talent and knowledge to help others tell their stories develops a certain aspect of your character that reading a book or workshopping stories by your classmates cannot. Taking creative writing into the community allows you, the writer, to understand how writing is indeed a service and meets a community need.

You might also discover while you're conducting your CBL project that you'd like to do more for community members who need help.

5. Provides structured time for reflection

The most valuable tool for handling challenges of any kind, or for understanding the self, for many writers is, of course, to write about them. I recommend you maintain a Structured Reflection Notebook, a Field Work Notebook—call it whatever you like—but keep some type of journal in which you really probe your reactions, observations, anticipations, and constantly evaluate your time at community sites.

Unlike a "journal" where you might simply react and respond freely to an experience, structured reflection asks you to dig a bit deeper—to assess your presentations, to explore connections of past experiences, to get uncomfortable with what you would say to your friends about your work. The essays in this book are structured reflections. Each writer has done the outreach work, but, rather than simply react to it, each writer has asked himself or herself challenging questions about the experience. Some explore how their community work connects with their personal histories, others explore how creative writing fits in a school curriculum that values standardized tests above all else, others explore the meaning of imagination.

The next steps

Once you have decided where you would like to conduct your CBL project, the next two steps include contacting the community partner and complying with any requirements the community partner site might have for volunteers.

1   Contact the community partner.
2   Complete CP volunteer requirements.

Contact the community partner

If your teacher, director, or coordinator has already arranged the partnership, you're in good shape to begin planning your residency. Or he may, as I do, offer you a list of possibilities that allow you to choose, based on your schedule and when the community partner can arrange for participants to attend. For example, if students in my classes wish to conduct their writing residency at the shelter for the homeless and work with adults, they will need to be available on either Tuesday or Thursday evenings from 7:30–8:30 p.m. This is the only time the shelter in our area has a space and time available for their clients to attend these types of activities. Most of the residents at the shelter for the homeless have jobs or are in other life-skill classes during the day. If students wish to conduct their writing residency at the foster-care facility, they must have some time available between 9 a.m. and 3 p.m. on weekdays.

If you wish to work in a school, contacting a teacher you know is perhaps the most successful way to get into a school. Otherwise, you should contact the principal, assistant principal, curriculum coordinator, or volunteer coordinator at the school where you are hoping to work. Obviously, you don't want to contact all of these people at once, but try to find out through the website which person is the one who deals with community partners or volunteers.

If you are interested in working at a shelter, prison, or other facility, you will need to call the facility where you wish to work and inquire as to whom handles volunteer programs.

In your initial contact, express your interest in volunteering for them, giving them a brief overview of what you plan to do. For example, I might say something like:

> My name is Terry, and I'm interested in offering creative writing workshops to your adult residents for one hour each week for 12 weeks. Could I talk with you more about this possibility? I am available on Tuesday and Thursday evenings and all day Friday.

Be sure to communicate directly with the community partner about the length of your CBL project. Don't leave it open-ended by letting them think you'll be conducting your project for the next ten years. For now, stick with the 10–14 weeks of the semester. Later, you can decide if you might want to conduct a second writing residency at that same location.

Complete CP volunteer requirements

Once the community partner (CP) agrees to your residency, you need to find out the procedures for being able to volunteer or work at that **site**. You may need to complete a volunteer application. If you are contracting with a school, or district, or other organization, there are certain procedures which you would need to work out depending upon the agency. If your project will be at a public school, you will most likely need to agree to a background check, and you may be asked to complete fingerprint checks. You may need to attend some type of volunteer orientation or interview.

If your CBL project is the first of its kind at a specific location, you may need to develop a more thorough description of your writing residency, which I'll discuss in the next chapter.

The site where you choose to conduct your writing residency is, most likely, eager and excited to have you working with their children, youths, or adults. It is also possible, if you're working individually, to encounter organizations or schools that don't feel they have the time for the fluffy stuff of creative writing. You may need to provide administration with some evidence that "creative writing" fits well within public school skill-building standards. You may need to provide assisted living facilities assurance that you won't be exploiting the residents living with dementia. You may need to sign a confidentiality form at the domestic violence shelter—promising that you won't disclose protected information of their clients.

Structured reflection

Personal

1 What is the value of your individual voice?

Academic

2 On the National Campus Compact website (www.compact.org), browse through the syllabi (located in Faculty Resources) for another course at a different university that incorporates SL or CBL. Where is it? What do they do for their service project? How does your project compare with the project on the other syllabus?

3 Locate Adrienne Rich's poem "North American Time" (1986). Relate Rich's poem to your own sense of being a writer in the community.

Civic

4 Visit the websites for the following organizations. You don't have to memorize the entirety of each website, but take notes as you read through them so that you can discuss various aspects of service-learning (community-based learning). Then, in your own words, describe service-learning or CBL.

   a *National Service-Learning*

   b *Florida Campus Compact*

   c *National Campus Compact*

5 How does your course's CBL project fit in with the larger national framework of service-learning? Identify a couple of things you discovered about CBL that you did not know before.

6 What does it mean to be a "writer off-campus"?

Readings

Julia Spicher Kasdorf

Julia Spicher Kasdorf has published three collections of poetry with the University of Pittsburgh Press, most recently *Poetry in America* (2011). Among the previous collections, *Eve's Striptease* (1998) was named one of *Library Journal*'s Top 20 Best Poetry Books of 1998, and *Sleeping Preacher* (1992) won the Agnes Lynch Starrett Poetry Prize and the Great Lakes College's Association Award for New Writing, and a 2009 NEA fellowship. She is the author of a collection of essays, *The Body and the Book: Writing from a Mennonite Life* (2001). With Michael Tyrell she co-edited the anthology, *Broken Land: Poems of Brooklyn* (2007). In addition to teaching poetry workshops, she established the Writer in the Community course in the MFA program.

What is an Author Off-Campus? The Writer in the Community and the Corporate University

Coming to terms with service-learning

More than a decade ago, I was hired to teach creative writing and to become "engaged" with the local community around the Pennsylvania State University. Following an "outreach initiative," the College of Liberal Arts searched for an author who wrote about "place," and who could develop "outreach" activities in the region. For years I had written poems and essays, set in central Pennsylvania, from my apartment in Brooklyn without considering any of the professionally-credible words I have placed in quotes in the first two sentences of this paragraph. In the job interview, the department head asked what ideas I might have concerning "outreach," particularly given that I had family in the area. I said I might take MFA students over the mountain to collect oral histories in the farm valley where my parents were both raised, a Mennonite and Amish community where gossip and storytelling remain lively arts. The head looked surprised and a little confused. Instead of something like that, he had imagined that I would take the creative writing graduate students out to read their own poems in the local area, he told me.

The moment passed. I got the job and pursued neither project, but the difference between the ways we had conceived of "community outreach" in creative writing reveals important realities about the role and authority of the public university. The department head's expectation reflects both historical and immediate experience. Penn State started out as an agricultural college and was later established as a Land Grant institution in 1862. The first college president tested new chemical fertilizers so that farmers would know what they were putting on their crops. By the turn of the nineteenth century, the school was devoted almost entirely to training engineers. In years past, Penn State faculty members have judged produce and canned goods at fairs around here; they have written local histories and lobbied for the preservation of vernacular architecture and natural areas. Now, citizens regularly turn to the Penn State Extension Service to learn how to remove Japanese beetles from their rose bushes or mold from their basement walls. Long before it was known for football, Penn State served as a beacon of practical knowledge: scholarly—usually scientific—research applied to local problems.

In more recent years, largely due to cuts in funding for public education, changes in patent law, and the professionalization and mobility of the professoriate, "outreach" has come to mean the cultivation of relationships between highly specialized research laboratories and private companies. The work that engineers and scientists conduct on campus—funded by industry or the government—launches start-up companies on the edge of university towns. Nowadays, when people speak of "engagement," they may be referring to the geological research that mapped natural gas deposits or the online assistance the university offers landowners negotiating with gas companies who seek to drill on their farms. Moreover, "outreach" has become a catch-all term for non-traditional, web-based instruction, from professional development for police officers and homeland security agents to entire online degree programs.

In this environment, I rarely say "outreach" or "engagement" because those words seem to be reserved for other purposes. When I speak of the wonderful but largely invisible work that graduate students in creative writing have done off campus, I say "service-learning," to signal the work that contributes to the lives of individuals who are not in a position to pay for the service; and to note the learning that students do as they read, write, construct new knowledge through teaching practice and collaboration, and write some more.

Our work at Penn State is not unique, as this collection well demonstrates. In many creative writing programs, community involvement typically takes the form of teaching creative writing in public schools and other off-campus sites. These activities are common enough to be included on the list of features that define a quality program by the Association of Writers and Writing Programs (AWP), the national professional organization for creative writing in the academy. AWP notes that teaching writing in the community builds audiences for contemporary literature in a nation that seems to be reading fewer and fewer books. Perhaps more importantly, community work provides vocational experience for MFA students who have little hope of securing teaching positions in a dire academic job market, no matter how talented, hardworking, and well-published those young writers may be. Indeed, several graduates from Penn State have gone on to teach creative writing in community settings in San Francisco, New York City, and elsewhere.

For the majority of the students, however, the most interesting "outcome" of this work is less tangible, impossible to measure or count. The Writer in the Community course I teach, like other forms of community engagement in the academy, is "a wonderfully complex and situated practice that truly disturbs and forces students (and faculty) to rethink their normal patterns of thought and belief," as described by Dan W. Butin in *Service Learning in Theory and Practice: The Future of Community Engagement in Higher Education* (2010, p. 133). This disturbance—not service to the community, no matter how consistent with our Land Grant tradition—makes the work a worthy activity for the intellectual agenda of the university. In other words, the production of new knowledge, the thinking and re-thinking of old understandings, and the sharing of those new ideas, makes service-learning an *intellectual* endeavor, valuable in its own right apart from whatever good it might do in the community. I borrow this argument from Butin, who refuses to take the bait in Stanley Fish's (2008) *Fix the World on Your Own Time*, wherein Fish argues that professors should focus on doing their jobs, which he defines as the production and dissemination of knowledge. As Butin points out, community work fulfills this mission in part because it is an "anti-foundational practice," that enables students "to question their certainties" and "expand their sense of the possible" (2010, p. 132). I will show *how* this happens in my course, but first a brief description of *what* the course involves and how it works.

The writer in the community

Through the Master of Fine Arts program in creative writing, the English Department at Penn State has offered the Writer in the Community course six times since 2000, and I was able to teach it five of those times. I adapted the course from a model project with the same name, created by Nicholas Coles and Catherine Gannon at the University of Pittsburgh during the late 1990s. My course description for the three-credit class reads as follows:

> Writer in the Community is a service-learning course that involves students in the teaching and practice of writing in non-university settings. It aims to increase student understanding of and appreciation for the uses of writing among diverse groups of people. In particular, we will study and discuss the uses of creative writing—poetry, fiction, creative non-fiction—as a means of developing literacy and promoting human growth and healing in various contexts. Students enrolled in the course will have a strong background in creative writing and must be committed to meet the demands of a service-learning course, including weekly visits to off-campus sites.

Graduate students typically work in teams of three and are required to meet off-campus with their writing groups for at least ten sessions. The teams design their own classes in response to the needs and goals of the particular populations they serve. Each class typically involves a writing exercise and sharing of members' work. Weekly, we all gather as a class of about 12 students for a couple of hours to discuss assigned readings from various common texts, such as articles from *Healing and Writing*, edited by Anderson and MacCurdy, and to share reports of progress and frustration at the off-campus sites. During the course of the semester, students are required to observe at least one other site and to discuss what they have observed with the group in charge. I visit all the sites at least once and meet with each group to discuss the observation. Each individual is required to keep a log of reading responses and teaching reflections, and to share that writing with the class and professor on a weekly basis.

Locations that have hosted Writer in the Community include the county jail, shelters for teenagers who are no longer able to live with their own families, the local literacy council, a public nursing care facility, private care facilities, a community center that serves disadvantaged children, and English as a second language groups for both adults and children. (I usually make a preliminary contact with the organization prior to the start of class, but sometimes students initiate contact themselves.) As a final requirement, students develop a publishable essay that explores an idea that has emerged from their practice and writing. (Two other articles in this volume—one by Silvi Alcivar, another by Sharlene Gilman—have their origins in this course.)

What is an author off-campus?

In a 1969 lecture, Michel Foucault used the term "author function" to characterize the beliefs and assumptions governing the writing and editing, circulation, classification, and reception of literary texts. For example, copyright signals a relationship with written materials that we believe to be the personal property and sole production of an author, and yet an author is not only a writer. Although it has operated differently at different times and places, "author function" makes us wait in line for a novelist to sign a copy of her new book, whereas we may not feel the need to get an autographed copy of a scientific article. "Author function" explains why we don't regard the writer of a letter, or contract, or poster as an author. I attribute to "author function" the frenetic energy that electrifies the stale air of the book fairs set up in the basements of conference hotels during the AWP's annual meeting.

MFA programs explicitly introduce student writers to "author function" and reinforce it through all manner of well-intentioned efforts at profes-sionalization. Students are encouraged to read contemporary literature, especially journals and magazines. Many are coached to submit their work for publication and to envision their final degree projects as first book manuscripts. But most of all, and in countless subtle ways, students are invited to try on the identity of author, not as amateur writers, but promising professionals (proof of their professional promise being admission into a competitive MFA program). Faculty members press them to practice their craft seriously, as aspiring members of a guild, and to conceive of themselves as specialized and special, creatures who are mystically different from their fellow graduate students engaged in literary study who also read and write a great deal, but who draft critical rather than literary writing.

Beliefs and assumptions about the author as a rare creature engaged in the individual production of special texts is precisely what the Writer in the Community work "disturbs." Consider Centre Crest, the public nursing care facility located about ten miles from our campus, where residents are largely drawn from rural areas and small towns in the region. When our graduate students first started leading a writing group there in 2001, they had to face the fact that most of the people who showed up for the first meeting could not hold pencils in their hands. Right then, in a quite literal sense, writing was no longer an individual product. Sometimes group members composed poems in their minds and memorized them until one of the graduate students could write them down. Others talked through an idea or memory, and a transcription of the dialogue, often led and shaped by the scribe, became a piece of writing to be discussed and revised the following week.

Through the efforts of students enrolled in the course every other year, and through the work of subsequent graduate student volunteers, some of them literature students, the writers' group at Centre Crest has continued since 2005. For the elders who gather each week in the recreational room, the group is a pleasurable and important alternative to Bingo and Bible study, the other regular events at the institution. The group has become a place where residents meet to listen to one another's words and to write their stories or poems from memory or imagination with the help of an engaged interlocutor and transcriber. After the invasion of Iraq, for instance, several of the men and women began remembering and sharing their own experiences at the start of and during World War II. At various points throughout the history of the Writer in the Community project at Centre Crest, graduate students have published booklets of the residents' poems, sometimes funded by grants obtained from the local arts council. The booklets are distributed to other residents at the facility and the writers' family members. The practices that have become routine at the Centre Crest site destabilize notions of what writing is, physically, but also unsettle the general sense of who gets to be called an author and what the production and publication of writing entails.

For the graduate students, the drive away from campus offers a sense of connection to life outside academia, away from the MFA program, to a realm where disabled bodies and confused minds are more common than ambitious, apparently composed intellects. This connection—because it exists in the context of study, analysis, and their own writing—can be quite destabilizing. Popular narratives that describe what it takes to become an author demand that the writer "can't go home again" like Thomas Wolfe, although his background was the literary subject. Like James Joyce, the writer becomes an author who works in "silence, exile, and cunning," physically removed, yet imaginatively situated.

Involvement in the local community makes it impossible for graduate students to maintain a distanced relationship with everyday life. For some, the work actually bridges back to home. Students write about the ways that working with the elders at Centre Crest cause them to reconsider relationships with their own grandparents, deceased or living. One student's mother was diagnosed with a fatal illness during her work at the site, and that student kept returning to serve as a volunteer through the next semester and summer and then the next year, as if the writers at Centre Crest could somehow help her to understand the failure of her mother's body and teach her to accept mortality.

By physically leaving campus and entering other contexts, students sometimes confront parts of themselves that schooling practices have asked that they minimize or omit. The summer that students taught at both Centre Crest and the county prison, several were struck by similarities between the two institutions, where residents remain confined to various locations, and visitors follow security routines upon entering and leaving. To what extent is campus also a policed, protected zone, they wondered, and what purposes get served through the creation of sequestered spaces? For some students, like "the scholarship boy" of Richard Rodriquez's (1982) *Hunger of Memory*, compartmentalization of one's background is an essential strategy for surviving and obtaining an education. One student, for instance, was frustrated that we would be conducting workshops in prisons. "Why do *they* get poetry?" she asked. In time, I learned that her brother was serving a jail sentence, and that she had been the exceptional sister who rose above a disadvantaged background. In another instance, a student inquired about enrolling in the course, and particularly about working with a writing group in a prison, because, he told me, his brother had been incarcerated at the other end of the country, and he thought this work might help him to understand his brother's life.

It is tempting but dubious to claim that service-learning enables the integration of those personal identities that are often marginalized in graduate school, and thereby helps the students to become "more whole." At the very least I dare say what I have already said in other ways: the experience of working with writers in the community disturbs the clean line that we all draw between school and the rest of the world: school and family or community of origin; school and local life, by which I mean the people who do not or cannot share the aspirations of those who are trying to gain a foothold in academia. Work in the community exposes values implicit in the academy and creative writing education, and sometimes calls them into question.

Only connect

In designing the Writer in the Community course and selecting our common textbooks, I deliberately try to guide the ways the students conceive of their community work. I want them to consider "literacy," that is not only the ability to decode and produce written texts, but also the ability to feel and think meaningfully about one's life and circumstances. I am especially interested in the ways writing can promote "emotional literacy," as described by Jerome Bump and others. I also invite them to think about writing as a means of "healing," broadly conceived.

The last time I taught the course, "healing" was the source of great controversy and even resistance. The first- or second-year graduate students, trained to teach composition, felt barely qualified to teach writing, and certainly not to heal. Teaching, with its focus on skills and techniques, they could manage. Healing, on the other hand, implies pain, mess, and human neediness that are impossible to meet. Anxiety about caring (and failure to care) surfaced repeatedly throughout the course. One student, poised to begin work at a teen shelter in the first month of the course, expressed his concern this way:

> Something I don't want to see is a poem about sexual abuse. I could say I don't want to see that sort of poem because I'm not trained to deal with it, or because I'm not an appropriate confidant. Both of these are probably true, but my real resistance stems from my distaste at the notion of becoming relationally involved and responsible for these girls. I don't really want to worry about these girls; I don't want my emotional reserves sapped by their problems. I don't want these girls to "open up" to me, and I don't want to "open up" to them. Yes, I believe I'd gain wisdom or humanity or humility if I engaged wholeheartedly, but I'm not sure it would be worth it.

By the beginning of the second month, resistance to the assigned readings was palpable. In graduate school, students told me, they are taught to deal with complex texts—whether in literature class or writing workshops—but this class asked them to deal with writers. Louise DeSalvo's (1999) work, in particular, asked them to consider themselves and all people as wounded or broken, and to see expressive or imaginative writing as a healing practice. This was something some were prepared to engage, given their own experience, and that others flatly refused. One student wrote, "… my reaction to DeSalvo bordered on outrage, but in truth, I think that strong reaction comes from my desire to connect myself and my acts of writing to some higher, more ostensibly meaningful ideals." While she admitted that she first turned to writing to describe the troubles of her teenaged years, since enrolling in graduate school, she had taken on an impersonal writing project based on historical research. Did "author function" dictate the need to distance from her needy writer within?

By month three, under the typically grim, grey skies of March in central Pennsylvania, things began to come undone. In response to an essay, one student finally blurted, "Why does the conversation always get around to caring? It's as if it's not really the writing that heals anyone, but the teacher's caring!" Her dark eyes flooded with tears as her voice faltered and trailed off. I noticed the intensity of her feeling, but did not acknowledge it. Instead, I turned to the class, asked a broad question and shifted attention away from the distraught speaker. Other students picked up the conversation. A few moments later, the only graduate student who was not studying in the English department, the one from clinical psychology, broke our conventional mode of seminar discussion and said that she noticed tears. She wondered what it is about the English department that makes people seem so disconnected all the time. "You read all those important books that are full of feelings; you write about feelings, but you seem unable to connect with one another!" (I felt the sting of my own pedagogical failure.) This student, who does individual counseling and works in groups as part of her professional practice, felt distance in her community work—with an English as a Second Language group—and between her graduate student collaborators. She wondered whether the distance she felt had anything to do with a failure to care.

Immediately others joined the conversation, describing their own feelings of alienation as graduate students in a highly stratified department, where they serve as instructors of teacher-proof composition classes—designed and determined by others—which no undergraduates want to take and no senior faculty members want to teach. "How do you care about 24 students who are hostile to what you do and love, who say they find writing pointless?" one asked.

The values of literacy and healing, and the moments that felt energizing in their work in the community, seemed counter to all they do in a composition classroom. One student said that she realizes she just hates teaching composition! She is shy, has enrolled in a graduate program far from her home, and hasn't formed many meaningful relationships here yet. Somehow this class seemed to highlight her inability to connect with people. Others articulated similar feelings.

The more we talked, the wider the conversation roamed, touching on the fact that our university had cut funding for future graduate students in creative writing, and few faculty members in the department expressed concern about that loss. The psychology student observed that people withdraw from others when they feel oppressed. Several confessed to feeling fraudulent—as authors and novice teachers—which made it hard to feel open to others. By the end of the class, one student formulated a challenging question for us all to contemplate the next week: How am I enabling the distance?

After that very vulnerable and disturbing conversation, the classroom climate shifted. Work in the community had not only caused the students to question their ideas about writing and authors, but to examine conventional teaching and academic culture. Authors off-campus cannot disseminate knowledge like county extension agents treating blight on apple trees, but they can facilitate small connections through tentative encounters. They ask questions and offer writing prompts to people who are rarely asked to speak or write about their lives. The writers listen and sometimes transcribe the words of others. They may care about the individuals whose stories they gradually come to know. They feel uncertain and cautious—emotions that their graduate training asks them to hide. They are often discouraged.

Much of the time, they wonder whether they are "doing it" at all, whatever "it" is—teaching, caring, making a difference. In that wondering, I am quite certain that they are.

* * *

Heather Fiedler

Heather Fiedler graduated from the University of Central Florida with a BA in English/Creative Writing in 2005. She participated in Terry Thaxton's very first Creative Writing in the Community Class, conducting her residency at the Coalition for the Homeless. After graduation she led a poetry writing workshop at the Women's Residential Counseling Center in Orlando, worked as a contracts negotiator for Lockheed Martin for five years, and is now living in her hometown in the Midwest to pursue a master's degree in Biblical Spiritual Formation at Moody Theological Seminary.

Birth of an American Scholar

I read with some joy of the auspicious signs of coming
days, as they glitter already through poetry and art.
Ralph Waldo Emerson "The American Scholar"

"Nametags must be worn in the building at all times," reads the sign on the entrance to the Women's and Children's Shelter.

There are two kinds of badges here: green for visitors, and blue for residents. I'm given the green because I will only be teaching creative writing here on Wednesday nights. Sheryl, the director of Orlando's Coalition for the Homeless, gives me and my three fellow student teachers a tour of the entire facility, beginning with the women and children's area, followed by the men's only section (known as the Pavilion). The Pavilion is appropriately named as it much more resembles a pole shed barn than a housing unit, consisting of a soccer field sized concert slab, where the men line up for food each night and sleep on the ground.

Upon entering the Pavilion, my visitor badge feels heavy and noticeable, like the Star of David during the occupation. Odd isn't it? Wouldn't any one of these men do anything for this badge, for a safety pin's assurance that this is only just another stop on the tour, not where they will be spending the night? And, like Pip in *Great Expectations*, I look down at my leather boots and suddenly feel disgusted and out of place, not because "my hands [are] so coarse and my boots [are] so thick," (Dickens, n.d., p. 50), but because they aren't. I am overdressed and, quickly realize, overeducated in irrelevant matters; for my geometry may be a little rusty but I'm sure that the 3 × 6 rectangle chalked out on the floor is simply not big enough to accommodate a sleeping man.

We are then escorted back to what will be our classroom for the next ten weeks: a small "conference room" in the Women's Shelter equipped with a pair of mismatched tables and assorted chairs; a long hallway lined with women waiting patiently for medications, tampons, and sheets, and an occasional conversation, as their children grab the legs of passers-by; a dark parking lot where a resident teen named Dana will follow me to my car and ask me to take her home; a strip of street along which grown men sleep; a gated entrance way.

This is a service-learning classroom and one that cannot be found on a college campus. In it you will find no books because the books we need haven't been written yet. We bring only blank paper and pens. You will not find some teachers and some students but *all* teachers and *all* students, writers coming together to celebrate "the survival of the love of letters amongst a people too busy to give to letters any more" (Emerson, 1957, p. 63). You will witness a response to Emerson's call for a new American Scholar.

Scholars, have we not become a "book-learned class, who values books, [but] not as [they] relate to the [present] human condition" (Emerson, 1957, p. 67)? Do we not regurgitate "past utterances of genius," passing them off as evidence of our own (p. 68)? What good are the eyes of man in shaping the future if they are buried in the words of the past? We must dispel this notion that "the scholar should be a recluse … a bookworm" and become active souls, for it is "the one thing in the world of value" (pp. 69–70).

Somewhere along the line, the scholar was appointed the function of intellect, but, in doing so, has been excused his responsibilities as a citizen, a member of his community. He has been marooned on the isle of his own intellect. He has "suffered amputation from the trunk … [making] a good finger, a neck, a stomach, [a doctor, a lawyer], but never a man" (p. 64). In order to call oneself a true American Scholar, one must "return from his own labor to embrace all the other laborers," re-commune with his community (p. 64). We read something of this in our American Literature classes, some Whitman perhaps, but do we actively experience his poetry? Have we actually taken the time to get to know each leaf of grass: "the carpenter," "the pilot," "the farmer," "the lunatic," the homeless? (Whitman, 1959, pp. 33–4).

On our first day of writing class at the shelter, we all look up as Sharon, our first student, enters the room. She pulls a few perfume samples (Burberry, Calvin Klein, Estee Lauder) out of her pocket and proudly places them in a neat line on the table. Taking notice to our observation, she explains, "I invaded Burdines today. Got them for my underwear drawer," she says in a raspy laugh. "Wouldn't expect homeless people to be so happy would you?" she continues, and I don't know what to say. No, is what I'm thinking, after all, I couldn't ignore the men sleeping on the sidewalk on my way in, but I say nothing. But I guess she knows I won't and ends with a smile, saying, "Well, I guess we should be considering rent is only one dollar."

So I guess I am supposed to tell you what I have learned from all of this, what I couldn't have been taught just as well in a classroom. Before we embarked on this project, our definition of learning was somewhat black and white, mere words on a page, the traditional classroom. This experience has served as a practical application of our learning. Being in the position of teacher, our knowledge of the craft is truly tested. In order to reach a skill, one must have a comprehensive understanding of the technique. And yet, "colleges and books only copy the language which the field and the work-yard made" (Emerson, 1957, pp. 71–2). This is where language is born and stories are made.

Some might see the two, service and learning, while equally valuable, as separate. While service feeds our sense of morality, what place does it have in our educational system? The answer to this quandary came to me during an interview with Chaunet, one of the homeless women in the class.

The question posed, "*Has* writing changed the way you see the world?" Her response:

Yeah, [because now] I can change [the world]. I can change it to the way I want it to be. That's one thing I like about writing: sometimes I'm not happy with what actually goes on, so yeah it does. I look at the world in a totally different way than other people do. I like to read between the letters instead of the lines. When I do that, I have a tendency to understand more. Writing is an outlet for me.

This Wednesday night Edie, another resident at the shelter, will write about the first time her little boy saw snow; Sharon about the epic tale of a journey through Yugoslavia; Chaunet about Sister Mary Vaughn; and I, I will write about them. And this, Emerson says, is the first sign of a new intellectual era in which, "that, which has been negligently trodden under foot by those who were harnessing and provisioning themselves for long journeys into foreign countries, is suddenly found to be richer than all foreign parts" (1957, pp. 77–8).

This is more than service, it is more than credit. It is about giving a voice to those who typically go unheard. It's about hearing stories we can't read in our textbooks. It's about coming together as a community to share our knowledge. It's about becoming an active soul, an American Scholar, a citizen.

Emerson states, "to the young mind, every thing is individual, stands by itself. [Yet] by and by, it finds how to join two things, and see in them one nature, whereby contrary and remote things cohere, and flower out from one stem" (1957, p. 65). It appears as though the young mind of our educational system has finally begun to mature, to recognize the value in a partnership between service and education, to take seriously the need for true American scholars if we wish to see a future different than our past, to provide the scholar with "an university of knowledges" (1957, p. 79), rather than the knowledge of an university.

CHAPTER THREE

Making a Plan

Envisioning your CBL project

Many nonprofit organizations such as Community Word NYC, Writers in the Schools Houston, Write Around Portland, Urban Word NYC, Write Girl, ArtsBridge, and InsideOut Literary Arts in Detroit, have developed procedures that help to guide and support writers who conduct residencies through their organizations. While specifics may differ, the general ideas are similar, and most of them begin with a question that is also vital to a CBL project for creative writing students: *What is the single most important thing you want your participants to take away/remember about your time with them?*

The answer to this question helps you develop an overview of what you hope to accomplish with the participants at your site. The overview will help you design your weekly sessions. Here are some questions for guidance as you design this overall plan. Once you develop this overview, you can begin planning your weekly sessions, which we'll get to later in this chapter.

- Make a list of several possible questions that you might want to learn about yourself, your participants, writing, the community, or a social issue.

- What *skills* do you want your participants to be able to have at the end of your project?

- What *knowledge* do you want them to have?

- What types of final/culminating products do you want to have (publications, performances, student work, etc.)? Set a date for this reading/celebration. How will you know your CBL project is successful? What evidence can you look for?

- How will you know that the community partner (whether this is a teacher, the administration/staff at a shelter, the caregivers at an assisted living facility) feels that the residency has been successful?

- How will participants explain what they did and how they did it?[1]

Here are a couple of sample project overviews and project goals. On the companion website for this book and in Appendix A, you can find complete semester-long CBL projects to help generate ideas for your own project. Once you develop this overview, work with your community partner to ensure that your plans are appropriate for the group of participants you'll be working with.

Aimee Campbell—STUDENT EXAMPLE OF PROJECT OVERVIEW (2012)

The ideal outcome of this project would be that the students gain a greater sense of self, and a greater sense of self-esteem, by learning to express themselves through writing. I want them to know that writing is powerful, and that being able to present what you have written in a powerful way can change the world.

Aimee's Project Goals

I hope that with this project I will be able to introduce the participants to writing as a means of self-expression, and help them to gain self-confidence as a result of being able to share their work with their peers. They will learn how to take everyday experiences and use them to express a greater idea through non-fiction writing and poetry. Group work will facilitate a sense of community among the participants, and as they work on their stories together they will become more comfortable with sharing them. I want to encourage illustration of stories. Elements of theater will help to teach the participants how to perform their work. The culmination of the semester will be an open mic night where students are encouraged to perform and to cheer on their classmates.

Katie Land—STUDENT EXAMPLE OF PROJECT OVERVIEW (2012)

The outcome I would like from this project is for participants to see literature as a source of adventure, knowledge, fun, and inspiration. If they gain an appreciation for reading and writing now, I believe it will help give them a richer future. I want them to see the positive way that the arts can reach people. I want them to remember the fun we had in class and all of the new concepts they learned and desire to bring that same enrichment to the world.

Katie's project goals
My project goal is for the children to gain confidence and creativity in their writing that will continue into other academic endeavors. I want them to be inspired to become positive world changers, to discover that life is an amazing story and we all have our own chapters to tell. The participants will practice writing their own short stories, monologues, and screenplays. By the end of the semester we are going to write, perform, and edit a short film that will be used by the school.

Designing 10–12 weeks of session (lesson) plans

Now it's time to break down that overall picture into weekly sessions, and to prepare for your first workshop. By this time you should know where you're going to conduct your CBL project and which of your classmates are going with you, or if you're going it alone. Students in my classes have access to a class blog where they can post their lesson plans. In this way other students or groups can "borrow" those plans and I can offer suggestions. Maybe you can use IM chat, or Facebook, or email. It's a good idea to discuss plans with the group of students you're working with prior to your first workshop on site.

At the end of the semester, you will find a way to publish the work of the participants at your site, and you will organize a reading and/or celebration. A good way to prepare for this is to type up the work of your participants each week, or with the help of the classroom teacher (if you're in a school setting) have the participants type them up. There are several different ways to "publish" the work of your participants. Include your preference in your residency overview and plan. Here are a few ideas:

- Record each person reading a story or a few poems they've written, and then post the reading online. Maybe add images and music to this recording.

- Create a private or public blog and post the stories and poems.

- Create a newsletter or newspaper of the stories and poems.

- Create a chapbook for each person or a chapbook anthology that includes a few of each person's writing.

- Ask each participant to select one piece of writing he/she is most proud of, and create a broadside of each piece.

Preparing weekly lessons

You know from your own workshops that there are many different ways to teach poetry and storytelling. For a CBL project, some lessons are more appropriate for a particular age group, but many of them can be adapted to fit different groups. You might find it helpful (or required by your teacher) to use a particular template or outline, as least for your first lesson/session in the community. The important thing is to have your craft lesson and writing prompts planned before you head out into the community for your first workshop.

Below is a useful template to help you to start with session (or lesson) design. You may need to alter the template to suit your overview of your CBL project. The idea here is to read about the experience of others and what has worked well for them, but to also make use of your creativity and adapt the structure and details to your preferences and to the needs and skill levels of your participants.

It's important to be flexible when you venture into the community. You may be expecting 15 participants, but the night you show up, only two people attend. This can be disheartening. Remember that your goal is to further develop your understanding of craft and to provide the opportunity to write to anyone who comes to your workshops.

Basic outline for weekly lessons:

1 Introduction of self/team and overview of lesson
2 Content: discuss craft topic (approximately 7 minutes)
3 Model: read samples of craft in a work (approximately 7 minutes)
4 Writing activity (20–30 minutes)
5 Read aloud (15–25 minutes)

Notice that most of the time is spent writing. This is, after all, your purpose: to provide your participants the time, space, and opportunity to write. At your first workshop session it's possible that none of the participants will want to read aloud. They might feel too self-conscious or afraid of not getting it "right."

If you're part of a teaching team, you might alternate who leads the lesson and who assists. If you're assisting, I encourage you to write with the other participants. Sometimes, especially if you're working with children, you might need to encourage them individually. Pick up your pencil and write with them! And read as part of the reading circle when it's time to read.

Anticipations, hopes, challenges

While developing your project overview and lessons, also consider your hopes, not only for the participants but also for yourself. A well-planned CBL project expands not only your academic knowledge, but you grow personally, and you develop a stronger sense of civic responsibility. Some of the structured reflection prompts that follow are intended to help you identify your hopes/outcomes in these three areas (academic, personal, and civic).

Brittany Osbourne worked with fourth graders at an inner-city school in Orlando.

> The first week I conducted my creative writing lesson you'd think I was preparing to defend my thesis rather than teach a group of fourth graders. I was nervous beyond comprehension. Would the students enjoy the lesson? Would they even pay attention long enough for me to teach it? Those questions and loads more swarmed in my mind, so I prepared. Over prepared. I finished my dense lesson on description, knowing it was a poorly wrapped UPS packaged lesson with a destination city called Disaster. When I read the children's stories, I was not surprised that some completely ignored the instruction and meandered away from the writing topic which was supposed to be something like American Idol meets the Ringling Brothers Circus ... don't ask. Over the next few days, I reread my lesson plan and studied the students' writing, desperately trying to diagnose what went wrong and how I could improve it. (Osbourne, 2008).

Wherever you work, you will learn something. You'll learn something about poetry, fiction, or nonfiction, but you will also learn something about yourself. And you will learn something about the value of having a voice. You will learn something about your community and your role in it. You will learn that your talents and knowledge mean something in the real world.

Throughout this book, you will read essays and comments from writers, community members, and community partners who describe the great variety of satisfactions from working in the community. Robert Coles, community activist, author, and child psychiatrist at Harvard University, discusses the satisfactions and "hazards" of service in his book *The Call of Service* (1993). But it is important to note that once you're out there— observing children living in generational poverty or adults with dementia or youth in foster care facilities because no one else wanted them to be aware that there are challenges. Coles identifies some of these as "weariness and resignation," "cynicism," "arrogance, anger, and bitterness," "despair," and "depression (burnout)." These challenges, or "hazards," usually happen when our idealism runs headfirst into reality (pp. ix–x). When our best intentions meet with the stark reality that children living in a homeless shelter might likely live their entire childhoods in shelters, we might experience a great sense of despair.

Now is a good time to think about what might be the greatest challenge for you. Are you nervous when you talk in front of strangers? Do you worry that you'll feel overwhelmed by some of the circumstances of the participants? What if you arrive at the site before any of your team members?

Structured reflection

Personal

1   What do you hope to accomplish during your residency for yourself and your own writing?

2   One of the key elements to community-based learning is the belief that college students learn as much—if not more—than the clients/students at the agency/school where they work. What do you anticipate learning out there? Make a list of what you hope to learn, dividing the list into goals for your 1) writing goals, 2) personal goals, 3) citizenship goals.

   a   Personal goals include those ways in which you might grow as a person. Examples include, able to adapt to unfamiliar settings, develop time management, learn to organize better, etc.

   b   Examples of writing (or academic) goals include, expanding my range of writing subjects, deepening my understanding of the elements of craft, learning to write on the spot rather than waiting for inspiration, etc.

   c   Examples of citizenship goals include, understanding what it means to be part of a democracy, be able to evaluate and advocate for persons living in different situations, become more tolerant of people who are different from me, etc.

Academic

3 When you first started to write, what did it do you for, and can you relate that to what you hope will happen to your participants in the community?

4 Who, what, when, where, how?

  a Who's going? Are you working independently at your site? If not, who else is going with you?

  b What are you going to be doing there?

  c When are you going? What day of the week? What time of day? Are there any days during the semester you will not be able to go that week? If you're working at a public school, are there any school holidays that will interrupt the flow of your residency?

  d Where are you going? Have you at least driven to the site so that you know how to get there?

  e How will you and your group deal with any miscommunications? How will you and your group handle participants who refuse to write?

Civic

5 What citizenship challenges do you anticipate during your CBL project? (Examples include, tolerating people who are different, cooperating with my community partner staff or my peers, compromising on lesson plans, etc.)

6 How do you think people in the community will respond to your presence?

Readings

Mark Powell

Mark Powell is the author of three novels—*Prodigals* (2002), *Blood Kin* (2006), and *The Dark Corner* (2012)—and has received fellowships from the National Endowment for the Arts, the Breadloaf Writers' Conference, and the Collegeville Center for Ecumenical Research. Educated at the Citadel, the University of South Carolina, and Yale Divinity School, he is an assistant professor of English at Stetson University.

The Lawtey Workshop

The long approach to Lawtey Correctional Institute is unsettling as much for its unbroken monotony as anything else. The highway is a plumb line of hot macadam. The slash-pines are in ordered rows. The prison, one of the largest in Florida, sits in the fly speck of Starke, an eye-blink of a town an hour west of St. Augustine, and there is little outside the walls but mobile homes and a railroad, all of it scattered along the edge of a National Guard camp.

Lawtey itself puts one less in mind of a prison than of a sprawling high school. Low cinder block buildings painted institutional yellow. A lot of uniformed people milling around the gate. And razor wire. Roll after roll tangles along the chain-link that bows inward as if shouldering an unbearable weight. It is the only soft shape to be found.

The gate buzzed and I swung it open, walked to a folding table where a man in khakis and a Florida DOC (Department of Corrections) hat sat with a clipboard and a Guardian hand wand. Early fifties, I guessed. A patchy beard and eyes closing down in the corners. I gave the man my name and emptied my pockets, took off my belt buckle and walked through a metal detector. The man handed me what appeared to be a small pager with a large gray button in the center.

"Clip it to your waist," the man said. "There's a little clasp there on the back."

"Panic button?"

"Something happens hold it down for three seconds. Somebody'll come running."

"I'm just here to teach a class," I said.

The man looked up from his clipboard. "I'll be dogged," he said. "I guess you're the guy from Stetson?"

That was January of 2010. A few months earlier the English department chair at Stetson University opened a faculty meeting by reading from a letter requesting help in starting and facilitating a fiction writing workshop at Lawtey Correctional Institute in north Florida. The letter was eloquent and poignant, and before anyone else could speak I asked for it. I wasn't sure exactly what the workshop might entail—in fact, I was new to Florida and had no idea where Lawtey Correctional even was—but the opportunity seemed too intriguing to pass up. That afternoon I began my correspondence with Larry and Reggie, the two men trying to start the class—and plenty of other prison officials. It took the entire fall semester to both hammer out the details and gain clearance from the department of corrections. And in January of the following year our workshop began.

My first shock was the four-hour round-trip drive to Lawtey, long enough that we met for two hours every other week instead of every week as I'd hoped. My second shock was the class itself. I went in, as you do with these things, with absolutely no sense of what to expect. Chris Hazlett, a University of Florida PhD student who was already teaching at Lawtey, accompanied me that first evening. I tried to look stoic. I imagine Chris saw straight through me. But by the end of the night I was at complete ease. I wasn't just at ease, I was hooked. Outside of my own private desires and ambitions, never had I encountered such enthusiasm for fiction, such a blinding desire to write. There's a desperate hungriness etched on the faces of those who have no choice but to write. It speaks as much to ambition, the need for and certainty of recognition, as it does to frailty, the almost equal certainty that nothing will ever come of so much lonely work. Now and again I find that look on the face of some quiet undergraduate who, for half the semester, has sat silently in the corner but now, having turned in her first story, has suddenly been revealed as a writer. That night, I saw that look all over the room.

I threw everything I had at the class. Made copies of stories by Alice Munro and John Cheever and ZZ Packer and Junot Diaz and Flannery O'Connor. Drafted lectures on setting in the work of William Gay or dialogue in Robert Stone. Because of the difficult logistics, we would read a story aloud for 30 or 40 minutes then spend another half hour discussing it. For the last half hour the students read their own work aloud and we made what useful comments we could.

It was wildly revelatory. Abilities varied, so much so that I was sometimes at a loss as to how to approach lectures. There were a couple of writers of the highest order. Others needed help with what we think of as the most basic concepts: what is a first person narrator? Why might the writer choose to use present tense instead of past? But gradually I found that I should approach class just as I approach my workshops at Stetson: with the highest expectations and the understanding that what we are collectively pursuing is art. This wasn't about self-expression. Or maybe: it wasn't *just* about self-expression. I once heard Margaret Atwood say that if you're interested in expressing yourself go stand in a cornfield and scream. If you're interested in writing get to work. We got to work and in our second year decided we wanted some record of it. It was then we began work on what became the first Lawtey fiction anthology. In a mad fit of coalescing, Chris Hazlett and I assembled the work into a scruffy marked-up pile. Along with the text were a number of photographs of original work we used to separate sections.

A bit of an aside here: prison writing, and I mean the actual artifacts, is often found art. To conserve paper men wrote in tiny cryptic print onto note cards and napkins and, in one singularly beautiful instance, the backsides of the sixteen foil rectangles that constitute a complete pack of Big Red chewing gum. It was invigorating work that gradually became maddening. A 90,000-word document had to be typed and line-edited. Outside of visits, my only contact with the class was via US mail. Thus there was something peculiarly antiquated about the revision process. I wanted permission to cut a line or reformat a page and felt trapped in the nineteenth century. But by mid-summer the manuscript was complete. The collection represented, of course, only a tiny portion of the work written in and out of class. But it stands as a testament to the men's two years of hard work. The stories (and occasional poems) are various, at times thrilling, sometimes mournful and elegiac, always moving. But most importantly they are the work of the men. Raw and honest and unsettling, they testify to the intensity of life. Reading and typing these pages often felt like swallowing a flame—I felt if I survived I would be changed on a cellular level, if not somehow purified.

Thanks to the generosity of the Sullivan Creative Writing Program at Stetson—who, I should say, has been ridiculously generous at every step—we self-published the book through the McNally Jackson bookstore in Brooklyn. In August we had a book launch: Little Caesar's pizza and two-liter Cokes. It was a signing party reminiscent of yearbook day in high school, except more rewarding and a lot more fun.

In January, my fifth semester at Lawtey, the prison workshop became a for-credit class for Stetson undergraduates. A 400-level creative writing course called "Creative Outreach," I am now accompanied every other Monday by eight seniors and one very precocious sophomore, all of whom have taken multiple courses in fiction writing and theory. The workshop itself has grown from 16 participants to 35. The Stetson students work in pairs: two Stetson students facilitating a workshop of six or seven inmates. The undergraduates are responsible for writing a syllabus and weekly writing exercises (which they also complete), critiquing the work of the inmates, and making certain that their group runs smoothly. It's invaluable training that serves a very useful end.

In April we will begin to assemble our next anthology. Stetson group leaders will be responsible for editing and introducing their section of the book. So they not only write and teach, they gather and edit. After class we drive to a local sub restaurant and talk about the men and the class and what works and what doesn't. It's the most fun I've ever had as a professor.

So I realize at this point I've made all of this sound somewhat magical—always rewarding, never tiresome—and while my experience at Lawtey has by and large been wonderfully positive, I haven't been completely forthright either. Once the initial buzz of adrenaline and enthusiasm wore off—it took, maybe, three months—I had to fight the two-headed monster of laziness and self-righteousness. There were a few early days I got into my car to drive to Lawtey exhausted from teaching at Stetson and only half-prepared. My feeling was: I've been teaching all day, I'm doing this workshop out of the goodness of my heart, I'll just wing it. I learned quickly how wrong-headed this attitude was. That I would never approach a class at Stetson ill-prepared should have been clue enough. But it took fumbling through a craft discussion to realize—simultaneously, and with a rapidly spreading blush of embarrassment—both how foolish I appeared and how serious the men took the class. It was a humiliating experience, and since then I have made certain never to enter the classroom unprepared.

There is also the negotiation of the department of corrections bureau-cracy. I've found the folks at Lawtey almost uniformly helpful. But that doesn't make the restrictions and rules any less of a burden. My best advice—which came from Chris—always use letterhead, the more official and pompous the better.

Particularly difficult is handling the logistics of the workshop. What is taken for granted in a college classroom—access to paper and pens and computers and copy machines—must be weighed and considered when teaching in prison.

The introduction of undergraduates has also presented a different scope of issues. Seven of the nine students in Creative Outreach are female. The prison population is all-male. I wish I could ignore this, but that simply isn't possible, and one of the things that had to be made explicit at the outset of the course was that the professional nature of our relationships must never be violated. This is tough, especially in a workshop. Stories are confessional. Men work through what are often difficult pasts. The atmos-phere can get charged. Which perhaps is why it's all the more important to acknowledge clear boundaries from the start. That's not to say things are clinical, far from it. But before we can begin to discuss fiction my job is to make certain these discussions take place in an emotionally and psychically safe place. This is new to me. I have developed lasting friendships with any number of students, both undergraduates and inmates, and to have to be conscious of this—to view it as a potential detriment as well as a boon—is something I am learning primarily through trial and error.

What else have I learned? First and foremost: to be flexible and patient. I've always felt it takes a high tolerance of ambiguity to be a writer. It takes as least as much to teach at a prison.

Second, but of equal importance, approach classes at prison with the same purpose and focus as one would carry into any teaching environment. Your mere presence doesn't help anyone. You have to be prepared to do the work. Doing the work has made me a better teacher and writer. It's also made me a more patient and less judgmental person. Lastly, I would stress how gratifying the experience can be. I've had a lot of fun. Working with the men at Lawtey has been (and remains) a great privilege and I value their insight and humor as much as their friendship.

*   *   *

Allen Gee

Allen Gee is an associate professor at Georgia College. He edits fiction and essays for *Arts & Letters*, and his work has appeared in *Ploughshares*, the *Crab Orchard Review*, *Lumina*, *Gulf Coast*, the *Rio Grande Review*, and elsewhere. He's represented by Gail Hochman at Brandt & Hochman, and he's served as the director of the Writers in the Schools (WITS) program at Georgia College for five years.

Linking the Creative Writing Program with the Community

A traditional WITS (Writers in the Schools) program works by placing one professionally trained writer with an entire classroom; the writer might be teaching 25 to 30 students with the support of the class's regular teacher. These arts residencies are often funded by the schools, and have relied upon Title 1 funding if the students are from low-income backgrounds, or if schools will allocate funds to pay the writer from an annual budget. WITS programs frequently train their writers with funding from arts education grants derived from private foundations, or, in some instances, NEA support. I was once fortunate enough to serve as the Director of Development at WITS Houston and thrived upon the sense of purpose each day's work instilled.

I loved Houston, but in 2003 departed to teach creative writing at Georgia College in the rural town of Milledgeville in my wife's home state. By 2006 I became involved with the WITS program that had been set up here by our MFA Director.

The Georgia College model is different, operating on a smaller scale than most non-profit WITS programs. There is a supervising professor, and two graduate students who work in tandem, instructing a class of from ten to 12 undergraduate creative writing tutors. Most importantly, there is a seventh-grade class of 55 students that we work with each Friday, during the fall and spring semesters. The large seventh-grade class is part of a Bill Gates-funded initiative called Early College, which is a seventh- through twelfth-grade public school situated on our campus. This arrangement could easily be substituted, though, with two regular public school classes from any desired grade level, or you easily scale down and work with one regular school class. Our fiscal model is set up like this: the supervising professor's time is considered as part of the faculty member's yearly course load. Our two graduate students include WITS as part of their teaching duties for their stipends, counting it as a class, but they also teach composition or introduction to creative writing, depending upon where they are in their degree progress. Our ten to twelve undergraduate creative writing majors are enrolled in our WITS program as a three credit hour class, which creates revenue for our university. This, you can imagine, justifies the program in many administrators' minds. Each of our undergraduate creative writing tutors works with five to six seventh-grade students at a time; the tutor-to-student ratio is kept low, so as not to overwhelm the undergraduates, and it's more ideal for the seventh graders. Since this structure doesn't depend upon funding from a target school to pay a professionally trained writer, the cost for a school is minimal; the school should be asked to pay for an annual print anthology, which can run from $2,000 to $3,000, but nowadays an online publication page can be produced at virtually no cost; therefore, a WITS program can feasibly occur without a public school having to incur any significant fiscal burden. This model is, in other words, entirely community-minded, drawing foremost upon the resources of the university.

I would not aspire to run a larger program. We have been teaching two seventh-grade classes for eight years now, through the midst of the recession, which demonstrates the strength of our fiscal model. My four years as the supervising professor have led me to fine-tune several aspects, but the people and their contributions have, of course, been more significant than any plan or model.

The supervising professor has to be community-minded, and have a genuine love for creative writing and service-learning. The graduate assistants, too, need to be public-service-minded, and often we have assistants with Peace Corps or Americorps experience. Our graduate students work with our WITS program for two years; one experienced second-year graduate student leads, helping to train the incoming first-year graduate student who assists; knowledge is always being passed on and shared. The two years is part of an overall three year MFA program.

Our undergraduate creative writing major tutors are selected from spring interviews for the following academic year. We look for students who have experience working with younger people, those who desire a future in education, or who are investigating teaching as a career. We have over 120 creative writing majors, so we are normally able to select juniors and seniors, but our main requirement is that the students have taken introduction to creative writing and that they have a passion for creative writing. More than 50 percent of our undergraduate WITS tutors have gone on to enroll in an M.A. in teaching. Several have headed overseas to teach in ESL programs, or they have been accepted to MFA programs. The tutoring they do, and the observations of their work, always result in strong recommendation letters for their academic and professional futures. If a university does not have an undergraduate creative writing major, a WITS class could still easily be conducted with invested English or Education majors. Our WITS class also meets one of the requirements for a senior capstone experiences which helps to assure the longevity of the program.

The WITS class is a year-long one because the pace is steady, not hurried, and because the majority of the seventh-grade students we teach are at-risk, so they deserve our attention from fall to spring. Each Friday, the graduate students meet with the undergraduates from 9 a.m. to 10 a.m. to go over the day's lesson plan and share strategies. Then from 10 a.m. to 11 a.m., each undergraduate meets with their five to six seventh graders. Each group is able to work in a separate classroom, since Fridays allow for more vacant space. While all the creativity is happening, the two graduate assistants are "on call," walking the hallways, glancing into classrooms, or carrying out individual teaching observations. Between the undergraduate tutors and their seventh graders, there is always some sharing time with work read aloud and praised, during the last five or ten minutes. From 11 a.m. to 12 p.m., the graduate students meet with the undergraduate tutors and the supervising professor for an assessment session, where teaching and successes or difficulties are discussed. The supervising professor is always in the building for liability, to help with any discipline issues or emergencies, and the regular seventh-grade teachers and their principal have to be available. Although I make suggestions for improvement, I'm careful to let the graduate students run the class as much as possible, providing them with the sense that the program is also theirs; they have to grow as teachers and administrators, as well.

Our whole year begins with three orientation Fridays, spread out over the first three weeks of the fall semester.

On the first Friday, there are enthusiastic introductions, and then we have three very important "sessions."

In session one, two returning senior mentors—selected undergraduates who have returned to help with the program for a second year—talk with the new undergraduates about what makes an ideal tutor or mentoring figure. This talk covers issues such as behavior, positive versus negative reinforcement for working with seventh graders, and how the tutors should appear and conduct themselves as "role models."

In session two, we go over the syllabus, which has a curriculum mapped out for a year. We want the undergraduate tutors to see how important and necessary planning is for working with a public school. If a college or university wishes to start a new WITS program, WITS Houston will share syllabi and curriculum (WITS Houston heads the WITS Alliance, a national consortium of WITS groups), and online databases are also currently being initiated by several of these WITS organizations. There are resources; a new program never has to feel alone. Here is a sample year's syllabus, in a nutshell:

Fall
8/20: Orientation Day One
8/27: Orientation Day Two
9/3: Orientation Day Three
9/10: First Day of Teaching: Color Poem
9/17: Haiku
9/24: Slam Poetry, with a visit from the performance troupe, Art as an
    Agent for Change
10/1: Flash Fiction
10/8: Flash Fiction Finishing
10/15: Field Trip Pre-writing
10/22: Fall Break, No Class

10/29: Andalusia Field Trip (Flannery O'Connor's home and dairy farm grounds)

11/5: Revision Day

11/12: Couplets and Meter

11/19: Best Choice: undergraduate tutors' selection of the best piece for each student to revise, and nominate best pieces from each group

11/26: Thanksgiving

12/3: Rehearsal Day: students read their work in an auditorium to initiate them to the idea and experience of reading aloud for an audience

Spring

1/14: Go over spring lesson plans/revisions with undergraduate tutors

1/21: Martin Luther King Day poems (We poems, poems that begin with "We")

1/28: Literary Devices

2/4: Symbolism

2/11: Sonnets/Love Poems

2/18: Dialogue, Perhaps leading to flash drama

2/25: Revision Day

3/4: Last Revision Day

3/11: Field Trip Pre-Writing

3/18: Field Trip to Lockerly Arboretum

3/25: Georgia College Spring Break

4/1: Rehearsal Planning/ Early College Spring Break

4/8: In-class Rehearsal, reading individual best works

4/15: Early College testing

4/22: Auditorium Rehearsal, Dr. Gee leading

4/29: Dress Rehearsal, Public Reading at 6:30 p.m. in the auditorium, reception afterwards

Through trial and error, we have learned that poetry is the best way to start and quickly build trust and good working relationships with our seventh graders; this is why the majority of the lessons in our syllabus are organized around poetry. When teaching fiction, we invoke flash fiction lessons, since young writers like the suddenness and the quick turns or leaps that often help to make the short form dramatic and successful. We tend to lean away from essay writing because we've found that not many seventh graders are poised to write memoirs, but who can say if another program hasn't discovered a cool way to teach it? The most important aspect when planning the syllabus is to consider the end results, which for us are a spring reading and an anthology. The spring reading highlights the hard work and creativity of all of the undergraduate tutors and their seventh-grade students; our program shows its best face, so to speak. And we have learned that poetry and flash fiction lend themselves to shorter readings, which are best when writers are reading to a large audience for the first time. Not only are poems and flash fiction easier to practice for students, but these shorter readings are also more appreciated by listeners.

During the third orientation session, we discuss the anthology. At WITS Houston, I frequently heard that there is nothing more meaningful or rewarding for a student to see his or her own work and name for the first time in print. The importance of the anthology, print or online, for any WITS program can't be over-emphasized; the anthology is the truest end result of a program, so it should be given ample time and attention. Building in significant revision time is one of the most, if not the most, important issues that should be considered when planning the year's syllabus.

To end the first orientation day, we have the undergraduates sign up for observation hours. During the next two weeks, they'll introduce themselves to the regular seventh-grade English teachers and then sit in and observe a full class period of activities, so they have a better understanding of the students they'll be working with and what their writing skills are. We also assign mentor groups on this first Friday, dividing the undergraduate tutors, placing them with one of the two returning senior mentors. Then they participate in get-to-know-you activities, before the day closes with having them write in "teaching journals" that will be kept for the year.

The second orientation Friday starts by having our two senior mentors take the new undergraduates through the logistics of a normal teaching Friday. This is session four, and no topic or question is insignificant, from cell phone and bathroom policies, to waiting for students or how to communicate with the regular seventh-grade teachers. Session five addresses individual classroom management; we discuss discipline, employing a three strikes model. If a student is disruptive or refuses to participate, or if they are rude or problematic in any unacceptable way to an undergraduate tutor more than twice, they are removed and sent to meet with the Early College principal. We let our undergraduate tutors know that they will be challenged, and that their limits will be tested, but discipline problems are not the norm. The majority of our seventh graders look forward all week to their Friday creative writing; they develop great respect and admiration for their undergraduate mentors.

To help foster this anticipation, we stress the importance of time management; this includes the importance of having materials and a prepared teaching strategy, as well as needing to challenge students by encouraging them and not being afraid to ask them to accomplish more. For session six, I like to have two new seventh graders drop by (selected by their regular teachers), and I'll work through a short poetry lesson with them (color poems or haiku), just to show the undergraduate mentors about how to ask prompting questions and to stress the importance of encouragement and praise. I tell the seventh graders when they've used a great word or found a unique way to describe something. Above all, I emphasize to our undergraduates how this might be the first time that a teacher has spoken to the seventh graders about their creative writing.

For the penultimate activities on that second day, the undergraduate students break into their mentor groups, and the two senior mentors teach a sample lesson plan and answer any and all questions. Then we pass out the fall semester's lesson plans. We emphasize that the plans are only a starting point; each undergraduate tutor is encouraged to find their own models or examples for each week's lesson, and they can choose different delivery models, using Xeroxes, the Internet, or reading aloud. We close again with journal writing.

The third orientation day begins with having the undergraduate mentors provide their feedback from their observations of the seventh grade teachers' classes. We want for there to be an understanding of how our creative writing lessons can best fit in with what and how the seventh graders are learning. The undergraduates then practice, teaching sample lessons to their mentor groups, followed by our giving out classroom assignments and their seventh-grade students' names. The graduate assistants follow up with a free- time activities segment, showing the undergraduate tutors how to challenge all the seventh graders by asking them to compile word banks, brainstorm for similes and metaphors, introduce them to new vocabulary words, and then use these creative bits and pieces in their poetry or fiction. This segment also emphasizes how the Friday hour with the seventh graders should always be enjoyable but vigorous; the tutors should know that there is always something else that they can be doing, or that an hour is never enough. Exciting things can happen, if the right atmosphere is being created. At week four, the undergraduate tutors start working in classrooms with the seventh graders. They have learned enough to begin well, but it's a given that they will learn more.

There are two field trips on the syllabus. We partner with a Georgia College biology professor who helps design lesson plans focusing on nature writing—like, say, the imagined life cycle of a plant, the voice of a tree or a fossil, describing the anatomy of a pond, or an hour from an insects' points of view. Collaboration is always helpful, invigorating, and best for the students; the burden doesn't always have to be on the WITS supervising professor to create an engaging hour in the classroom. It's also intriguing for us to see how different students behave and react when they're being asked to write in other places. The pre-writing for these lesson plans can stem from research in books to watching videos. There can be brainstorming, drafting, listing, free association, word play, or idea making. It can be silly or serious. I tend to favor literary writing, becoming the most enthusiastic when a young writer surprises us with their own new or unique way of seeing or expressing something. In fact, I have been fortunate, becoming used to seeing how capable young writers are of creating their own brand of high art.

Here is a poem by Isaiah Person, one of our Early College seventh graders, that exemplifies this:

The Sky is the Ocean

As the steamy sun
approaches
I see my
face in
hollow water.
Cold winds slap
my face. The
green grass makes
a crackling noise
as wind whips
by it. The black
spider crawls
through the silky
blades of grass. As I
look at the sky
I see an
ocean, but
really, it's not
moving. As
I look, the sky
is on the ground
and the ocean
is in the sky.

Isaiah's poem, its use of metaphor, was written without intrusive prompting or heavy-handed revision; the idea for the poem was all his. For the last three years, though, we have asked a few additional students from our MFA program to volunteer during the 10 a.m. to 11 a.m. class hour for set aside revision days. These graduate students provide yet more one-on-one time, working with those seventh graders who are struggling, who our undergraduate mentors have identified as their weakest writers. The graduate students are able to quickly assess where the seventh graders' poems or stories are, and then ask questions to help guide the students toward greater clarity or specificity. Of course, there might be greater ambiguity or outrageousness to revise for, if that's the aesthetic.

Our collaboration with the seventh-grade teachers differs from some traditional WITS programs because the regular classroom school teachers can't possibly be in ten to 12 rooms at once with five to six seventh-grade students; our undergraduate mentors truly have to make the classes happen. And, although some WITS organizations offer professional development for public school teachers, that's an endeavor we haven't taken on; we provide teachers with our syllabi, so that they know what our lesson plans are, and so that the teachers can provide additional creative writing time for the seventh graders during other days if they wish (if this matches with their curriculum needs), but we don't mandate that the regular teachers actively participate or circulate from room to room to constantly check on their students. Most often, the regular teachers use the WITS hour for planning time, or their own grading.

If I was to initiate a new program now, I would probably work with just one class, emphasizing quality over quantity. You need to: identify who your creative writing tutors will be whether they're MFA students or undergraduates or a combination of both; decide what grade you want to work with; design your syllabus and train your tutors carefully; and then, once you have gained the support of your college or university, take the leap. It's much more advantageous to contact an existing WITS organization, and join with other community-minded creative writing proponents, before the first class is taught.

Approaching a new public school is actually not that difficult. Most schools are eager for literary arts programs; keep in mind that you'll be offering an enrichment activity that they will probably not otherwise have. The easiest first contact to make is with an English teacher, simply emailing or telephoning, and the teacher will help arrange a meeting with the principal or other administrators. If you have the program mapped out, the school will view you as professional and be more accommodating, and the issue of budgeting for an anthology can, as I've already mentioned, be avoided by having an online version.

The end of the year reading is the final public link. Friends and family of all the students are invited. Each student takes the stage, reads their best work, and receives applause. You can see on the sample syllabus that adequate rehearsal time needs to be figured in. We make sure to invite university department chairs, deans, and other administrators, as well. Planning is again foremost; the auditorium has to be reserved months ahead. University communications generates publicity. The regular teachers need to know the date and time far in advance so that they can help to notify parents and others. I have enjoyed making the reading more of an "event" by having students recite poems as a group by writers such as Gwendolyn Brooks or Elizabeth Bishop, in-between the readings of their own work. We have also taken the best student MLK Day poem and had the entire seventh-grade class read the work; it's a celebratory evening, featuring, most of all, students' talent and achievement. And each time there is a reading, each time when pride and the sense of accomplishment can be seen on a students' faces, you know once again that any efforts taken to build or continue a program have been worthwhile, all of your time well-spent, the initial leap worth taking.

CHAPTER FOUR

Taking the Leap

Creative writing and life experiences

You may be planning on working at a public school, nursing home, foster-care facility, prison, or shelter. Whatever your participants' current situation and background, it's a good idea to conduct some research to understand the link between creative writing and their experiences. In your research find out about the specific site you'll be working at, the demographics of the participants, and the larger social issues that touch the lives of those you'll be working with.

Whether you'll be working with young children, youth, or adults, many of them might lack the self-confidence to attempt to write anything. They might need constant encouragement. They might need to sit in the back corner and not show their writing to anyone, including you. They might have been waiting their entire lives for someone to hand them a pencil and a blank piece of paper, thrilled that you want to see and hear their stories.

Apprehension, resistance, fear

Even in a course titled "Creative Writing in the Community" or "Poets in the Schools," you might have some apprehension about leading creative writing workshops on your own, or even with a small group of classmates. You might be surprised to know how often your own teachers are anxious or apprehensive at the beginning of each semester—even those who have taught for decades. You might be flat-out excited and ready to go to work. You might feel unprepared. All of these feelings are normal.

In traditional workshop courses you are usually not required to take a leadership role in your community. For many students this added CBL assignment to a *workshop* may seem far too time-consuming. You might worry that you won't get enough attention to your own work if you and your classmates are conducting a CBL project. Sometimes students in my workshop classes resist this assignment so much that they drop the course, which is unfortunate. Some are so nervous and/or resistant that I pair them with a student who has already completed one semester-long CBL project. But, every semester when I require CBL and I ask at the end of the term if I should eliminate this requirement, 99 percent of the students tell me I should keep the assignment in the course. They tell me that even though they hated the idea at first, and could not imagine giving up any of their time to meet this requirement, it has the best experience they've had in a college class. They tell me I should *always* require it. Not just because it teaches them about poetry and storytelling, but because it helps them consider many more options about their futures. CBL helps students consider career possibilities they had never considered.

Brittany, the student I mentioned in an earlier chapter, reflected on her first session:

> I recognized two things. My long-winded lesson plan focused too heavily on teaching the fiction elements, and I glossed over a writing assignment that the kids could relate to. Because of this oversight many of the students wrote and drew about what they wanted. What startled me most about their work was that they were either writing or drawing about each other or things they heard or experienced in their community, some of it good, some of it bad, but none of it had anything to do with elephants or clowns auditioning to become the next new star. They were bored and inattentive. I knew I had to shift my teaching approach.[1]

It's quite natural to doubt yourself after your first visit, and that's part of the learning process. You learn to teach in the same way you learn any skill—trial and error, or trial and success. Reflecting each week after your session will allow you to examine your approaches. You are serving, and you are learning.

CBL provides a way for you, as a creative writer, to share your craft with others in your community. And it allows you the experience of being in the world, of seeing the world up close, of watching and learning things you would not learn within the walls of a classroom.

One of the effects of CBL is that you begin to see writing in a larger context, as part of society's collective story. Getting a college education is not just about the academics, but also about learning to be engaged in your community. CBL educates the whole person, the whole writer.

Service-learning vs. volunteering

You are not simply volunteering. Volunteerism is great, and in fact, one of the long-term effects of doing a CBL project is discovering the importance of community involvement. CBL means that you are using what you learn in your course for the purpose of bettering your community. While community service and service-learning projects have some things in common (providing a service free of charge and being engaged in your community), service-learning is directly linked to the content of your course.

Service-learning history

Service-learning has gained momentum in higher education over the past couple of decades, connecting classroom learning to real-world problems. According to an article in *The Chronicle of Higher Education*, service-learning "was kick-started in 1985, when several college presidents decided to counter the popular image of college students as disaffected, materialistic, and self-absorbed. That year the presidents of Brown, Georgetown, and Stanford Universities started Campus Compact to promote—and publicize—volunteer work on campuses" (Ashburn, 2009, pp. A25–A26). Campus Compact has, of course, grown; in fact, more than 1,100 colleges and universities are members. "Membership has grown by an average of 70 campuses per year over the past five years, a trend that reflects both an increased commitment to the civic purposes of higher education and greater awareness of the value of our work" (Campus Compact, n.d.).

Obviously, nonprofit agencies need volunteers to meet their needs and the needs of their clients. As a college student, you are learning an academic discipline and need to understand how your discipline applies to the world around you. Higher education becomes not only the source for academic knowledge, but an advocate of democracy, of citizenship.

Service-learning in other disciplines

Nursing students might apply their classroom knowledge in the community by educating families living in poverty about well-care or providing basic well-care checkups. Business students might design fund-raisers, and marketing students might develop promotional materials for nonprofit agencies. Sociology students might learn about the details of research by working with the local homeless shelter. The students design research methods, holding focus groups and interviewing homeless people living in the woods. With the results of their research local social service agencies can better serve the homeless population. English composition students might tutor children in after school programs.

Service-learning in various creative writing classes and programs

College faculties around the country have designed different types of CBL projects for their students. Some of these programs are long-standing, others are more recent, others depend entirely on funding, which in higher education can be a challenge. David Hassler is the director of the Wick Poetry Center at Kent State University. Professor Hassler developed a Poetry in the Schools course, which is similar to the CBL project that I'm guiding you through in this book. Allen Gee at Georgia State College and University also has developed a program which he details in his essay in Chapter 3. Julia Kasdorf designed a Creative Writers in the Community course for the MFA program at Pennsylvania State University.

Other teachers have found different types of service projects to teach creative writing to their students, like collecting oral histories at local nursing homes or writing and making books for orphanages in third world countries. Creative nonfiction writers might use service as the immersion experience that students will use as the basis for the essays they write in class.

Before I developed a course that focused entirely on CBL, I integrated CBL projects into my creative writing workshop classes. In addition to the traditional workshop—distributing their original work for class critique—students work in small groups and lead creative writing sessions at various locations throughout our community. This book was borne of that integration.

Perhaps you are in a course focused entirely on CBL and its impact on you as a writer, thinker, and community member. Or you might be in a creative writing workshop course, and, if so, you will most likely spend most of your class time discussing the original work of your peers. In order to articulate what is working and what is not working in any given piece of writing, you need to not only know the terminology for discussing your peers' works, you also need to fully understand how each element functions within the piece. The best way to learn something, to really synthesize it into your writing process is to explain and describe it to someone else.

Community partner staff as co-educators

If you have encountered too many hurdles in getting your CBL project going, you may need to get your teacher involved to help move the process along. Sometimes students in my classes choose a site on their own (rather than one I have pre-arranged) and discover how very long it can take to get approvals, not only waiting on their applications and background checks, but also waiting on approvals and paperwork from administration who have the ultimate say in allowing college students to work with their clients for a few weeks.

Some agencies may require a year-long commitment from all volunteers. In cases like this, it's possible that your teacher might be able to talk with administration at your site about how service-learning works, and suggest that the agency allows you to conduct your semester-long CBL project there with the added incentive that your teacher will be able to provide them another student or group of students the following semester.

At UCF, since we have a Service-Learning Program with a director who supports faculty across the university, the director will go with the faculty member and give a short presentation, showing them the projects that started out as a one-semester project but have turned into sustainable projects over several years.

Even without a service-learning director, your teacher might reach out to the agency and discuss the possibility of a short-term project. In fact, your teacher will most likely want to be in contact with the agency staff to ensure a successful CBL project. Links to service-learning forms are located in Appendix A of this book that ask for the community partner's signature so that the partner knows and understands your intentions and goals, and so that you understand what the agency expects from you. You should make sure that you, your teacher, and your community partner all agree on the project.

Structured reflection

Personal

1 Describe your initial reaction to the CBL requirement. Uncertain? Anxious? Hopeful? Excited? Perhaps you have been involved in community service for a long time; perhaps this is your first go at it. How do you perceive this project as being different than other volunteering or service projects?

Academic

2 Locate and read one novel, collection of stories, or memoir about the environment in which you're working. Before reading the book, discuss why you chose the one you did.
3 How is creative writing an art?

Civic

4 Locate the website of your community partner. Describe the agency's mission in your own words, noting the demographics of the participants.

5 Locate statistics and information on the demographics of people you are working with. For example, if you're working at a shelter for the homeless, find information on your state's homeless population. If you're working at school, how many of them receive free lunch? What is the average cost of a home in that area? What are the hindrances to the education of the children who attend that particular school? If you're working with the elderly, how much does it cost to live in an assisted living facility? Who pays for the person to be in the facility? If you're working at a foster-care facility how are the youth/children referred there? How long do they stay? Here are some national organizations where you can find statistics and information about specific populations in the U.S.:

a National Institute for Mental Health

b Bureau of National Statistics

c Bureau of Prisons

d National Coalition for Literacy

e National Literacy Project

f U.S. Department of Education

g National Foster Care Coalition

h National Coalition for the Homeless

6 How might your project differ if you were working with a different population?

Reading

David Hassler

David Hassler is an award-winning author and poet, and director of the Wick Poetry Center at Kent State University. His poetry collection *Red Kimono, Yellow Barn* (2005) was awarded Ohio Poet of the Year 2006. His nonfiction works include the play, *May 4th Voices* (2013), based on the Kent State Shootings Oral History Project; *Growing Season: The Life of a Migrant Community* (Harwood and Hassler, 2006); and *A Place to Grow: Voices and Images of Urban Gardeners* (Hassler and Gregor, 1998).

He is also co-editor of *Learning by Heart: Contemporary American Poetry about School* (1999) and *After the Bell: Contemporary American Prose about School* (2007).

The Prayer Wheel

The unicycle

The unicycle my grandfather bought me for my twelfth birthday had a cracked, red vinyl seat and a wide tire. He found it used at Eddie's Bike Shop. It was the only present I wanted that August my mother was in the hospital. I learned to ride the unicycle by leaning against my father's station wagon with both feet on the pedals, then pushing off, leaning forward, and pedaling to keep my balance.

I practiced every day while my mother was in the hospital. I rode around Leppo's trashcans and Bobby's basketball hoop. I rode through the streets of our neighborhood, while my friends ran alongside me cheering, timing my ride with a stopwatch.

A month later, the afternoon we were waiting to go to my mother's funeral, I rode my unicycle, dressed in coat and tie, in circles on our driveway. My father, brother, and grandparents were in the house. No one came out to tell me that people didn't ride unicycles at times like this. At that moment, all I could think about was pedaling my unicycle.

That memory of my unicycle and odd sense of calm in the driveway would come to mind years later, and I would feel confused: guilty, as if I had behaved improperly, but somehow good, proud of the skill I had learned, as if riding my unicycle then was something necessary, something I needed to do.

In my mid-twenties, after returning from a year in Japan, I felt my grief for my mother resurface. I had no balance. I couldn't go forward with my life. I needed to speak about my mother in order to reclaim her. My most vivid and persistent memory, the one I could not stop playing over and over again in my mind, was of riding my unicycle in our driveway, which I connected somehow to the prayer wheels I had seen while traveling in Asia.

I learned that prayer wheels are usually placed outside of Buddhist temples. The wheels vary in size and material. Some are made of wood and painted with bright-colored emblems. Before entering a temple, one inscribes a prayer on a piece of paper, attaches it to a peg on the wheel and spins it. By spinning the wheel, you animate your prayer. Other wheels are large metal drums, inside of which can be thousands of small slips of paper printed with mantras. The most common of which is "*Om Mani Padme Hum*," praying for the "peace and prosperity of the planet." Some mantras are printed on a prayer roll, a small, coiled sheet that looks like the paper roll on an adding machine.

In some Tibetan and Nepalese villages, giant prayer wheels are placed in streams like water mills, so that the wheels continue to turn all day and night, praying incessantly. Or they are placed on giant posts held high above a village, like windmills turning in the wind, blessing the village. One doesn't have to read the prayers inside the wheel. It's a mechanical form of prayer. Though I did not know what I was doing at 12, pedaling my unicycle, I was a prayer wheel, praying for my mother to see me.

I cannot tell my story of teaching poetry to students without telling the story of the prayer wheel. What I lost as a child was set in motion and comes back to me now in new, unexpected ways every time I walk into a classroom. I see myself in my students, and they know that I will listen. We offer each other a kind of recognition, a listening eye.

Reaching to a sky of soba

I worry about what I'll say to the fifth-grade class at St. Sebastian School in Akron. They are my first assignment for the Ohio Arts Council as a Poet-in-the-Schools. I assume these students are growing up with electronic teaching aids and interactive computers, their lives immersed in media. Will they be wired differently? Will we speak the same language, be able to listen and respond to each other? Can I have an experience with these kids that will measure up to my memory of fifth grade?

My fifth-grade teacher, Mrs. Kouba, had the softest voice I'd ever heard. She told us listening was a skill—it was something we needed to learn. I remember at my mother's funeral she walked up to me and said in nearly a whisper, "If you ever need me, David, I'll be here for you." Once, in our fifth-grade class she put us all in a circle and told us to close our eyes. We took turns walking around, tapping the heads of those we loved. I remember hearing her footsteps, waiting for her to come to me. Years later, I realized she must have tapped all our heads.

Now when I walk into Ms. Brown's fifth-grade class, the students crowd around me. They want to know how tall I am and if my hair is real. I hold out my hands to measure their heads. I tell them I'm eight-feet tall. "Wow!" one boy says, "the tallest man in the world is only eight six!" "Well," I say, "he's my father." He frowns, pulls back, and then smiles.

I've lied, but I haven't lost his trust. I have reflected back to him his own wonder, given him an "emotional truth." Without realizing it, I've set a good tone in class, one of trust, respect, and playfulness, a feeling between us that the Japanese call good *kimochi*. Before I read them poems about my experience living in Japan and teaching English, I ask if anyone knows any foreign words. Many of the students raise their hands. I ask them to say these words without telling the class their meanings. We practice pronouncing the words, feeling the way they shape our mouths, then guess at what they mean, sometimes agreeing that the sound conveys the meaning. Then I take the words *ugly* and *beautiful*, and ask them to say each word in a way opposite of its meaning. I demonstrate. They laugh and giggle, wooing each other: "you're so uuugly!"

Before I read my poem about eating soba, they try to guess what soba is. I explain it's a long noodle in a big bowl of broth; when you eat it you can slurp as loud as you want, and the air cools the noodle between your lips. The louder you slurp, I tell them, the greater the compliment to the chef. They giggle again. We all practice slurping.

I tell them a raw egg in a bowl of soba is called a "Full Moon," because it looks like the full moon reflected in water. And if you want an egg in your soup, you order a "Full Moon Soba." I say the Japanese language is full of such beautiful images and expressions. Then a girl raises her hand: "But in our country we order our eggs 'sunny-side up!'" "That's great," I say, laughing at myself for being deaf all these years to that expression. I tell them that when I arrived in Japan, I couldn't speak Japanese, but when I ate soba, I felt fluent. Then I read my poem, "Eating Soba:"

> I speak your language when I eat—
> the silence of steam and scent
> rising to me; red pepper, ginger, and soy.
> This bowl's heat in my hands.
> I snap apart chopsticks,
> break the yoke of the raw egg
> they call Full Moon that drifts
> in the center as though in a pond.
> I pull the soba noodles to my mouth,
> un-making their long strings
> and hiss. This is the sound
> of eating soba, sucking in air,
> loud and energetic.
> I hear wood rasp and tap
> inside the bowls as they are drained
> and clacked down on the counter empty.
> Customers come and go through
> the heat and steam of these small
> kitchen shops, ordering soba,
> "soba o-kudasai!"
>
> I bow over your bowl
> your body, your broth.
> These are my hands that hold you.
> This is the sound of my lips, warm
> breathing you in
> saying soba!

When I finish, one boy, who the teacher tells me later has never spoken in class, raises his hand: "Could you say the sky is a bowl of soba?" I hear his question and I am thrilled. "Yes!" I say, not expecting him to go on. But he does: "Then the sun is a raw egg floating in it!" There is an audible gasp. Another boy shoots up his hand, squirming in his seat, impatient to release his idea. "And trees are chopsticks!" he shouts. The class applauds. Heads turn to look out the window, then back at me.

Perched on the edge of their seats, the students listen to each other, one idea sparking another, their hands waving in the air. They wait for me to call on them, one student speaking at a time. They are all natural, respectful critics, applauding lines they know feel good.

At one point I say: "Do you guys know you're making incredible metaphors?!" They don't care. "Yeah, we know we're making metaphors," one boy says. It doesn't matter what it's called. They aren't concerned about a literary term, what meaning might be ascribed. They're in the moment, fishing the lower layers of consciousness, listening for the emotional truth of the image. They don't try to see what's down there before they pull it up. It tugs on their lines and their hands shoot up. They dictate their poem to me, and I write it on the board:

Reaching to a Sky of Soba

The sky is a bowl of soba.
The sun is a raw egg floating in it.
Trees are chopsticks.
And clouds are steam rising above.
Planets are onions.
The moon is a bump at the bottom of the bowl.
Stars are spices.
The Milky Way is a row of bowls.
Earthquakes break up the noodles,
their rumbling is slurping.
Our mouths are Black Holes breathing it in.
God is the chef.
Meteors are coins we throw down to pay.
The universe is a giant bowl of soba.
We keep eating and eating until the last explosion.
When the universe ends, our bowl is empty.

The bell rings, their hands still reaching in the air, one boy pleading: "I have two! I have two!" The room is a force field, its energy palpable. When we rise from our seats, all of us, that day, stand eight-feet tall.

Two red marking pencils

"No one perhaps has ever felt passionately towards a lead pencil," begins Virginia Woolf's essay, "Street Haunting: A London Adventure" (1930). But today, I do. I feel passionate about one, perhaps as passionate as Virginia Woolf felt seventy years ago strolling through the streets of London to purchase her lead pencil. Only I'm not looking for an adventure; my pencil is not a pretext to go street rambling. I'm in a suburb of Dayton, Ohio this November afternoon, and I need a red marking pencil—not to mark my students' papers with red circles and slashes, as mine were once marked, but to proof the pages of my manuscript, an anthology of poems about school.

I imagine Virginia Woolf setting out on her early winter evening ramble, as I drive down Far Hills Avenue, past feeder streets that lead to a Macaroni Grill, an Applebees, and Damon's, past the bright-lit green oasis of a BP Mini Store. These are not the lamplit streets of Virginia Woolf's London, nor is there a "champagne brightness" in the air, nor have I stepped out from "the solitude of one's own room." I've taught all day at the Miami Valley School, listening to my students read their poems, and now I'm anxious to begin my own work. I feel the excitement I felt as a teenager buying my first car. This is a turning point in my life. This little red marking pencil promises to take me places.

I pull into a CVS pharmacy, and the girl behind the register says she thinks the Krogers supermarket at the end of the strip mall might have these pencils. As I step into the bright fluorescent light of Krogers, I see two ladies who appear to work there, hanging out by the front registers. One of them flicks her wrist, says "aisle five," and returns to her conversation. There, in aisle five, hanging on the shelf at eye level, is a packet of two red: Colorific Marking Pencils. And only 99 cents!

Virginia Woolf might have been able to purchase just a single pencil from a stationer's shop in The Strand, but I know I'll never find a packet with only one pencil. So I grab the packet and walk up to the front registers. I pass through the funnel of magazine racks, gum, and candy shelves hanging with bags of chips and nuts—any last minute, spontaneous purchase a shopper might want to make. Unlike Woolf, I don't see everything "miraculously sprinkled with beauty," and these are not the shores of Oxford Street whose "night cast up nothing but treasure." I see that Hillary Clinton on the cover of *Talk Magazine* is going to "Tell All." And Tom Cruise and Nicole Kidman have an exclusive interview about their newest film. And there's the blotched, teary face of Elizabeth Taylor, whom I've seen in checkout lines for as long as I've been shopping.

But today there's no one in line to hold me up, and I'm not interested in these treasures. The only other customer is a woman in the aisle next to me, her shopping cart filled to the brim. The man behind the register, probably about my age, in his mid-thirties, is waiting for me to hand him my purchase. I place it on the conveyor belt—one 99-cent packet of red pencils. Nothing more. No six pack of diet cola to go with it, or party-size bag of tortilla chips, or gallon of milk.

"That's all you need today?" asks the check-out guy. I say yes, that's all and smile back at him. He's in no hurry to ring up my purchase. He looks at the packet and then at me. "So are you a teacher?" he asks, probably thinking of his own school days, his papers handed back to him screaming with red x's and arrows and a big number or letter grade at the top.

"Yes, I'm a teacher."

"What do you teach?" he asks.

I was hoping he wouldn't ask me that. I know how often the mention of my job prompts a long explanation and then a conversation in which I hear of someone's poetry experience in third or fourth grade, and how they memorized and will recite for me now the poem they had to learn. I usually enjoy these conversations, but today I just want to begin my proofing. I already have a coffee shop picked out. I tell the cashier that I teach poetry in schools all over Ohio to encourage students to write their own poems, and that my job is sponsored by the Ohio Arts Council.

He's not heard about my job before. "Tell me a poem," he says, smiling.

I know he's asking me to show him what I value. Not to prove that I'm a poet, but to show him my treasure. He's holding my red pencils and turns his back to the register, leaning lightly against the drawer, and says again, "Come on, recite me a poem. I'd like to hear a poem."

The cashier in the line next to ours, who is still ringing out her customer with the loaded cart, pauses to look over at me. I think they have a right to hear a poem. My job, after all, is funded mostly through tax-payers' money.

I think of my shortest poem, "Morning Ride on the Yamanote Line," about riding the trains in Tokyo each morning to work. A long title, but a short poem. I recited it once in a parade in downtown Cleveland for the opening of the Rock-n-Roll Hall of Fame Museum. With five other poets I marched behind the Pinball Wizard float, while people dressed as giant silver balls roller skated around others dressed as bumpers and flaps. We poets stepped right up to the crowd along the street and recited our poems to anyone within earshot, shouting out our words, as people cupped their ears and leaned forward.

But now I worry this cashier won't like my poem. And though I know it by heart, I worry I might forget a word and freeze in the middle.

Instead, I ask, "Would you like to hear a poem from one of my students?"

"Sure, let's hear it." He crosses his arms in front of his chest and narrows his eyes, as though he might, at any moment, close them.

I tell him that this poem is called, "Lilac City," written by a second grader in Lima, Ohio. The cashier nods, without saying a word. I explain that it was the first poem this student wrote, after several weeks of my residency. The teacher had warned me that this girl might never speak in class. But one day, after we had filled the board with new names for spring, she wrote this short, little poem and read it aloud to the entire class:

I'm going tulip crazy in this lilac city.
Dandelion faces smiling all around me.
I'm going daisy crazy in this mud-delicious world.

I finish and wait for his response. "Thanks," he says, smiling. He swipes my packet across the light that reads the bar codes. "That's a pretty cool job you have."

The other cashier turns around. She's been listening with her back to us. "Wow, if that's a second grader, imagine what she'll be writing in tenth grade!"

My cashier hands me my pencils, and I suddenly feel like I'm in no hurry at all. I want to ask him to tell me about his experience with poetry in school. Maybe he'd like to hear another poem. This time I'll recite "Morning Ride on the Yamanote Line." But he appears content to have heard just three lines from a second grader he'll never meet in Lima, Ohio.

Perhaps when he returns home from his shift, he'll tell himself the story of his encounter with me and of this second-grader's poem. Just as Virginia Woolf, walking home, could tell herself the story of her stroll through the streets of London, her encounters and moments of perception, to give herself the illusion that she was not "tethered to a single mind," but could "put on briefly for a few minutes the bodies and minds of others."

I give the cashier a dollar and some change. He gives me a few pennies back. As I walk beyond the bagging station, I see Mrs. Priest by the shopping cart area. She's a third-grade teacher at the Miami Valley School. She's talking to someone, another teacher, perhaps. Or a parent or friend. She's smiling the way I've seen her smile with her students. I consider going over to say hello, but instead, just hold up my red marking pencils and wave. In a moment I'll settle into my favorite table at the coffee shop to proof my poems, just as I imagine Virginia Woolf returning to her room with "the china bowl and the brown ring on the carpet" to examine her pencil and settle into the comfort of her old self.

General Sheridan

In Somerset, Ohio, a statue of General Sheridan, a civil war general who came from this once-frontier town, stands in the center of the traffic circle where State Route 22 and Route 5 intersect. In his time, he fought for the abolition of slavery, for creating a proper law and order in our country. Now the traffic going east and west and north and south must slow down and circle around this statue covered in a thick, green patina. He waves his hat, while his horse rears up. He looks as though he would leap over the town and away, if he could break loose of his stone pedestal.

But General Sheridan is going nowhere, as are most of the children who live in this Appalachian town in southeastern Ohio, whose families are fighting to hold onto their family farms or their houses in town in need of repair. After having taught in many suburban communities, whose middle-class families can afford unique experiences for their children all year long, I feel Somerset Elementary needs me and will not forget me when I leave.

In other communities I often have trouble scheduling my residency between the school's many events. In one school, I remember packing up to leave, just as an inspirational rock band arrived and began setting up their huge amplifiers and speakers in the gym. I could hear the walls shaking to their bass beat and saw the whole school filing into the gym clapping their hands. Hadn't we just heard the quiet voices of third graders reading their poems earlier that afternoon in that gym? And now this would surely shake loose and sweep away any of those lingering thoughts and impressions. The third graders in that school carried large, bulky day planners, their after-noons and evenings as tightly packed with tennis lessons, French tutoring, and homework assignments, as their parents' days were scheduled with meetings.

Here in Somerset, this isn't the case. Mrs. Nelson, the third-grade teacher, tells me these kids have no special events scheduled before or after me—I am it. I arrive at their school, an old three-story, redbrick building, with red and yellow tulips planted around the flagpole in the spring of 1999. It is just a week after the tragedy at Columbine High School, where two high school students in a suburban, middle-class community, shot and killed twelve students and a teacher before killing themselves. We are all talking about this tragedy and feeling its effects even here in this rural area of Ohio.

I tell the students that the Chinese word for poetry is written by combining two characters: *word* and *temple*. Perhaps our poems will make a shelter, a *word temple* for our memories and feelings. I want our poems to offer healing words. I don't care so much about their literary quality, but rather, what energy will be released when we write and speak them. For there is no prayer wheel spinning its blessing over this town. Only an old gas station with its two full-service pumps and its Marathon sign slowly turning on its pole, and, of course, the cars steadily circling around the statue of General Sheridan.

I tell the students that in Japan it's not a custom to honor generals with statues. Instead, I remember the statue of the famous dog, Hachiko. I tell them that all the schoolchildren know the story of Hachiko—how Hachiko waited in front of a train station in Tokyo for his master to return home from work every day, and continued to return to the station to wait faith-fully for ten years after his master died. The Japanese tell this story to their children, so they will grow up to be faithful and persevering. I read my poem about Hachiko and tell the students that I often felt like Hachiko, waiting for something, though I didn't know what, to return to my life.

I say you can write a poem dedicated to someone or something you care about—a friend, a parent, a teacher, or even for General Sheridan.

One third-grade boy wants to dedicate every line of his poem to his mom and dad. But when he finishes, he can't read his poem aloud. Mrs. Nelson touches his shoulder and asks him if he wants to step out of the room with her. Later, he comes back quiet and calm. Mrs. Nelson tells me after class that his parents have just announced their divorce.

One girl, Mindra, writes a beautiful poem for her dad, and reads it so well to the class that I have no idea her dad lives in California, and that she rarely sees him.

> I am a door and you are my hinges opening the door to happiness.
> I am a piano and you are my keys playing a love song.
> I am a pencil and you are my eraser, erasing tears from my eyes.
> I am your daughter, and you are my #1 dad.

I fear what some of these children face at home. I remember a tall, burly high school principal once said to me, as we stood in a crowded hallway between bells and watched the students slam their lockers: "These kids don't get enough love. But how can we give them at school the love they're missing at home?" Here, one teacher tells me she wishes her students could stay at school 24 hours a day. She says whatever she tries to teach them at school, they unlearn at home.

I have met many teachers like this, who, in the face of so many obstacles, angry parents, lack of funds, and exhaustion, continue to give of themselves, who appear like heroes in their students' lives. One student writes a poem for Mrs. Nelson and gives it to her:

> Man, she
> Really
> Smiles
> Naturally
> Every day and
> Leaves
> Some
> Of her happiness and
> Niceness in our hearts!

We teachers continue to smile, although we listen to the news of Littleton on the TV and radio every day. Despite the tension we feel, these students have the spark of childhood that can be fanned into a frenzy.

One day I ask the third graders to write poems about their own shadows. The April sun feels warm and refreshing. When it peeps out of the clouds, they all look down at the ground and become mesmerized by their companion. They begin a serious play. Some dance with their shadow, holding out their arms to embrace it; others chase it in circles; some tilt forward and backward to make their shadow grow and diminish; they bump into each other's shadows. Even Mrs. Nelson, in her flowery dress with billowy sleeves, spins around in the schoolyard giggling. She has long arms that can scoop up and pull any child to her side. But now she waves them in the air humorously trying to hug her shadow. Suddenly the sun goes behind a cloud, and our shadows dissolve. Like wind-up toys losing their power, each child slows down and slumps into disappointment. Some stand there looking empty-handed, as though I had just taken away their ball or turned off the music. The sun goes in and out of the clouds several times before we file back into our classroom to write. One student, Brandon, writes:

> My shadow can run, ride and wrestle.
> My shadow will cheer me up when I am sad.
> My shadow knows secrets about me.
> My shadow gets grass stains and they never show.

Except for our shadows, which perfectly obey the sun, all law and order seems to be crumbling around us: two fourth-grade boys have been caught stealing money from their teacher's purse; the front page of the local newspaper prints the picture of a three-year-old girl who has been missing for several days from her suburban home outside Lancaster; each day the radio announces several more copy-cat bomb threats in schools everywhere; our principal is attending special emergency meetings at the board of education office every day. And on Thursday of that week, one fourth-grade teacher learns that her husband's friend, who had been the best man at their wedding, has just committed suicide. It was his thirtieth birthday, and he left behind his three-year-old daughter.

Yet the poems the children write continue to be hopeful and resilient, even though they brush up against their own personal tragedies. One day we walk toward the center of town just three blocks away, holding notebooks and pencils in our hands. The students all follow Mrs. Nelson in a single-file line. It's a little dangerous leading 28 students alongside the traffic of Route 22, but nobody disobeys Mrs. Nelson's command. Nobody steps off the sidewalk.

I want the students to write a poem about their community, to observe their town in a new way and to appreciate its many details. We walk past General Sheridan, but none of the kids know why he is there. He's "the green statue," one girl writes. Later, after we return to our class, Mrs. Nelson combines lines from different students and arranges the phrases into a group poem. She ends the poem with one girl's line, "A happy day," as if to convince all of us and the parents, too, who will hear this poem at our final assembly, that it is so:

Somerset Community

Bright blue bells giving bellows

Wind chimes chiming
Old shaking window in the breeze
People voting at the fire department
Antenna with yellow ball on top
Noisy engines
Green statue
Flags blowing breezily
Crooked breaks in the sidewalk
A happy day

But it isn't a happy day. On Friday morning before the buses leave to pick up the children for school, the board of education receives an anonymous phone call, threatening a bomb in the high school. That morning we teachers arrive at the elementary school, but no students file in after us. We stand in the hallways with the doors to the school locked. The principal, Larry, explains that we may not have school that day. The board of education has delayed the buses, while the high school is being checked for a bomb. In the meantime, he asks us to each carefully inspect our own rooms and other areas nearby.

Mrs. Nelson and I stand in the hall talking; we don't feel like standing in her empty classroom. She tells me something this morning that I won't forget. I already know that this will be her last year here after teaching for over 30 years. I know that she has always used poetry in her classroom. Whenever her kids are getting hostile or are unable to focus, she has the students recite one of the many poems they have learned by heart. That week, I'd heard many of these poems. They weren't necessarily good poems. They had a sing-song rhythm and always rhymed. But the kids loved reciting the words. Like mantras, the language had a mesmerizing effect. Each day when I stepped into her class a little early or a little late, Mrs. Nelson would turn to the students and call out a title. They would greet me with a poem in a loud chorus.

"Poetry," Mrs. Nelson tells me this morning, "has always been the best way for me to bring my students together. It establishes a good feeling in the class and encourages kindness and respect. Somehow, it creates a kind of law and order." This love for poetry is Mrs. Nelson's gift to her students, her blessing. But next year, no third grader will be held in her spell. She will be gone, although the cars will still be circling around the green statue.

I used to be … but now

We put a box outside the art room, where students can drop their poems for me to read. I feel like Santa Claus at the North Pole trying to read all my mail. But unlike Santa I don't have to answer the letters—the excitement for the students is in knowing their poems are being read and their voices heard.

One boy, Michael, who, I'm told, is learning disabled, always invents a new line to tell me every time he sees me in the hall. I've introduced one of Kenneth Koch's writing prompts in class, "I used to be … but now …," a kind of fill-in-the-blank writing exercise that some writers have criticized for being too formulaic. But I find it to be a good beginning exercise to get kids writing: *I used to be a baseball, but now I'm a shooting star. I used to be a bowl of soba, but now I'm a full moon in the sky. I used to be a unicycle, but now I'm a prayer wheel spinning.*

Each time Michael sees me, instead of saying hello, he uses that phrase, imagining a new thing to be: "I used to be a sunflower," or, "I used to be a caterpillar … but now I'm a cloud in the sky …" Serious and intent, he says his line in a loud, clear voice as he approaches me in the hallway then keeps walking. He doesn't stop for me to comment on his poem or reply in any way. He just wants me to acknowledge that I've heard him.

After teaching for two weeks in Michael's school, I leave and return five months later in spring. My first day back, I hope to see Michael and wonder if he'll remember me. We spot each other in the hallway, and when we get close, he says, "I used to be a giraffe, but now I'm a tree"—as if no time has elapsed, as if he were reciting one long poem that can last the length of a class, a day, five months, or a lifetime.

CHAPTER FIVE

Writing and Being

Statistics and real life

The research I recommended you do in the previous chapter helped you become familiar with some of the complexities of the social issues you encounter at your site. The statistics might correlate with what you see each week, or they might contradict what you see. While there are therapeutic effects in writing—in fact, it is quite often these effects that draw us to take writing into our communities—it's important to keep our focus on writing and helping our participants use the tools of writing to share their stories in their own time, in their own way. Coming face-to-face with generational poverty, homelessness, neglected children and youth, or the elderly can be overwhelming. I'm not suggesting that you avoid acknowledging the challenges your participants are living with; rather reminding you that your expertise is writing, not therapy.

Safety issues and boundaries

The site where you are conducting your CBL project might be in an unfamiliar area. It is important to prepare for safety issues—such as, making sure your car has sufficient gas to get you to and from your destination, ensuring your phone is fully charged. It is important that you dress appropriately: you want to dress casually and comfortably, but professionally. Additionally, each site might have its own dress code for volunteers, and you'll want to adhere to their requests.

You must be able to set firm but sensitive boundaries with your participants. Children living in poverty might ask you to buy them things.

Teenagers might ask you to help them get jobs, or want to get your phone number or email.

Adults living in a shelter for the homeless, whether they don't have a high school education, or if they have a college degree, or if they were successful business people, might feel embarrassed or ashamed of their current situation. Women in a domestic violence shelter may still be reeling from trauma, or they may feel guilty that they've left animals at home or that they've taken their children away from the only home they've ever known, only to live in a dorm with several other women and children.

Incarcerated adults might also feel ashamed that you're seeing them at this time in their lives. They might be angry that you're coming to "do creative writing" with them when they're focused on their parole hearing next month. They might be embarrassed if they can't spell, or can't write at all. They might be angry that you, "some goody two-shoes," have come to do your good deed. They might be angry that, after each session, you get in your car and drive away. They might offer to buy you things. They might ask you to give them money or to help them get a job. They might suggest you run away with them after they are released.

Youth in foster care facilities may pout each week when you come. They might refuse to write. They might challenge your knowledge. One teen may have just ended a romantic relationship with another teen. One teen might have cheated on another. One teen might scream at another teen.

Children in low-performing schools most often crave the attention that comes with someone "from the outside" coming to their classroom. These children might cling to anyone who will let them cling. Other children might be withdrawn and refuse to talk to anyone, let alone write.

Certainly I've not covered every single boundary issue that could arise; the examples above are actual reactions I've experienced in some of the community workshops I've led. This is why it's important to have your CBL project planned out prior to your first workshop on site. At your first workshop you'll want to be confident in your lesson plan so that you can get a feel for the reactions, anticipations, and fears of the participants, whether they are children, youth, or adults. And it's important that you understand your role in their lives, to remain professional while being personable, and to maintain healthy boundaries

If you've done your preparation work—envisioning the CBL semester-long project, laid out your weekly session plans, done some basic research on the types of people you'll be working with, communicating directly with the community partner staff—you'll be ready to head to your site or that first workshop.

When you enter the room, you are hoping you'll be met with open arms and willing writers, but you might also be met with uncertainty, mistrust, or outright hostility, which can make you feel deflated, thinking you should forget the whole thing.

For additional safety information, please see Appendix A, or the companion website for this book.

Writing and imagination

In public schools, writing is too often tied to school performance, teacher pay, and school funding. Even children in the classroom are aware of the pressure of standardized testing. Incarcerated persons may have gone their entire lives thinking that writing is only for the elite and educated. For whatever reason, many people learned that writing is for business, not for the creative mind, and that only certain people are granted creative minds.

All of that hostility, mistrust, insecurity, and uncertainty that you might encounter during your first workshop can be lessened through your creative writing prompts that will inspire each participant to tap into his/her imagination. Quite often participants are accustomed to working alone, not sharing any of "self" with others. This is why I like to send my college students in pairs or teams. While one student is "leading" the session, the other student can be among the participants, doing the prompts alongside the others, sharing what she has written based on the prompts and lesson.

The first semester I required a CBL project, my students and I worked at the homeless shelter. Our class, which was a small advanced poetry workshop, met from 6:00–7:15 p.m. on Tuesday evenings at our university's downtown campus in Orlando, just blocks from the shelter. I'd arranged for our CBL project to be on Tuesdays from 7:30–8:30 p.m. Each week, after our poetry workshop, we walked over to the shelter. One student was the leader, and the rest of us participated with the adult residents. The first night of our scheduled CBL workshop, we spent the last half of our class time talking about our expectations, fears, concerns, hopes. I reminded my students that the only person who would not be writing would be the student leader for that night.

Our plan was, as yours might be, that after the writing section, we'd invite participants to read what they'd written. During our discussion ahead of time, a few of my students were concerned. They wanted to know if they should read their writing based on the writing prompt. Of course, they should. Why not, I thought. The students were concerned that since they'd already had three semesters of college that their writing was probably better than what the participants would write. And they didn't want to make the participants feel bad. I encouraged them each to "be a participant." Write with them, share with them, and be vulnerable with them.

At the end of the CBL workshop, when my students and I walked back to our cars, they were beaming. They couldn't believe the great stories they'd heard and the image-focused poems. A few of the students noted one or two pieces written by the participants that were better than anything any of them had written.

Also during that first workshop, the residents hackled us at the beginning: "Are you getting your good-two-shoes points for coming here?"; "Are we the subject of your research?"; "Research this!" one said, fist raised. These questions and statements could have devastated my students; instead my students empathized. Because they had done some basic research on poverty and homelessness, they understood why people living in shelters might view college students in this way. The students handled the remarks with honesty and respect. We assured our participants we were doing this because we love writing and we believe everyone has imagination and a voice. And we wanted to share some of the tools of creative writing with them. We assured them they could write stories, essays, or poems with our lessons and prompts. During that session one or two participants got up and left. We just kept moving forward.

Throughout the semester, participants came and went, but we had five participants who were with us every single week, and these five participated in a coffee house reading of their work at the end of our semester. I'll talk more about creating end-of-semester celebrations in later chapters. I mention this here because some challenges we will encounter can throw us off-guard, and may hurt our feelings at first, but we haven't all been encouraged to write from our imagination. You're in the community to open that world for your participants.

Checking in with self

While you must certainly acknowledge that your time with participants is valuable and affects lives, you might also be realizing that you cannot change the world in four months, going once a week to a shelter or school. All you can do is the part you are doing at the moment. It's common to feel frustrated, hopeless, and/or cynical. What often starts out as idealism and hope can quickly turn into frustration, hopelessness, and cynicism. The emotional shifts give you opportunities to write, to write about your experience, to work it out on the page.

Brittany, the student whose reflections we've looked at a couple of times already, spoke with her aunt who was a long-time teacher who told her she needed to care about the students more than cared about her lesson. As she planned her next lesson, she contemplated what topic would engage these fourth graders.

> I chose slavery as a topic we would discuss over several weeks. Rather than lecture, I encouraged students to engage in discussion. Students were less resistant when they were enlightened as to the assignment's

significance. If they think the assignment is stupid, they will tell you. If they don't want to write about the topic, they will tell you. If they don't see the point to what you're teaching them, you guessed it, they will tell you. Class discussion not only gave students the opportunity to voice their opinions, but it allowed me to better understand their needs and meet them. (Osbourne, 2008)

Brittany's willingness to adjust to her preconceived notions about how to teach creative writing opened up her students to the idea of writing, which they'd first met with resistance, and allowed Brittany to use her academic knowledge of creative writing and of anthropology.

Structured reflection

Personal

1 What types of boundaries do you need to have with the participants at your site?
2 Make a list of safety precautions you should take while getting to your site, being on site, and leaving your site.

Academic

3 Make a list of *five* possible general topics for a reflective or analytical essay you might write at the conclusion of your project. The topics should somehow connect community-based learning with creative writing. In creative nonfiction, this essay might become a literary journalism essay.
4 Describe the connections between "creative writing" and "imagination."

Civic

5 Do an online search for other community-based creative writing projects/programs. You may look at the ones mentioned throughout this book, but I encourage you to find others. What other ways could creative writers become engaged in their communities? Identify two of these projects/programs.
6 Do a search in the college library database for research on creative

writing in community settings. Locate one article, read it, and discuss the research.

Readings

Anita Skeen

Anita Skeen is Professor in the Residential College in the in Arts and Humanities at Michigan State University where she is the Arts Coordinator for the College and the Director of the Center for Poetry. She received her MA and MFA from Bowling Green State University and her BS from Concord College in Athens, West Virginia. She is the Coordinator of the Creative Arts Festival and the Fall Writing Festivals at Ghost Ranch in Abiquiu, NM. She is the author of six volumes of poetry: *Each Hand a Map* (1986); *Portraits* (1992); *Outside the Fold, Outside the Frame* (1999); *The Resurrection of the Animals* (2002); *When We Say Shelter* (with Jane Taylor, 2005); and *Never the Whole Story* (2011). Her poetry, short fiction, and essays have appeared in numerous literary magazines and anthologies. Her forthcoming publication, with visual artist Laura DeLind, is *The Unauthorized Audubon,* a collection of poems and linocuts of imaginary birds.

A Red Wheelbarrow, a Hammock, and a Pomegranate: Why So Much *Does* Depend Upon Poetry

When I was a child I don't recall anyone ever asking me what I wanted to be when I grew up. Someone must have, at some point, but obviously it was not memorable. Looking back on those years of skinned knees and infinite possibilities, I don't know how I responded to the question. Fighter pilot, astronomer, and coal miner were out—because I was a girl. Texas Ranger, Viking explorer, Confederate soldier were out, too, because, well, they were history, and history, I thought then, was in the past. Nurse, schoolteacher, legal secretary, housewife—those were things women grew up to be in the 1950s, and though I knew girls grew into women, I couldn't imagine myself growing up to be one of those creatures who wore nylon stockings, girdles, and pillbox hats. And they carried purses. So, like Peter Pan, I planned not to grow up. I didn't want to be X or Y. I just wanted to *be*: outside in the woods, inside a book, up in a tree, down by the river, off with the dog. In retrospect, I see that this simply *wanting to be* is, in some ways, describing the life of the poet. Poets *be*. Archibald MacLeish in his famous poem, *Ars Poetica* (1968), writes "A poem should not mean / but be" (lines 333–4). The same could be said for many poets: they also want to *be*. To be in the actual physical world and in the world of language. To be given the space and time to transform experience to text. To be a voice to which others listen as they make their own meaning. If someone *did* ask me what I wanted to be when I grew up, I'm 100 percent drop-dead, knockdown sure I didn't answer "a poet."

But I did become a poet, and then I became a teacher of poets. In a similar vein, I don't know when I first became aware of the number of other people who felt they had unwritten poems dwelling inside them, that they had experiences (that they thought of as "feelings") to share, unique perspectives to offer. This, however, was not something that they often were likely to discuss in public. I did hear, on a number of occasions, the man standing beside me with a drink in his hand say, "When I write my novel …" or the woman sitting beside me in a committee meeting taking notes offer, "When I write my memoirs …" These people were not writers by profession but accountants, doctors, legislative representatives, teachers, and social workers. I don't recall hearing anyone say, "When I write my collection of poems …" What did these people do with the impulse to explore language, to let the language of poetry take hold of their experiences and transform them into art? Many kept journals. Some took photographs. Others listened to music that tapped into personal and private space. And just a few were looking for a workshop. They had come to the same realization as the speaker of James Wright's "Lying in a Hammock at William Duffy's Farm in Pine Island, Minnesota" (1987): there was much around them to observe, there was a world to *be* in, and not to take notice was to risk wasting their lives (p. 114).

I think of Randall Jarrell's comment: "The public has an unusual relation with the poet. It does not even know that he [or she] is there" (quoted in Winokur, 1986, p. 44). For the most part, that's true *before* the poem is written, *during* the process of writing the poem, and, unfortunately, *after* the poem is published. Poets are invisible to the general public. We don't wear uniforms that distinguish us, as police or firemen do; we don't carry identifying equipment, such as the cameras that photographers do, or drive around in little white boxes like mail carriers do; we do not perform in specific venues as do baseball players and Congressional representatives. What we do is, for the most part, private. What we do is *be*. I be; therefore I write. And if I write, I am not writing only for myself (despite what some of my undergraduate students tell me). I am thinking to be validated. I am speaking to be heard. I am writing to be read.

But who will read my work besides my family and my best friends if I am not connected to a writing community? Where can I find a writing group, a writing workshop that will give me feedback? Now that we're in the age of blogs and Facebook, there are ways to get a poem or story out into the public conversation that were not available ten years ago. Will people write back about what I have posted? Can I trust what those people have to say? Will they be compassionate and critical readers, or will they respond with axes to grind and chips on their shoulders? How do I know what kind of writers they are? How can I discover what they've written? The element I find missing from this kind of response is face-to-face human interaction.

As a poet, as someone for whom language is the way to take a private vision into the public realm, I am aware that I am translating my personal experience—anger, love, frustration, grief, disbelief, uncertainty, moral outrage—into community narrative. "This is what happened to me," I say, "this is what I felt." Or, "Here is what I witnessed." Or "Look at this mystery. What do you think?" Or even, "Surprise! How funny is that?" Edward Hirsch comments in *How to Read a Poem* (1999) that the poem speaks "out of a solitude to a solitude" (p. 4). Reading poetry, he says, "is an act of reciprocity, and one of the great tasks of the lyric is to bring us into right relationship to each other" (p. 4). How many readers of modern poetry have been bewildered by William Carlos Williams's small and unassuming poem, "the red wheelbarrow"? Here relationships are critical: "so much depends / upon ..." There is the writer, the reader, and the all-important "red wheel / barrow / glazed with rain / water / beside the white / chickens" (p. 256). It is a poem of external solitude whose *be*-ing depends upon the inner solitude of the reader. The poet begins the experience of "poem"; the reader completes it. There is a profound intimacy here. One to one, we are both changed by the experience of the poem.

As the director of the Creative Arts Festival at Ghost Ranch in Abiquiu, New Mexico, every summer, I have, for the past 33 years, worked at bringing together many different artists—poets included—and everyday, ordinary folks who for at least one week in the summer come to be transformed by art. Some are already artists. Others hoped to get into the hiking class, but because they didn't register in time and their second choice of river rafting also was full, they found themselves in their third choice, the poetry class. For many of them, this probably was a lot like hiking to the top of Pedernal, Georgia O'Keeffe's inspirational mountain, or shooting the rapids in the Rio Grande. My challenge here as a teacher of poetry and other genres is to show them that access to the inner life can come as much through language as it can from cresting a mountain or struggling with the current. In the Fall Writing Festival at Ghost Ranch, which I developed in 1997 in response to the increasing number of people who wanted to take a writing class in the summer when we had no spaces left for them, the participants who come are already attuned to words and know that when you read and understand a poem, you come closer to mastering chaos. I have a job to do during those weeks in New Mexico that involves everything from setting up chairs in the Lower Pavilion to picking up mail in the office to plucking the drowned mouse out of the elderly lady's toilet in Pine 1. Most people would not feel that this is the stuff of poetry (except maybe for the mouse). But it is the mundane work of helping to provide that room of one's own for someone whose life might be changed forever by encountering, on the page, the voice of Lisel Mueller, Robert Hass, June

Jordan, Garrett Hongo. It is my performance of Robert Hayden's "austere and lonely offices" (2003, pp. 173–4). What I take away from those weeks of hard work is the knowledge that delight, and sometimes even wisdom, have gone home with the participants in the Creative Arts and Fall Writing Festivals and that I, too, have been given gifts that will work their way, like an underground stream, through future poems.

In 2005 I began teaching a creative writing workshop to accompany the city of East Lansing, Michigan's annual One Book, One Community (OBOC) literary event, which was initiated in 2003. Each August and September the freshman students at Michigan State University (MSU), all 7,000 to 8,000 of them, are required to read the One Book, One Community selection that area book clubs, individuals, and organizations agree to read and come together to discuss. This year we will be reading Katherine Boo's *Beyond the Beautiful Forevers* (2013), and she will come to town to talk with both students and community members. Among the past selections have been Dave Eggers's *Zeitoun* (2009), Jeanette Walls's *The Glass Castle* (2005), Steven Lopez's *The Soloist* (2010), and Khaled Hosseini's *The Kite Runner* (2003), all books that pose provocative questions about social issues, about the nature of narrative, about the power and precision of language. As part of the month-long schedule of activities, I offered to teach a two-hour writing workshop once a week for four weeks on themes that grew out of the selected text. We limited the class enrollment to 15 participants. The first year the workshop was offered, it filled. The second year, it filled, with a waiting list. The third year, the waiting list was almost as long as the list of enrollees, and the fourth year I offered to teach two classes, one from 4:00 to 6:00 in the afternoon, and a second one from 7:00 to 9:00 in the evening. We cut down the enrollment to 12 people in each workshop, as I discovered that with 15 folks there was not enough time to give all participants their share of time to talk about their work. Both workshops filled the first year they were offered, and that has been the trend ever since. There is still a waiting list. I have toyed with the idea of offering a third workshop but have yet to be altruistic enough to do so.

The workshops are designed to be broad enough so that even if participants have not read the book (and, unfortunately, many have not) they can draw on their own life experiences to struggle with the same issues that are presented in the book. To illustrate this point, I would like to offer a couple of examples of the specific workshop description that accompanied the books. The following is the description that was circulated in connection with Dave Eggars's *Zeitoun*.

The Way I Remember It

... the art of losing isn't hard to master
though it may look like (Write it!) like disaster.
Elizabeth Bishop, "The Art of Losing"

There was no photo of the house the way I remember it from a distance, wholly intact. I did not understand, taking those pictures, that history must be collected while the subject exists. If not, what goes unrecorded can fill an ocean. (*Susanna Daniel, Stiltsville*)

Fifty years from now, when people want to know what happened to this once-great city during a shameful episode of our history, they will still be talking about a family named Zeitoun. (Timothy Egan, *The New York Times Book Review*)

When Hurricane Katrina struck New Orleans in August 2005, there were as many histories of that event as there were people in the city. Writer Dave Eggers recorded one of those, the story of a family named Zeitoun. He recorded it while the subject still existed, before people, memories, and experience vanished. Every day history occurs around us, whether it is the death of Robert Byrd, the longest-serving senator in U.S. history, or the birth of a first grandchild. What is happening around you that may go unrecorded? What small chip of the mosaic do only you hold? What photo should you snap because no one else will? In this workshop we will take the time to rescue the people and events we don't want swept away in the ocean of oblivion and, through the art of writing, honor them.

The next description accompanied the workshop for Jonathan Saffron Foer's *Extremely Loud and Incredibly Close;*

Missions: Impossible ... and Possible

In Jonathan Safron Foer's novel *Extremely Loud and Incredibly Close*, we meet nine-year-old Oskar Schell, who is on an urgent, secret search through the five boroughs of New York. His mission is to find the lock that fits a mysterious key belonging to his father who died in the attack on the World Trade Center. All of us have undertaken searches, quests, journeys that others might have labeled "crazy," "bizarre," or "obsessive." Sometimes those searches were public; sometimes they were conducted in secret. In Oskar's case, it is grief and loss that propel him forward. What of the adopted child searching for her birth mother, the grandson searching for someone who knew how his grandfather died in the war, the scientist searching for the rogue gene? Or, on a smaller, more ordinary scale, the child looking for the lost toy, the cook searching for her mother's potato salad recipe, the unemployed carpenter looking for a job. In all of these searches there are stories, hilarious or heartbreaking, that link us to Oskar Schell: our mission, ultimately, has to do with the inscrutable and with our desire for human connection.

In the workshop we will explore such quests, through fiction, poetry, memoir and that vanishing genre, the letter, in order to tell our own tales.

Finally, the following is the workshop description for the most recent *Beyond the Beautiful Forever.*

On the Street Where You Live: Place, People, and Possibility

We are all, in some way, shaped and influenced by the neighborhood or community in which we came of age. The East End, the West Side, South Hills, the Triangle District, or up Elk River Road all had characteristics that encouraged people to define, and often stereotype, the residents in certain ways. If you live in the Flowerpot District, the Bailey neighborhood, the Allen Street neighborhood, Urbandale, or White Hills, you are part of a community with alliances, jealousies, heartbreaks, secrets, sacrifices, and shared experiences. Writers, through their words and images, have brought us Sesame Street, Esperanza's Mango Street, Mr. Rogers's Neighborhood, the West Side of Tony and Maria, Hogwarts, and Yoknapatawpha County. In Katherine Boo's *Beyond the Beautiful Forever,* we enter a half-acre slum in Mumbai, India, where 3,000 people live in 335 huts. Even here among the trash sorters and scavengers there are dreams of upward mobility, political aspirations, a desire for home remodeling. But, as is so often the case in neighborhoods, the fiery temper, the ill-chosen word, the precipitous act have disastrous consequences. Yet in the midst of all this squalor and tragedy, we still find sensitivity and hope, tenderness and courage.

Although most of us did not grow up, nor do we live now, crowded in chaos on the edge of a lake of sewage, the characters in Boo's book have resonance with people in our own lives. Our desires for our own happiness and that of our children are not so different from Zehrunisa and Abdul. In this workshop, let us reflect upon and write about the communities that shape/have shaped us, the seemingly inconsequential events that turn out to be pivotal, the diversity in human personality that leads to courage or collapse.

I include these three workshop descriptions to illustrate how creating broad topics related to the themes of the book selections encourages a wide range of participation and welcomes people into the discussion who might not have read the book or, as is often the case, did not like or agree with positions they felt were advocated by the author. I also encourage participants to write in whatever genre they feel best suits the topic: poetry, fiction, memoir, essay, or even a ten-minute play. As each participant will write three pieces during the three weeks of workshop, he or she has the opportunity to experiment with different genres during the course of the month.

Having done these workshops now for a number of years, I feel I can make some significant observations about these sessions and the people who attend. There is a core group that returns year after year to take the workshop. Pat Miller (2012), a many-year participant, says that,

> As you listen to people read what are often very intimate and life-changing secrets, perhaps for the first time revealed, you realize how much every person contributes to your own thoughts and opinions. That is the magic of the group in my opinion. It is very satisfying and emotionally bonding to work in such an atmosphere and who would not want to come back again and again for more sustenance and reflection? Your group is a classic outreach experience from the knowledge and power of the university to the reflective capacities in the community, each with their own skills and experience.

Carol Myron (2012), also a returnee, adds,

> The OBOC writing workshops have given me a chance to step outside of my everyday life and be a writer again. For three weeks in the fall, I can dedicate time to writing and share that writing with others in a workshop setting. This allows me the opportunity to gain insight from others and puts me in a local community of writers who are not judgmental. I can write for the fun of it. I look forward to the OBOC writing workshop every year like a kid looks forward to summer camp—it gives me a chance to reunite with a group of people who share a passion for words. While my daily life doesn't always allow time for me to sit down and write, while I'm in the workshop, I make the time.

The participants make sure they call the East Lansing Public Library on August 1, the day enrollment begins, to get their names on the list. They sign up for the same session with friends they have made in previous workshops. They bring along people they know out in the community who are writers but who have no workshop or writing group to participate in. Some do have a group; still they add this one. When the second workshop was added in the evening, it became clear that when the 4:00 session ended at 6:00, there were people who wanted to hang around and chat because they were friends with writers coming to the 7:00 session. So, the library provided us with what would be called in most churches a "fellowship hour," a time to share coffee, cheese and crackers, and veggies, and conversation between the two sessions. Sometimes just a few folks come to the 6:00 to 7:00 hour, sometimes more. But it has provided yet another link between participants, another place to share stories, another place to build community.

It is clear to me that in this community, and I am sure in others like it around the country, there is a hunger to write. Not just to write, but to be heard. To become part of the larger narrative of our culture and our time, to line up Margarita's story alongside Glenn's, to meet Barbara's family as well as Evelyn's, to watch Mary's children grow up in ways so like, and so unlike, Sue's. The Irish poet Evan Boland, in her poem "The Pomegranate," tells us "the only legend I have ever loved" is the story of Ceres and Persephone, a story of love and blackmail, a mother and a daughter. "The best thing about the legend," she says "is / I can enter it anywhere" (2003, pp. 264–5). We do that often in these workshops. We write the poems, the stories, the essays and they open up a dialogue about love, about parenting, about loss, about death. In an article in *Newsweek*, the poet Jorie Graham wrote, "For every lie we're told by advertisers and politicians, we need one poem to balance it" (quoted in O'Driscoll, 2008, p. 115). These writings balance out the lies that pervade the airwaves and batter our psyches. These workshop writings say, "Here's what happened to me. And that's the truth. Maybe it's happened to you, too."

After several of these workshops, I felt that writers needed a larger venue than just the classroom in which to share their stories, so we now end each September's classes with a public reading. We hold it in a small theater on the MSU campus. Class members come and bring their friends and families. Friends who have ended up in different time slots for the workshop this year come to hear what their colleagues wrote in the class before or the class after. We have become familiar with the peculiarities and idiosyncrasies of some people's voices. We know Rita will always make us laugh; we know Bruce will always look through the analytical lens; we know Marilyn always has psychology in mind. We advertise the public reading along with all the other One Book, One Community activities. Students from some of the university classes come. It's an enjoyable and rewarding night. More importantly, it affirms how the power and richness of individual voice and experience come to enrich the entire community. Workshop participant Sarah Fryer (2012) wrote to me:

> I appreciate ... the opportunity the workshops afford to create community within community. People who like to write come together for an opportunity to write together and share their work in a safe and supportive environment. We enter with common interests (in reading and writing) and the shared experience of living in the same community, as well as the shared context of the book selected for the community read, but we have vastly different life stories. Many of us have difficulty creating spaces in our lives to write and to share our writing with others, but the short-term nature of the workshops allows us to make a short-term commitment through which we create a lasting experience as well as concrete written work. By writing together and sharing our work within the group, we broaden our own experience and—in some cases—make new friends. ... We build connections with each other through our work, and we learn more about life in general through listening to the work of others. I particularly enjoy observing the development of other writers'

voices over the years; there are many ways to write well, and writing and listening well can create lasting bridges.

When the month-long workshop ends, it is not the end. One of the writers from the very first year, Telaina, keeps a workshop going throughout the year. Writers from the One Book, One Community sessions attend, but other people in the community are also welcome. When I run across someone out in town who is looking for a writing group, "Call Telaina," I say, "I've got the perfect group for you." Participants in these writing workshops have gone on to get a master of fine arts degree from Antioch University; have been published in well-known literary magazines and anthologies, and with small presses; have written plays that have been staged; and have gone on to do readings in other venues. One poet became a writer-in-residence for two weeks in another Michigan community. These workshops opened doors. I was the facilitator, but it was the participants who encouraged and kept each other growing, reaching, and striving to write better and better poems, essays, stories. I watched them take on an identity as the One Book, One Community Writing Workshop and look forward to it each year in the same way I might a family reunion. I watched them bring to the workshops their own wheelbarrows, hammocks, and pomegranates. I watched them go out as writers.

I feel it will be useful here to include a few comments by some of the participants who have come back to the workshop through the years. Their voices should be heard as much as mine. Fran Lewis (2012) spoke to the friendships formed, and the sense of community:

> It means a great deal to me to participate in your One Book, One Community writing workshops. Whenever I meet another of the writers from the workshops around town, we always stop and chat like old friends. The workshops help to link us together as a community of writers. And, when I listen to what the participants have written, I am impressed by how good the writing is. It deserves our respect.

Al, who came into the first workshop wanting to write a novel based on some Civil War letters that were in his possession, sent me this when I asked him if he had any comments to make about how the workshop had influenced him:

> After meeting Anita at the One Book, One Community workshop, I started to attend her poetry workshops at MSU. Anita asked everyone to introduce themselves. At my turn I said I was a retired professor and admitted, "I don't really like poetry." Gasps all around and faces that said, "Then why are you here?" I explained, I don't like poetry and I don't like olives. But I keep trying them in hopes that my tastes might change. And today, I like some of each.

Dorothy, a retired teacher, among other things, responded this way when I asked why she kept coming back:

> I appreciate the fact that *this is a free workshop* series! Many of us are retired, and not having to pay tuition is really remarkable. I like this because I think it is so admirably equitable: writing (and all the arts) should be accessible *to everyone* and the fact of the matter is that in many instances it has become a luxury that is prohibitive because of cost of participation.
>
> For example, I moved back to East Lansing twelve years ago for the main reason that I would be next to a major university and I could take advantage of coursework there because I love to learn. But MSU has priced me right out of the market. I can't afford graduate tuition, which is what I would be charged, even taking undergraduate courses, since I have a graduate degree already. My whole dream of filling up on an entire smorgasbord of courses just across the street from me has been dashed. I have no patience for the fluff courses of MSU's Evening College. I wanted so badly to sink my teeth into substance, not amusement. ...
>
> I make the above point because it underlines how really *significant* it is to have a full professor from MSU teach the workshop at a level that is neither casual nor thrown together, but beautifully prepared with exemplary handouts, examples, teaching strategies and writing prompts (and also why the Center for Poetry means so much to me).

Dorothy's comment is the perfect segue into a short discussion of how the Residential College in the Arts and Humanities (RCAH) Center for Poetry at MSU took the One Book, One Community concept and created its own series just for poetry. I knew that the One Book, One Community selections would never include a collection of poems, as the organizers felt the readership for poems would be too small. Given that fact, four years ago we began a reading/writing series called Read a Poet, Write a Poem during the last two weeks of January (when no one in Michigan wants to go outside and nothing is on TV but basketball). In the first year of the series, we began by reading Theodore Roethke; moved on to Kay Ryan, the sixteenth U.S. poet laureate, in the second year; followed her with the late Irene McKinney, the West Virginia poet laureate, in year three; and last year chose Nikki Finney, who had just won the National Book Award for Poetry for *Head Off & Split* (2011). These sessions take place in the RCAH at MSU, although the audience is primarily community members, both readers and writers.

We say at the Center for Poetry that our mission is this: *to encourage the reading, writing, and discussion of poetry and to create an awareness of its place and power in our everyday lives.* We can do this as individuals; we can do this as members of a community. One of my personal goals as director of the Center has been to break down the barriers between the university and the community, to have members of the East Lansing community come to the Center for readings, workshops, events like the Edible Book Contest, and to get MSU students out into the community into public schools, art galleries, bookstores, and neighborhoods. In the first of the two weeks' sessions of Read a Poet, Write a Poem, we read the book we have selected and discuss it. Some people come to only this session, and do not come to the writing workshops that are held the following week. Likewise, some people do not attend the discussion session (which always baffles me) but show up the following week for the writing workshops. We encourage people to attend both, but never in the four years we've been doing this have we had all the same people for both weeks. In these writing workshops we write only poems, using themes, structures, and subjects we have discovered in our discussions of the poet's work the week before, always drawing on our own experiences, always finding connections among our lives and the life of the particular poet we have studied.

Red wheelbarrows, hammocks, pomegranates. A New Jersey poet, an Ohio poet, an Irish poet. A cultural observation, an individual epiphany, a Greek myth. Commonplace items and the meaning they make are exactly what poetry depends upon. Likewise, the community, however defined, however small or large, depends upon the poet for articulating its truths; the poet depends upon the community for inspiration and sustenance. By reading and writing, we see how to *be* in the world. "Poetry is a dividend," writes Polish poet Czeslaw Milosz, "from what you know and who you are" (Driscoll, 2008, p. 3).

CHAPTER SIX

Discovering the Pleasure of Poetry and Storytelling in the World

Building confidence as a teaching artist

Whether you started your CBL project feeling apprehensive or enthusiastic, after two or three on-site workshops, the participants are probably having some sort of impact on you. Usually after my first session with participants, I'm very excited about the possibilities for the project. In the next few visits, I find myself getting to know the participants as people, people who happen to be living in different situations.

Hopefully you're also feeling confident about the work you're doing in your community. The hour or two you spend with your participants each week is probably a weekly highlight for you and for them. Most community participants are happy that someone from outside their typical daily activities comes to do writing with them once a week. Just as you are, your participants are spending the rest of the week living their lives. I hope you're finding "service" a doable part of your life. And I hope you're gaining confidence that you *are* capable of teaching and mentoring others. I hope you're realizing how much goes into teaching, and how rewarding it is to share your knowledge with others.

Observing your surroundings

With the Internet as our current center of social interaction, it's easy to forget that as writers we must practice using all of our senses. Writers must use sensory details to convey experience. Poets use things we can see, taste, touch, smell, and hear to describe experience and emotion. Prose writers use specific, concrete, and significant details, and make distinctions between significant and insignificant details.

As a writer in the community, you have the great opportunity to practice this skill of observing life in ways you may not have observed it previously. You also have a chance to see writing as part of another thing—your CBL project. William Carlos Williams, a poet who earned his living as a medical doctor (who made house calls), gathered much of his poetic material from his career as a physician in Paterson, New Jersey. He viewed his medical practice as service and education—the very definition of service-learning. In his *Autobiography* (1951), he says, "As a writer I never felt that medicine interfered with me but rather that it was my very food and drink, the very thing that made it possible for me to write. Was I not interested in men? There the thing was, right in front of me" (p. 357).

His job made it *possible* for him to write! We write to discover something, to find out what it is we don't know—either about ourselves or others. We are interested in the human experience. The good news is that the human experience is so vast and complex that, regardless of where you are, you'll find some new perspective, some new experiences, and people that you will not meet by just sitting at your desk in isolation. "My medicine," wrote Williams, "was the thing which gained me entrance to those secret gardens of the self. I was permitted by my medical badge to follow the poor, defeated body into those griefs and grottos ... to be present at deaths and births, at the tormented battles between daughter and diabolic mother." He said that poetry "fluttered before me for a moment, a phrase which I quickly write down on anything at hand, any piece of paper I can grab" (1951, p. 288).

Whether you're gathering oral histories, teaching poetry, or mentoring young children in reading, there are moments that will flutter before you, that you'll want to write down, something that might become a line in a poem, the ending of a story you're working on, or the be the opening to a poem, a story, or the beginnings of an essay.

Coles greatly admired Williams, and recalls Williams saying about his home visits, "Those house calls are giving me an education. Every day I learn something new—a sight, a phrase—and I'm made to stop and think about my world, the world I've left behind" (1993, p. 147).

I hope that you're keeping a good notebook full of "sights" and "phrases" from your CBL project, not as a way to exploit or use people who are in troubling situations, but to explore more complexities of the human spirit, more ways to get at what it means to *be*.

The immersed writer

Literary journalists use *immersion research* for many of their writing projects. Immersion is about using experience as a way into a subject. While it does not always involve service, you could, with a little tweaking, create an immersion project that is also a service project.

Writer and teacher Philip Gerard teaches a graduate course at University of North Carolina—Wilmington, Research for Creative Writing. He says, "To me, research is a habit, an attitude of open-minded alertness, a way of being in the world, of being alert for *knowledge* in any form—knowledge defined as some clue I didn't have before about how the world works" (2012). One purpose of CBL is to get a better understanding of "how the world works."

The next time you're on your way to your site, take note of the different types of building as you drive or ride on the bus. What types of surroundings do the children you work with see every day on their way to school? What do the people living at the shelter for the homeless hear during the day and night? How far away from the foster care facility is the nearest mall? In one rural area of central Florida, where some of my students conduct their CBL project, the children all live in dilapidated trailers, most of them next to a dump pile of some sort. On one side of the street are several trailers (mobile homes one might say) and on the other side is a car dump, where cars are stacked 10–20 high. What does this do to a child's understanding of the world? Observing these things can lead to researching city records about zoning, safe water conditions, environmental issues, and more. Gerard knows that, for writers, we must get out of our isolation and into the world:

> Research takes you the writer out of yourself, frees you for a time from paralyzing self-absorption, while offering endless fascinating subjects. It entices you into the public arenas of history and politics and catches you up in the shared public memory of a place, a community, a region. And ultimately, of course, leads you back through a new route into yourself, your deepest writer's heart, teaching you what you truly care about and why.

A CBL project is not the only way to get out of the self, but also enables you to find out "what you truly care about and why."

Lee Gutkind is a teacher, editor, and writer. In his essay, "The 5 Rs of Creative Nonfiction," he discusses how involved writers become in their subjects through five "Rs": Real Life, Reflection, Research, Reading, and 'Riting. CBL provides a chance for all five of these. Your on-site activities serve as the "real life" component, and of course you're doing structured reflection after each visit. He encourages you to read about the people you're working with, finding out the background of the organizations, reading as much as you can about other things that interest you. And, of course, writing about your experience in a focused way.

He says, "As a writing teacher, I design assignments that have a real-life aspect: I force my students out into their communities for an hour, a day or even a week so that they see and understand that the foundation of good writing emerges from personal experience" (Gutkind, 2004).

While a semester of CBL work might not be enough time to produce a publishable piece of writing, you will learn the challenges and pleasures of immersing yourself in a subject. You can begin to imagine what other types of projects you might do in order to either write about them or just to train yourself to observe. You might also discover that writing comes easier for you if it's not the only thing you do. William Carlos Williams said that medicine and poetry were, for him, "two parts of a whole" (1951, p. 359). Perhaps you will need two parts to make a whole of your own writing life.

Connecting your project with your own life experiences

Writers connect experiences. During your project, you can begin to connect your past experiences with what you see and hear each week. Each week focus on observing something different and ask yourself how it connects to your life experiences. Do a little research about these connections. Find ways to connect your CBL project with your own life as a writer and person. Williams said, "I lost myself in the very properties of their minds. For the moment at least I actually became them, so that when I detached myself from them at the end of the half hour of intense conversation, it was as though I were awakening from a sleep" (1951, p. 356). Later, in an interview in *The Massachusetts Review*, Williams recalled how he quite by default became a doctor and what benefits it brought to his writing: "there I was, I didn't know what else to do, and it was put into my head, [and so] I became a doctor. Lucky, too, for me, because it [being a doctor] forced me to gets get used to people of all sorts, which was a fine thing for a writer or potential writer" (1973, p. 133). I hope you're starting to feel lucky.

Christine Dye (2008), an undergraduate in my Creative Writing in the Community course, conducted her CBL project at the Women's Residential and Counseling Center (WRCC)—a domestic violence shelter. Here, Christine considers what she thought her role would be (as a teacher of writing) and what how that role connected to her own experiences.

Once I accepted that planning and hosting a creative writing class workshop might involve more than writing, and improving literacy skills, going to the WRCC became a fulfilling experience I looked forward to. Though we [my group mates] continued to introduce writing and reading activities, our focus shifted; more important than our workshops was our commitment to the children at the WRCC. The children at the WRCC anxiously awaited our arrival each week, happy that we came back for them—not because we had to, but because we wanted to. I began to understand that my relationship with these children was far more important than teaching creative writing and experiencing productive workshops.

Initially, my involvement at the WRCC was entirely influenced by my decision to take a creative-writing class that required I teach a creative writing workshop in the community. However, as I became personally involved with the children, their mothers and the staff at the WRCC, my involvement had little to do with completing a course or attempting to teach creative writing. Creative writing is no longer what motivates what I do and what I want to continue doing at the WRCC. I still value creative writing and believe that it has the ability to bring about positive change—and I definitely understand that education is vital to individual growth and necessary to ending the cycle of poverty—but for me, more important than successfully using tools and methods to promote change is having good intentions, a desire that come from within, that is honest and sincere, because dedication—and that which we lend ourselves to—must come from the heart, if our words and actions are to have any meaning.

Structured reflection

Personal

1   There are many satisfactions when you go into the community and use your talents and skills to mentor and help others. Describe your favorite moment from your first visits.

Academic

2   Locate at least literary one poem and one literary story that would be appropriate to use with the participants at your site. If you can find it online, post the URL; if not, give us the title and the author's name.

3   Using the techniques of "scene," describe a short scene at your community site. If you have not been there yet, imagine a scene.

Civic

4   One way to think of your relationship with the children, youth, or adults at your site is that you are a writing mentor. Imagine that you are one of the participants at your site, how would you perceive college students coming in to do what you're doing? Why might they be skeptical of your presence? Why might they be hesitant to attend?

5   Describe the reaction of at least one person at your site to your presence.

6   Discuss at least three things you have in common with the participants at your site.

Readings

Robin Mello and Anne Basting

Dr. Robin Mello is the director of the K12 Theatre Education Program and an Associate Professor of Theatre, Peck School of the Arts, at the University of Wisconsin-Milwaukee. Her research focuses on storytelling, myth and archetype, and how arts-based approaches impact student knowledge, identities, and development.

Dr. Anne Basting is author of numerous articles and books and nearly a dozen plays and public performances, including *Finding Penelope* (2011). She continues to direct the award-winning *TimeSlips Creative Storytelling* Project, which she founded in 1998. Basting is Director of the Creative Trust and the Center on Age and Community at the University of Wisconsin-Milwaukee.

"The Sublime, the Unsettling, and the Exuberant": Changing Students' Attitudes Toward Aging through *TimeSlips* Creative Storytelling

TimeSlips Storytelling

We (the authors) are committed to the power of teaching through creative engagement. Despite our separate professional trajectories, we both have come to understand storytelling as a learning paradigm. As artists, both of us seek to help our students explore what Gardner,

Csikszentmihalyi, and Damon (2001) call "the struggle for relationship between high-level [arts making] and social responsibility." It is our understanding that, as professors, we can assist in changing academe with new approaches.

To create opportunities for students to be involved with engaged-practice in their classroom and community, we created a curriculum built around the *TimeSlips Creative Storytelling Method*,[1] an improvisational method that replaces the pressure to remember existing stories with the freedom to imagine new stories.

TimeSlips originally emerged out of the desire to support growth and learning with people with dementia and their caregivers. It was first used in a Milwaukee nursing home in 1996, and replicated in four adult day centers in 1998 (two in Milwaukee and two in New York City). The replication process included training undergraduate students as facilitators in the method. Students worked side by side with staff during the storytelling sessions. Students from the University of Wisconsin-Milwaukee (UWM) joined the project from departments of nursing, education, English, and theatre. In New York, undergraduate students from New York University and Hunter College joined the team, representing interdisciplinary programs and departments of education, theatre and social work.

All the student facilitators received training in the method and joined a team that would visit one of the two day centers each week. Over the course of ten weeks, the students facilitated some two-dozen stories. At the end of the ten weeks, the team of students designed a celebration—an opportunity to share the stories back with their elder storytellers. Both celebrations included gathering the stories into a "book" (simply copied and bound). In one celebration (in a day center in Park Slope, Brooklyn), students presented a retelling of the stories through puppetry—something the storytellers and their care partners enjoyed tremendously.

The *TimeSlips* method itself is built on ritual and improvisation techniques. Facilitators invite people to participate in a special event and welcome them individually. They provide a prompt to initiate the story, most commonly an image. Facilitators practice active, full-body listening—watching for and echoing back contributions to the story in words, sounds, gestures, and facial expressions. Like improvisation's guideline of *"yes—and,"* TimeSlips facilitators invite and accept all responses to the prompt—and emphasize this fact repeatedly throughout the storytelling session—to encourage people to step into the world of imagination. *"There are no wrong answers—we're making up a story together,"* is a common, reassuring phrase among facilitators. *"You can say anything you want, we're just making it up!"* is another.

As a way to prove to the storytellers that they mean what they say, facilitators write down every word on an oversized piece of paper. This is usually done on a flipchart to enable all the participants to see their words being captured on paper. Facilitators also refer to the flipchart when they retell the story. Throughout the storytelling session, which can range from 30 minutes to an hour in duration, facilitators repeat the story several times to bring storytellers to the moment of creation. When a facilitator feels the group starting to lose the thread of a story, she simply goes back over what they've built so far and the group is typically ready to offer more responses.

A crucial element of the story facilitation process is to let go of preconceived notions of story structure and follow the lead of the storytellers. This can be particularly challenging for writers, therapists, or teachers of creative writing who are sometimes married to rigid structures of beginning, middle, end, rising action, climax, and denouement. But the key to the method is not to drive the story, but to ask open-ended questions that put the power of creativity into the hands of the storytellers. This takes practice for students and for staff, who are often trained to *answer for* their clients. "*What do you want to call this person?*" or "*Where do you want to say they are?*" are examples of open questions. "*Do you think his name is Bob?*" or "*Which of the Great Lakes do you think that is?*" are both examples of closed questions that give the power of creativity to the facilitator, not the respondent-storyteller. In this way *TimeSlips* is more akin to improvisation than some story-generating programs that rely on conventional story structure.

TimeSlips is *not* intended to be a social-science inquiry protocol—rather a way to engage the imagination. Open-ended questions are used so that all participants may explore a range of imaginative possibilities. If, as sometimes happens, a participant does not answer a particular question, the facilitator often repeats the question, uses wait-time, or offers another question. Remember, the absence of data is data. If there is no response to a question this silence can, and often does, become part of the story itself.

TimeSlips processes are intended to challenge the more traditional approaches to creative writing and storytelling, (where the endpoint—a piece of writing—becomes the goal). It is designed to override the impulse of facilitators to write for respondents or edit so that the resulting written work has formal grammar, mechanics or flow. It is intended to allow all participants to write imaginatively and engage in a world where the imagined spoken thought becomes primary.

If four storytellers provide four different names for a character, then the story has a character with four names. If two storytellers disagree on a course of action, the facilitator will retell the story with two possible courses of action. *TimeSlips* stories are full of possibilities. In addition, storytellers often respond with sounds or gestures and even words that facilitators don't understand. When this happens, facilitators echo the response (with full body echoing) and write it down as best they can. *TimeSlips* training suggests they draw or spell it in a way that enables them to read it back to the satisfaction of the storyteller who originally said it.

In effect, facilitators are creating a safe space in which people with cognitive challenges can practice communication in a safe space where creative responses are not judged or denied. *TimeSlips* facilitators are encouraged to provide people with dementia access to meaning making, a sense of belonging, and feelings of pride and purpose. Facilitators learn how to open the storytelling process, freeing themselves from rigid structures, including spelling rules. It is an open, supportive space for experimentation.[2]

Over the 15-year history of *TimeSlips*, the method has been incorporated into classrooms in a wide range of disciplines. At Lehigh University, English professor Elizabeth Dolan used the *TimeSlips* method as part of an exploration of memory and identity in works of literature. At the University of North Carolina at Wilmington, *TimeSlips* was woven into a sociology class. At the University of Wisconsin-Oshkosh, psychology professor Dr. Susan McFadden incorporated *TimeSlips* into undergraduate psychology classes and an honors course that focused on identity and dementia.

Along with one of her students, Dr. McFadden created a measurement tool to assess student attitudes toward people with dementia. This scale has been used to capture the change in attitudes among students in classes that use *TimeSlips* as part of service-learning. Using this scale, professors at UW Milwaukee and Lehigh University implemented a study of the *TimeSlips* service-learning and found significant improvement in student attitudes toward people with dementia. The hope now is that, by improving attitudes and reducing fear, students can potentially improve the quality of their relationships with seniors (not to mention coming to terms with their own aging process).

To test this idea further, build on existing findings (described above), and examine undergraduate learning more deeply, we collaborated on a two-course *TimeSlips* program while also researching[3] its impact on student learning.

Teaching *TimeSlips*: Collaboration as pedagogy and practice

In 2010–11 we designed a *TimeSlips* curriculum at UWM by building on lessons learned from our past projects (*TimeSlips*,[4] *Elder Tales*[5] and *Milwaukee Stories*[6]). Anne is the faculty of record for THEATRE 359, a playwriting course. Robin teaches THEATRE 460, a storytelling course. We wanted to give our students a deeper and fuller experience for creative engagement. To do this we created a two-course offering designed to enhance literacy and writing skills and provide students with opportunities to learn and engage with intergenerational ethnographic storytelling (i.e. *TimeSlips*).

It was quickly apparent (at the beginning of our course-design phase) that using the standard undergraduate model, which requires offering each course at different times and in separate spaces, was not going to work. This conventional course delivery system was a problem because students' schedules were already committed and credit heavy (65 percent of UWM students work part or full time while attending college). We needed a format that mirrored the interdisciplinary nature of the project itself and decided to offer the courses simultaneously, in a process referred to as "stacking." Students could take both courses, (for six credits), or one course, (for three credits). Half of our students enrolled in the six-credit version. We used two adjoining classrooms (one a studio for group work, the other a classroom with tables, chairs, and learning technologies) and team-taught by moving both our classes back and forth between rooms or by traveling and swapping instructors when needed.

Our service-learning site was Luther Manor (LM), chosen because of its long association with *TimeSlips* and the Center on Age and Community at UWM. LM is an accredited continuing care retirement community. Our collaborator on site was Beth Myer-Arnold, Director of Adult Day Services. Beth has been a partner on many previous projects. Her leadership and focus on person-centered care have proved an invaluable resource and some of the success of this project is certainly due to her vision.

To solve the question of how to separate student groups when they needed focus on course-specific information, students in THEATRE 460 and THEATRE 359 were uploaded into our online course management system (Desire2Learn, a.k.a. D2L). As a hybrid course we were able to meet with students both online and face-to-face, as needed. The students in Theatre 359 had the opportunity to work with Anne on their playwriting skills (e.g. writing a scene or dialogue) while 460 students could "meet" with Robin to address improvisation, oral history, and storytelling techniques. At the end of the semester 359 students wrote scripted presentations that dramatized the material that was collected in the TimeSlips storytelling sessions.

The culminating capstone project was a script that was inclusive of the experience and contained the storytelling work. These scripts were then rehearsed and presented at a celebration at LM.

A note here about collaborative instruction: While university administration at UWM encourages innovative teaching (like sharing courses and materials) the practice still has little *structural* support. University mechanisms for assigning instruction, tracking the profitability of courses, locating classrooms, etc. continue to encourage one teacher per class—isolated from other instructors and divided by subjects or fields of study. We feel that the fact that we prevailed in our collaboration—and succeeded—is testimony to the way that *TimeSlips* demonstrates (and requires) collaboration at all levels.

The 359 and 460 courses were open to any qualified student (Sophomore-Senior status) attending UWM. Enrolled students were invited to participate in the research study and all agreed to do so. In early October our students began to work collaboratively with LM staff and residents in small groups with the goal of creating a final inclusive presentation (we have since made it possible for students to take *TimeSlips* online training and have incorporated the training as an online module in courses).

Groups were identified by their location within LM—The Courtyards, Day Center, Health Center, and Terrace—and each was overseen by the Life Enrichment Specialists assigned to these areas. Subsequently, every Tuesday afternoon we met on campus to review, explore new concepts, and plan next steps. Then, on Thursday afternoon, we would board the LM bus and work on *TimeSlips* implementation. These bus rides became an important part of our course experience. It gave us all time to socialize and exchange ideas, problems, concerns, and perspectives. At LM students worked collaboratively in groups and the remaining half-hour was spent debriefing (at the Welcome Center reception area)—then a bus trip back to campus.

Difficulties we encountered at the start of our service-learning had to do with the experience that most of us have when theoretical plans meet reality, i.e. cognitive dissonance. The first two service-learning sessions at LM were especially stressful, as students were encouraged to freely focus on individual participants' insight and ideas. Some undergraduates discussed their apprehension and fear. They reverted to thinking there might be a right answer and wondering if they were earning a "good grade." These were legitimate questions. Fear of failing and trepidation over what the stories might be like soon gave way as the processes led to tangible results. This intergenerational engagement actually invited new learning from both students and elders alike. As one Luther Manor resident noted: "My overall experience was 'hooray for young people!'"

Impact on learning

The 359/460 students participated in a pre- and post-survey tool that was adapted from McFadden's protocol (described previously). A pre-survey (designed to provide a baseline and identify perspectives and attitudes prior to engaging in *TimeSlips* activities was administered at the start of formal 359/460 course work, before engaging in *TimeSlips* activities, and prior to going to LM. The same survey was administered after the final presentation at LM. Overall, these data suggest that the students' (whose median age was approximately 19 years old) comfort, conceptions, and empathic perspectives were enhanced by their experience (see Table 6.1).

Comparisons of pre- and post-survey (gathered in the fall of 2010) data show *significant* changes in attitudes (see Table 6.1). Before participating in any service-learning activities the group was split between positive and neutral/negative ideas and dispositions toward the elderly. By December the majority of our students surveyed said that they were more likely to visit an older relative, be comfortable around older adults, and be interested in assisting and support elders.

Notable changes in attitudes can be seen in responses to the prompts: *I enjoy talking to old people, I enjoy being around old people, and I enjoy*

Table 6.1 UWM student survey results.

Survey question/prompt	Pre-survey (9/11)			Post-survey (12/11)		
	Disagree/ strongly disagree	Neutral	Agree/ strongly agree	Disagree/ strongly disagree	Neutral	Agree/ strongly agree
I enjoy being around old people	19%	25%	56%	14%	14%	72%
I like to go and visit my older relatives	19%	13%	69%	145	14%	72%
I enjoy talking to old people	19%	6%	75%	0%	7%	93%
I feel very comfortable when I am around an old person	50%	37%	13%	7%	14%	79%
I enjoy doing things for old people	0%	31%	69%	0%	7%	93%
I believe that I'll still be able to do most things for myself when I am old	6%	13%	81%	14%	29%	57%
It is rewarding to work with people who have Alzheimer's disease or dementia	13%	56%	25%	14%	28%	57%
People with Alzheimer's disease or dementia can be creative	0%	31%	69%	0%	7%	93%

doing things for old people. In September, there was a range of responses. A little over half of 359/460 students reported enjoying *"being around old people."* By December, 72 percent of those surveyed now *"liked being around"* older adults and 93 percent enjoyed conversing with them.

Also significant are the responses to the prompt: *"People with Alzheimer's disease or dementia can be creative."* Prior to their service-learning work, 31 percent of respondents were neutral. By December, 93 percent *strongly agreed* that elders with dementia were able to create and engage in creative activities, while only 7 percent reported neutrality. Students' experience of storytelling helped shift their dispositions toward elders in a positive direction.

Data indicate that the experience of talking, storytelling, and reflecting on the stories of self and others gave our students chances to engage empathically. As one student observed: *"What are the benefits of this? For me it's discovering how many of us [students] have so many things in common with the group of (elders) we are with!"*

Life and death

Discussing, considering, facing, and reflecting on death was a topic that kept cycling through the course discussions and reflections. One of the themes embedded in students' writing was the avoidance of the idea of death—a majority of undergraduates discussed being fearful of being near persons who were terminally ill and/or close to death.

Most students entered the course with a strong sense of invincibility. They made the assumption that the young do not die young; that the old are both close to death and unable to engage in activities that the young enjoy (e.g. sexual intimacy, romantic love, innovative action, seeking adventure, consuming contemporary music or media, etc.). They articulated youthful and avoidance-oriented ideas about their own aging. This feeling may be why a small minority of them reported feeling uncomfortable around old people at the beginning of the academic year while at the same time expressing optimism toward their own old age. By the end of the semester their positive approach to their own end-of-life had shrunk from 81 percent to 57 percent. At the same time their comfort in being around older adults increased!

As the courses proceeded, students felt better prepared to share perspectives and actively listen to others' ideas and responses. They also developed a more nuanced, realistic, and practical impression of aging and dying. One student observed: *One of the things I keep thinking about is talking to David who died just after we talked to him! About sharing his memories of private airplanes.* Another observed: *We tried to do something different every time so when we went to LM and lost a group member [who died] it was somehow OK.*

Building community and relationship(s)

This has been the best educational experience in university—ever! (UWM Student survey)

The students in this study grew empathically and intellectually. Two students commented: "I am learning about the way I can now interact with the elders in our Milwaukee community" and "Now I've formed a deep respect and deep respected relationship with [people in my group]."

They gained a deeper sense of being "part of a way bigger community" than they had previously. The courses also expanded their ideas of community engagement. Especially significant was how the coursework, including their service-learning experiences, encouraged them to improvise and develop material—iteratively and over long periods of experimentation.

Most students felt that the coursework was intellectually beneficial as well. They gained information and knowledge from the *TimeSlips* experience. Responses on the D2L discussion board included statements such as: *Amazing to work with the people at Luther Manor. Hearing their stories changes my day and my thinking for the better* and *This has been an excellent experience. I think that every student [in this university] should be involved in a project like this at some time.*

Students requested that UWM create more opportunities like the 359/460 collaboration. They sought more *TimeSlips*-like experiences and asked for engaged, applied, and community oriented course work in future: *I love the applied theatre that we are learning. I hope I can create similar ones in the future.* A fairly typical response came from 460 students who noted: *It is amazing being around these women [at my LM group] an enlightening experience. At first I was terrified. Now, it's funny to think I was. I want to do this again. Are there other courses like this?*

What we would do differently

Students were enthusiastic, hard-working, and always ready to experiment with course materials. The fact that there were few, if any, absences from the class is another testimony to the positive impact of *TimeSlips*. In reviewing liabilities and problems with 359/460 the overwhelming student response was that it was "*much too complicated*" and, at times, there was *too little discussion in [face-to-face meetings] about the online assignments and work.*

The only thing that could have made it better is having the content in the syllabus synthesized and D2L content organized differently. The framework of this made it clunky at times. *(UWM Student survey)*

Instructors concur. We are currently reworking the curriculum model for future dissemination. One other problem was mentioned—one that the instructors struggled over for some time: transportation.

The lack of reliable transportation was finally solved by LM, which generously offered a free bus service so that students could engage at their service learning site. The problem with getting to and from LM, which is essentially across town from campus, was so problematic (at least six different solutions were sought before finding a positive outcome) that the next project Anne will be addressing is the lack of public transportation in the Milwaukee area. This project is entitled "Islands of Milwaukee."

Conclusion

Clearly, things went well for all participants. Auxiliary data from this study, which we have not reported here, suggest that the intergenerational nature of the work, literacy components, and the enthusiasm of the undergraduates had a profoundly positive effect on LM staff and residents. Success was also due, in part, to the community-oriented and creatively engaged nature of the work. Planning, collaboration, and a willingness to explore the improvisational nature of *TimeSlips* also played an important role in the efficacy of the experience.

The results of our shared teaching experience show us once again what a powerful mode storytelling itself is: as a creative and active literary process that benefits brain function as well as higher-level thinking skills. Additionally, storytelling—especially the creative nature of the *TimeSlips* process—turns out to be more efficient and productive than passive experiences such as watching videos, television, or viewing a film (activities that are popular with both undergraduates and at long-term care facilities).

The TimeSlips curriculum allowed students and residents to build interpersonal connections that were immediate and imaginative. Our research suggests that by engaging elders and young adults in the processes of telling stories, students established uniquely interactive and relational first-person experiences. Then, through the writing, repeating, and "editing" of *TimeSlips* work participants had opportunities to deepen their response and reflect on shared worlds of meaning.

The storytelling process is easy to learn and to fit within the semester framework. The greatest challenges tend to be logistical—transportation and organization of information. Within the method itself, the greatest challenge is for the facilitator to release the temptation to drive the story, and instead open themselves to inviting, confirming, and really hearing the creative expression of those they might otherwise never have known.

※   ※   ※

Robin Reagler

Robin Reagler is the Executive Director of Writers in the Schools (WITS) in Houston, Texas, a program that serves over 20,000 students annually. She leads the Writers in the Schools (WITS) Alliance, an international consortium of 25 organizations engaged in teaching creative writing to grade school students. She is a poet and published a chapbook, *Dear Red Airplane*, by Seven Kitchens Press, in 2011. In 2012 she won an Individual Artist Fellowship from the Houston Arts Alliance.

Teaching, or How to Fall in Love

I met Claudia more than 20 years ago while teaching for Writers in the Schools (WITS) in Houston, Texas. She was extremely shy. That first day, I made it my goal to get her to read her writing aloud to the class. It took all year, but she finally did it. The story she read to the class was about a trip her family made to a volcano that had recently erupted in Mexico.

Toward the end of my time at the University of Houston, I'd won a fellowship to support me while writing my dissertation. Since I'm not the type to write nonstop day and night for weeks on end, I asked the WITS director to give me an assignment with a big challenge. She assigned me a residency, teaching every sixth grader in a public school. At this middle school, I taught 200 children each week, including Claudia, Clay, Raquel, Guillermo, and many other children, visiting them every Tuesday and Thursday.

The school served two neighborhoods: one with single-family homes, the other with large apartment complexes. Houston is the quintessential American melting pot, and this school was its microcosm. Half of the students were immigrants and spoke native languages including Spanish, Arabic, Polish, and Russian. Other children came from families who owned boats, second homes, and expensive cars. The mission of the school was to create community amidst difference, and although this was a tall order, they were generally successful.

The school building itself was old and small—too small to serve the children they were expected to serve. Half of the classrooms were in temporary buildings similar to mobile homes. The culture of the school was generally positive and nurturing, and I admired the mutual respect between teachers and students. The hallways were always decorated with amazing student art, and the children had designed and created gardens with mosaic tiles.

My middle-school residency lasted two semesters, and together we had many marvelous adventures. We learned to write dialogue by talking into a banana, and we created huge colorful broadsides of our best poems. We took a fieldtrip to an art museum. Each visit brought surprises. One day our discussion somehow drifted to teeth. Everyone shared what traditions and rituals their family practiced when children lose their teeth. Children talked about placing the tooth under their pillows, the tooth fairy, or, in some cultures, a mouse, that took the tooth and replaced it with a gift. In one culture they threw the tooth on the roof, and if a bird stole it the child would have good luck. It was unplanned but wonderful when this kind of conversation came up. The WITS classroom valorizes our cultural and individual differences. Good writing celebrates these differences.

When I reviewed the students' portfolios (simple manila folders containing their writing and revisions from the year) in May, I found myself tracing the journeys of each student. For new immigrants it might be transition from their own language to tentative English. For native speakers, it might be learning the power of verbs. I hadn't realized it, but over the course of that year, I'd fallen in love with each of my students. I remembered Claudia—the shy girl I mentioned earlier, who was an excellent writer, even though she hadn't realized it at first. When she read aloud the story of her family's trip to Mexico, many of her classmates made effusive comments to her about her vibrant story. Her teacher and I could tell that she felt proud of herself. She smiled into her lap.

Although this first residency took place almost 20 years ago, I treasure the details of each child's story simply because I fell in love with teaching writing to children. This middle-school experience is what made me decide to devote my career to WITS. What I discovered was that the WITS process helps children regardless of their circumstances or abilities. WITS helps students tell their stories with strength and grace. Of the 200 students I taught that year, I think each and every one experienced the pleasure and power of reading and writing.

The creative process brings out our uniqueness. By sharing our stories in the classroom, we honor one another by listening carefully, noticing details, and asking good questions. Sharing brought students and teachers together. I had fun with the students, and I learned probably more than they did. As I continued with WITS, I learned to trust the process of falling in love.

1   Look before you leap

Every school has its own culture, and as a visiting writer, it helps to get a sense of that culture before beginning to teach. If possible, try to visit the classes you will be teaching before you begin your residency. After many years of visits, I have become a regular Harriet the Spy. Look for clues as you visit each teacher's classroom. Look for clues about her values, her teaching style, and the way students interact with the teacher and each other. What rituals are in place? Do students have weekly "jobs"? How do they decide who is next when taking turns? What kind of student work appears on the walls and bulletin boards? Knowing how the class works will help you adjust to the culture so that you understand a little about the world you are about to enter.

2   Do the Cupid Shuffle

Your relationship with the classroom teacher is paramount to your success. Yes, you want good lesson plans, you want to learn the students' names, you want great writing to come out of each session. But a good relationship with the teacher secures these goals. Like any healthy relationship, this one requires weekly nurturing and respect. For a writer in the school, this means always remembering that you are a guest in the teacher's classroom. This is her space; these are her students. When you enter the classroom each time, she should be the one you greet first, if possible. Following the rituals and rules of the classroom are another way to show your respect. Being a teacher is a difficult and hectic job. Your classroom teachers are your collaborators. You want to ally yourself with the teacher. Help her carry her load and credit her when her students succeed. I try to remember that the teachers are pulled in all sorts of directions and deal with multiple issues at every moment of every day. Rather than become one of her issues, I strive to be her assister.

I remember Guillermo during my first semester in the middle schools. He turned in a story was jumbled and confusing, and there was something about the symbolism that worried me. It seemed to me that he might be referring to an abusive situation in his home life. I did not discuss it with him; instead I consulted his teacher because I thought she'd know what to do. She talked with the school counselor who began meeting with Guillermo. I'm not sure what transpired exactly, or whether my suspicions were right or wrong, but at the end of the school year Guillermo gave me a painting he'd made in art class. In the school art show this painting had won the first place ribbon for "best in show." I still have that picture framed in my office.

The effort you put into the writer/teacher relationship will pay off. And the silvery lining is this—by the very nature of the WITS collaboration, the writer and the teacher share the same goal—for the students to improve their skills and discover the joy of writing.

3   Make a plan, Stan

The WITS lesson structure is based on the writing process itself. If you are teaching for the first time, it may take practice to adjust to the rhythm and timing of your lesson. The typical WITS lesson has three parts—cultivating, writing, and sharing, and in the classic WITS format, each receives more-or-less equal amounts of time. Within this framework the possibilities are endless.

a   Cultivating

I like the word cultivating for the first part of the lesson because I am a gardener. In a garden you cultivate the land before planting a seed, and the same is true with falling in love. In gardening you turn the soil, fertilize it, and let it "breathe." You plant the seed and water it. In a relationship, you give space and time to discover new things about the other person. During the first part of the lesson you get the students excited about the project and help them choose their subject matter. You introduce new terms and often you guide the group in brainstorming or writing together as a group before asking them to write independently. You ask interesting questions that help rev up their imaginations. One thing to keep in mind is that during most of the school day, a student is asked to produce the same answer as everyone else in the room. Students are accustomed to a world of right and wrong answers. When a teaching artist enters the scene, suddenly the rules change. Students are expected to produce something *unlike* everyone else in the room. Originality may be an unexpected request for some students. It may take some time for them to trust that you are genuinely interested in their personal stories. So the beginning of the lesson helps students to make a transition to a more creative frame of mind.

Most of my lesson lessons involve some sort of prompt. It might be a short story or an essay, a poem, a reproduction of a Rene Magritte painting, a Gregorian chant, an old bowling trophy, or a pineapple. Because students have different learning styles and levels of ability, I always appeal to at least 3 of their senses. If I'm teaching "Someone Puts a Pineapple Together" I might give students a handout of the poem, read it aloud, while an actual pineapple is passed from student to student. Passed, carefully, of course. The poem has twelve numbered lines, and each one is a metaphor representing the pineapple. We might reread the poem one line at a time and try to figure out what aspect or perspective of the pineapple Wallace Stevens is describing in each line. Studying the pineapple, turning it around so that we can observe it from different angles, we discuss which part of the fruit is like "nailed-up lattices"? How is the pineapple "yesterday's volcano"? Where are the hundred eyes? We could discuss the term metaphor, how a metaphor is a comparison of two things, how metaphor is a double whammy that writers use to make a powerful impression. As they say in the comics, Ka-pow!

Pre-writing is part of cultivating; it can help them understand metaphor-making by giving it a test run or it can be guided brainstorming for their own poem. Perhaps we would try to write poem made of metaphors as a group. Choosing an object in the classroom or one I've brought with me, we study it carefully using all five senses. Let's say the object is a tennis ball. Ask students what they notice. Encourage them to use all five senses. Feel the texture. What happens if you drop it on the floor? What does the ball remind you of? By writing the class examples on the board, student get to see how to get from an observation or impression to a metaphor, step by step . In this way they learn how metaphor works. Pre-writing can be done solo as well, in the form of brainstorming, listing, drawing, map-making, and so on. But the idea is to practice the new skill, in this case, creating metaphors, together. By the end of the cultivating period, the students should be ready to write.

Clay, a student from that middle school residency, was a preppy, well-dressed blond boy with an amputated arm. He'd begun the school year writing nonsense, "My hair is fluffy like a flat table." But eventually the creative process won him over. By the second semester he wrote what I'd call flash fiction or in some cases flash nonfiction. All the stories began in the world as we know it but by the end something had inexplicably disappeared.

b Writing

During the writing portion of the lesson, the seed unfurls, sprouts, and grows—the relationship begins to mature. During each WITS session, I am sure to give the students uninterrupted time to write. First, I ask, "Who already knows what you are writing about?" I answer questions and check in with students who want more guidance. Then I enforce a long block of time in which there are no questions. The silence might be uncomfortable at first to a new teacher, but I remind myself that this is what I'm here for: to give them time to write creatively. I find this reassuring. Some of my colleagues actually set a timer or use an hourglass to demarcate this sacred time dedicated to writing. During that time I check in with the teacher and sometimes I even do a little writing myself! After the minutes are done, students continue to write, and I check in with students who have questions or may be stuck. As you continue your residency, you may find that you can increase the amount of writing time. Since students finish their work at different times, I always post a "bonus" on the board for the early birds. The bonus is actually a mini-revision, a tweak, often echoing a lesson we've done before. Examples might be, find a "be" verb and replace it with an action verb, or review your story and make sure to use words representing all five of your senses. For students who struggle with the blank page, sometime the solution is as simple as offering them choices. Sometimes using colorful paper or writing with a special pen or looking at a photograph can help unleash a student's creativity.

c Sharing

The WITS lesson generally ends with students sharing their writing with one another. The purpose of this part of the lesson is not merely to share, as the name suggests. It is also a time to teach children to begin to analyze writing, which is essential to revision. Also it is a time for the group to come together and support one another. Many of the WITS writers designate an Author's Chair in the classroom for the reader. It can be a different type or color of chair and place it in a central location in the room. This shows the importance of the student's writing and helps focus the group's attention on the child who is reading. If no special chair is available, you can choose a "magic square" on the carpet or floor.

I remember Raquel from that first residency, 20 years ago. She'd begun the year with a descriptive and evocative "Ode to Mangoes." Her teacher said it was positive attention that she had lacked until WITS came to their classroom. As the year ended, I'm not sure that any of her writing was as strong as that first poem, but the experience gave her new confidence, which she held onto throughout the year. On the final day of my residency we did a performance for parents and friends. Raquel came dressed in a beautiful floral dress, jewelry, and high heels even. I'd never seen her wear a dress at school. The teacher whispered to me, this is Raquel's way of saying thank you.

The sharing session should be a positive experience for each student. Therefore, you will have to explain your expectations clearly before you begin. Often the WITS Houston writers let students come up with the rules by imagining what they would want when they are the featured author. To teach students active listening you can come up with one or two routine questions so that they know what to listen for. The questions will vary based on the ages of the students. With young children, writers often ask for "two stars and a wish," meaning two things that are amazing (stars) and one question about something you'd like to know more about (wish). With older students, the WITS writers often ask for favorite phrases or sentences in the author's own words. This trains students to listen for specific words as opposed to general content. Writers sometimes do this using sticky notes. While the students are working on their stories, the writer places four or five sticky notes beside each one. Each student writes phrases that impressed them and records them on the note paper. The notes are passed to the author, and *voila*—she has 25 suggestions indicating what is strong in her work.

The structure I've described is the basic one used at WITS Houston. Once you feel comfortable with it, you will begin to discover all the many wonderful variations.

4   Try this

Think of a teacher who made a difference in your life. What was it about that experience that made this particular teacher memorable? How would you describe that teacher? (See Figure 6.1)

Find the three words that best describe the teacher who came to mind. Then try to "unpack" each word you chose, remembering a specific example for each one.

5   You are not alone

Trying new things may cause anxiety and other side effects. Please note: you are not alone. There are thousands of other writers teaching young students, and you can find support when you need it. There are resources in book form and on the web. Teachers & Writers Collaborative (twc. org) has published dozens of books for teaching artists, including *Poetry Everywhere* (1994) by Jack Collum and Sheryl Noethe and *Third Mind*

attentive challenging
understanding
joyful supportive
humble curious
quirky kind decisive funny
organized knowledgeable
loving driven demanding
fair tough
certain respectful loyal
enthusiastic
calm

FIGURE 6.1 *Word cloud of favorite teacher.*

(2002) by Tonya Foster and Kristin Prevallet. Teachers & Writers has launched its Digital Resource Center, a searchable collection of lessons and articles from their magazine.

The WITS Alliance (witsalliance.org) is an organization headquartered at WITS Houston (witshouston.org) that provides mentorship, training, and resources for individuals and organizations engaged in this type of teaching. The WITS Alliance presents a strand of panels, meetings, and events at the annual AWP Conference (awpwriter.org) that specifically supports teaching writing. WITS Alliance members organizations such as WITS Houston (witshouston.org), Community Word Project (communitywordproject.org) in New York City, and WITS Portland (Literary Arts) offer annual training events for colleagues in other cities.

But wait, there's more!

Most learning happens through practice. WITS teaching, when it's done well, helps students find their own personal voices. Most of the writers at WITS Houston admit that they are often inspired by their students' writing. I'll end with an excerpt from Jennifer's (fifth grade) poem which came out of a lesson that we call "Blessings." I hope that the practice of teaching writing brings you showers of poetic magic and a spirit of giving. And, of course, love.

May your house never be blue.
May the rain kiss your eyelids.
May starfish protect your dreams.
May music blossom into flowers.

CHAPTER SEVEN

Creative Writing as Social Activism

Art as resistance

Art—whether it's creative writing, visual art, performance art, film—is a form of resistance. None of us wants to be invisible, unseen by our community, cast off, marginalized. Art gives us a way to say, "I am here." Many people who have been labeled as being "in need" tend to have learned to take what they can get, and to not ask questions. Art asks questions, prods for the individual's dignity and social rights.

Jessica Rueter Dawkins worked with elementary students at an inner-city school, and designed a lesson teaching the narrative epistolary form.

> I asked Sechua who her letter was being written to, and she told me it was for her father, "because he's in jail." Sechua made the confession without even blinking an eye. On a personal note, my own father has been to jail, and I haven't told anyone except my fiancé. In the world of students like Sechua, jail is a commonplace topic. There wasn't any embarrassment in her voice when she continued to tell me that she couldn't visit him because her mother didn't have a car. I asked her how long her father had been in jail. "Three weeks," she said without hesitation. When I asked her when he was coming home, she said she didn't know. She told me that hoped that God would bring her father back home. She asked me how to spell God. My heart sank. (Rueter Dawkins, 2008)

While none of us likes to hear that Sechua took her father being in jail as "commonplace," this experience certainly demonstrates that her life—where she was in her life at that moment—mattered. This is also an ideal example of a child teaching a college student a thing or two about acceptance of one's life.

Beyond your project

Each semester I have students who, once introduced to taking creative writing into the real world, want to continue doing this type of work. Imagination and creativity are vital to community building, and there are numerous opportunities for you to continue after you graduate.

In the United States, there are formal programs within university settings as well as individual teachers who offer or require service-learning projects similar to what we're talking about in this book. In Great Britain, the National Association of Writers in Education (NAWE) provides numerous programs and support for writers in schools, in community settings, and universities. They publish pamphlets and booklets and provide training for writers interested in getting involved with taking creative writing to school children and community members. The Australian Society of Authors connects authors with K–12 schools that request creative writing instruction. Wherever there are writers—in every city, every country—you'll find community based writing projects.

Many universities in the U.S. have volunteer programs for any university students to conduct different types of service projects. Many nonprofit organizations, as I've mentioned before, hire writers or use volunteers to conduct writing residencies. And there are hundreds of individual writers who support themselves through arts grants and foundation support to do this type of work for many years. The lists provided here are in no way exhaustive. There are more colleges and universities, nonprofit organizations, and individual writers doing this kind of work than I could possibly list here. More and more universities, organizations, and writers begin new projects all the time.

Many programs within a university operate on small scale; however, depending upon administrative support and funding, some can develop into larger programs. For example, at Arizona State University, The Young Writers Program is supported by a foundational grant through the Virginia G. Piper Center, which relies on grants from a trust. Numerous universities and colleges offer undergraduate and graduate students opportunities to provide creative writing opportunities to persons in their surrounding communities. Here's a list of a few of those universities. If available, I've provided the name of the faculty or contact person. Please see Appendix C for more detail.

University programs/faculty

Arizona State University, Young Writers Program
Georgia College and State University, Allen Gee
Kent State University, Wick Poetry Center, David Hassler
Michigan State University, Anita Skeen
New York University, Literary Outreach Fellowships
Pennsylvania State University, Julia Kasdorf
Sarah Lawrence College
Stetson University, Mark Powell
University of Arizona
University of New Mexico, Connie Voisine
University of Wisconsin, Center for Community

Nonprofit organizations often grow out of an individual writer's desire to provide creative writing to underserved populations. These organizations rely on a Board of Directors and eventually a staff to help raise funds in order to pay writers to keep programs going. Robin Reagler, Executive Director of Writers in the Schools Houston (WITS Houston), created the WITS Alliance, which encourages communication and collaboration among numerous literary arts programs around the country. Here are a few organizations. There are hundreds of organizations like these around the U.S. where writers interested in community based creative writing.

Nonprofit organizations

826 National
Community Word NYC
InsideOut Literary Arts Detroit
TimeSlips
True Ink
Write Girl
Write Around Portland
Writers in the Schools Houston

Many writers prefer to work independently of a university, and may or may not use the nonprofit model to keep this work going. These writers often put together a living through freelance writing and consulting, as well as receiving grants through state arts councils, school districts, individual schools, community organizations, and individual donors.

Individual writers[1]

Silvi Alcivar
Christopher McIlroy
Allan Wolf
Glenis Redmond
Michael Beadle
Mick Fedullo
Marge Pellegrino
Sherwin Bitsui

One of the most well-known and earliest formal creative writing CBL projects in a university was developed by Frances Payne Adler at California State University, Monterey Bay. Her essay, which follows the structured reflections, not only describes how and why she implemented this project, but also reflects on the project's impact on herself, the university, and how these projects address social justice issues.

Structured reflection

Personal

1   Choose one of the individual writers listed in this chapter, review her/his website. How to you think they got started? How do they support themselves in order to do the work they love? What obstacles do you think they've encountered?

Academic

2   Locate one literary poem or one literary story that relates to creative writing as social activism (for example, the Adrienne Rich poems you read during the first week). How do these pieces relate to the work you're doing at your site?

3   Identify aspects of your project or lesson delivery that you need to adjust or change?

Civic

4 What changes are you seeing in the participants?

5 How has your view of "community" changed since you began your project?

6 In Chapter 4 "Structured Reflection," I asked you to locate statistics and information on the demographics of the population you are working with. How do those statistics compare with your own observations at your site?

Reading

Frances Payne Adler

Frances Payne Adler is the author of five books, *Making of a Matriot* (2003), *Raising the Tents* (1993), and three collaborative poetry-photography books and exhibitions that have shown in galleries and state capitol buildings across the country. She also co-edited *Fire and Ink: An Anthology of Social Action Writing* (2009). Her current collaboration is *Dare I Call You Cousin*, poems, photos & videos about the Israeli-Palestinian conflict, with Israeli artists Michal Fattal and Yossi Yacov. Adler is Professor Emerita of Creative Writing and Founder of California State University Monterey Bay's Creative Writing and Social Action Program. She lives in Portland, Oregon.

Activism in Academia: A Social Action Writing Program

Try telling yourself
you are not accountable
to the life of your tribe
the breath of your planet ...
Adrienne Rich (1984b, p. 325)

My work is rooted in the notion
that art can provoke social change.
Willie Birch (1990)

You are the soothsayer with quill and torch.
Write with your tongues on fire.
Gloria Anzaldua (1987)

Witnessing is especially necessary
when the reality of a lived experience
is denied by the culture at large,
the culture to which the witness is brought.
Judith McDaniel (1987)

I think that the job of poetry, its political job,
is to refresh the idea of justice, which is going
dead in us all the time.
Robert Hass (1997, p. 22)

"The life of your tribe." "Tongues on fire." "Witnessing." "Social Change."
Writers' voices, invoking justice and peace. The Creative Writing and Social
Action Program at California State University, Monterey Bay (CSUMB)
honors and teaches this kind of writing. We come by it honestly, as my
mother used to say. It is in sync with our origins as a university. Since 1994,
we have transformed CSUMB from a military base into an educational one.
With the guns gone, we brought out the books and committed ourselves
to "diversity, particularly low-income, working-class, and historically
underserved students." We regard social action writing as an act of critical
inquiry, the domain of academia. Social action writing teaches students
to break silences, to witness their lives, to be engaged and responsible
members of their communities, to bring together craft and critical inquiry.

The program is now six years old, and if I were to choose one word
to describe its evolution—the vision, implementation, impact—it would
be collaboration. Everyone who has been involved with the Program
has contributed her or his own lived experiences, skills, creativity, and
commitment to social action. For each of us, the collaboration began long
before we came to CSUMB. In the following, I will tell my part of the story,
about the evolution of the vision for, and the founding of, the Creative
Writing and Social Action Program. And I will tell you stories about some
of the process of building the Program, our institute, and the university, as
well as stories about our students, and what you can do at your university
if you are interested in social action.

Evolution of a vision for a creative writing program committed to social action

Although I could not have known it, for 13 years before coming to CSUMB
in 1996, everything I was doing was training me for this work. Let me begin
with a story. It is 1986, and I am about to teach my first creative writing
class. I have spent years learning the craft, and I am here to teach students
how to write poetry and fiction—rhythm and meter, metaphor and simile,
how to create characters, how to develop setting and plot. I am set, right?

"What shall I write about?" a student asks. "I have nothing to write about, nothing ever happens in my life." This is a central question, asked by many students in the class. Students are moving toward writing well-crafted poems and stories, but anemic ones. I try every writing exercise I know, yet students are still not inside their work. Many words, many pages, and they are silent within their words. Where is the passion, the energy in their writing, where is the *"duende,"* as Federico Garcia Lorca said, when "the blood burns like powdered glass" (1973, p. 93)?

The nothing-ever-happens-in-my-life student becomes my teacher. After several visits to my office, she writes a story about her two brothers she has lost to suicide within the past year. All this is going on in her life at the same time as she is saying she has nothing to write about. OK, I get it. Hear: nothing she is *allowed* to write about, talk about, reveal.

She brings me her story. "Do I have to read it to the class?" she asks. "It is a secret, I'm not supposed to tell." Such a large pain, and she is not allowed to tell. In how many ways has she been silenced? In whose interest is it for her to be silent? What would be the cost of breaking her silence? What might have happened had she broken her silence earlier?

Purposeful silencing is the hood that so often cloaks students' writing. As Tillie Olsen said, "the leeching of belief, of will, the damaging of capacity begins so early" (1978, p. 27). And the ways in which they have been silenced is what we began to study within my 1980s creative writing classroom. "Live the questions," Rainer Maria Rilke said (1934, p. 35). Writers who had assisted me years earlier in my feminist awakening, in my own writing breakthroughs, flood through me; their voices enter the classroom and take a seat. Adrienne Rich: "What if I tell you, you are not different/it's the family albums that lie" (1984a, 323). Muriel Rukeyser: "Write what burns in you, what you can't forget" (1987, p. 203) "Your silence will not protect you," Audre Lorde 1984a, p. 41). "Of what had I *ever* been afraid?" again Audre Lorde. "The will to power ... is the will to write," Henry Louis Gates (1991, p. 4). Voices move from my own writing desk to the classroom. I use my own path to help students come to their full voices. It feels, at this time, somehow dangerous, not "legitimate creative writing pedagogy."

Theory about rhythm and meter, imagery and objective correlatives, that is what I had learned in graduate school, this is how to teach creative writing. Yes, and this method is not enough to peel away the constructed silencings; this method does not begin to deal with the gender, class, and race issues that bind the tongue. I see that a different kind of theory is needed. While I am inventing—with my students in the English department—a way to teach creative writing that is holistic, that feels right, that breaks silences, I also begin to teach women's literature in the Women's Studies Department. Feminist pedagogy cross-pollinates and reinforces my creative writing pedagogy. I am teaching Rich, Lorde, and Rukeyser in both my literature classes and my creative writing classes. Essays and poems about undoing silences, peeling away the censors, witnessing. Judith McDaniel's voice enters: "Witnessing is especially necessary when the reality of a lived experience is denied by the culture at large, the culture to which the witness is brought" (1987, p. 128). Gloria Anzaldua: "You are the soothsayer with quill and torch. Write with your tongues on fire" (1987, p. 73).

Carmen, a student in my creative writing class, who is from the Imperial Valley, reads McDaniel and Anzaldua and writes at last, about her father, picking grapes, years in the fields, dying of cancer. "The pesticides scratch, poison his lungs/clog his breath," she writes; for years she has held her anger, knowing without knowing until she reads the environmental reports, her voice now sharp as steel.

Years later, in 1993, I will hear Toni Morrison on PBS radio, after she has received the Nobel Prize in Literature. "The master narrative is the story as written by the master. It's telling us who has value and who has not." I will think of Carmen, and so many other students, and my own experiences as a woman. But in the mid-1980s, I have not yet heard the term "master narrative," though I am certainly living in one.

I am listening to my body, outrage streaming through my body at the silences I recognize around me. I am a new teacher making it up as I go along; I have a pedagogical challenge here, and I am inventing from this need. I worry this may not be the "right" way to teach creative writing, and I do it anyway. I title the class, "Woman as Witness," and I bring feminist theory into my pedagogy. "Poetry is not a luxury," Audre Lorde said. "Poetry is the way we help give name to the nameless so it can be thought" (1984b, pp. 36–9). Students are lit up by retrieving lost voices, writing them, reading them to each other. Sandra MacPherson's voice enters: "Your story can help someone else to live" (1986, p. 30). Students are breaking long-held silences, and are not struck dead by lightning. They are claiming what they know to be true, their wisdom, their perceptions, their authority. It spills over into their public lives. They become aware of another overlay of silence they have been keeping about what is going on in the world around them, concern they have had about the environment, war, homelessness, and work conditions. The collaboration continues: the voices of writers speaking their process of coming to voice, students writing their lived experiences, reading them to their colleagues in the workshop, voices churning the classroom.

I long to collaborate in my creative writing classes with colleagues who are not solely focused on craft. I go to creative writing conferences. At one such conference, a white male colleague beside me says, "I wouldn't touch that stuff (breaking silences). I'm no psychologist." "Neither am I," I say. "But I am a human being. Women have been doing this for each other for thousands of years." Somehow, I am confident. Students' writings are luminous, their lives transformed. I know this is the right path. I envision teaching creative writing in an integrated way with colleagues who are dealing with gender, race, and class issues. I propose teaching creative writing in the Women's Studies Department, but, in the mid-1980s, creative writing is taught solely in English Departments. I write and publish an article in the *AWP Chronicle* calling for creative writing to become part of Women's Studies, African American Studies, and Chicano Studies. I call for "creative writing as representation, the building blocks of this multicultural house we're building" (2001, p. 10).

As Adrienne Rich has said, "Poems are like dreams: in them you put what you don't know you know" (1978, p. 40). In the mid–1980s, years before I am to build the Creative Writing and Social Action Program at CSUMB, I write a poem, "Raising the Tents," which envisions my future work. "In the first years of the twenty-first century, it was discovered / that voices, all the unheard ones, didn't die at the end of life. / Instead, they spent thousands of years, wandering underground … / It was an earthquake like no other" (Adler, 1993a, p. 64). This is the glimmer on the horizon, the early vision of future work. Ten years later, I will found the creative writing program at CSUMB and, with colleagues from diverse disciplines, teach students how to retrieve their lost voices and those of their families and communities.

But I don't know this then. I do know I am doing the work I am meant to do. This knowledge is a body thing. Like the time in the early 1980s, a few years before I began teaching, my mother, dead 15 years, comes back to me in a vision. *"Listen to what you know through your body,"* she says. This is years before I read Helene Cixous, years before I read her feminist theory about writing from the body. So I listen to my mother's advice, and my body becomes my compass.

When Edwin Meese, our attorney general in 1983, says, "there is no hunger in America," and a month later, a Presidential Task Force concludes, "there is no documentable hunger in America," I cannot ignore my body reaction. This is where my social action story begins. "Someone needs to do something," I rail. "Someone?" a friend asks, "Why not you?" "Me?" I say. "What can I do? I am just a student."

It is not long before I know he is right, and I know the answer. What I can do is write. I call Kira Carrillo Corser, a friend who is a photographer, and ask her if she wants to collaborate, to document the homeless. "Yes," she says. "I've already taken some photographs; let's do it." We research homelessness, need to understand what we are seeing and hearing, understand the causes, the spoken ones, the unspoken ones. We interview people living on the streets, early mornings before going to work, evenings after work. They spill over into our dreams. They enter poems and photographs. We produce an exhibition, and call it social action art. It is 1984. There are 3,500 homeless people living on the street. Ten years later, there will be 23,000. We do not know this then; we believe we can make a difference. A year later, to support the passage of legislation for services for homeless people, we are invited to bring the poems and stories and photographs of "Home Street Home" to the State Capitol Building in Sacramento, then to the Capitol Building in Washington, DC.

We work in collaboration with the community, who tell us our art helps break through denial surrounding homelessness. Our work is a catalyst for coalition building. It assists in passage of legislation, assists in a community organization receiving additional staff, more funding. We go on to do three more exhibitions about lack of access to healthcare. We are concerned about the 37 million people in the U.S. without healthcare insurance then, about the need for healthcare reform. One of the exhibitions is titled, "A Matriot's Dream: Health Care for All" (Adler, 1993b). "Matriot is a word I invent during the Gulf War in 1991, when our defense forces create the "Patriot" missile. That evening, I ask myself, what does a "matriot" look like? And I create the definition. "Matriot: One who loves his or her country. One who loves and protects the people of his or her country. One who perceives national defense as health, education, and shelter for all of the people in his or her country." The exhibits travel the country, showing in galleries, at community organizations, in state capitol buildings, on Capitol Hill.

I am asked why I do this. I cannot say. Only that I am compelled. Years later, I will understand part of it. I will come to ask myself core questions: as a Jew, had I lived in Europe during the Holocaust, would I have recognized what was going on early enough to get out? Or would I have looked the other way until it was too late? If I were not a Jew, would I have stood up for someone who was? My former mother-in-law, who survived the Holocaust, once told me that, as a Jew, you couldn't survive unless someone who wasn't a Jew helped you at some point along the way. For me, the question has become: What is happening today—that may or may not be happening to me—that I need to stand up for? That we all need to stand up for? As Elie Weisel has said, "I learned that in extreme situations when human lives and dignity are at stake, neutrality is a sin. It helps the killers, not the victims" (Weisel, 1987, p. 132).

Questioning the taboo: Activism in academia

This brings me to activism. There I said it. Activism in academia. There I said it again. As faculty, in an early part-time position in the Women's Studies Department at San Diego State University, I am told by our Chair, "Fran, you can't bring your activism into the classroom." I am collaborating again with Kira, we are producing our second exhibition about lack of access to prenatal care. Six hundred women a month are being turned away from prenatal clinics, women who wanted to have their babies. We are opening in the State Capitol Building in Sacramento, and I am writing a letter to a state senator, inviting her to the opening. I am writing on department stationery. "Fran," she says, "you must keep your activism and your teaching separate." She is a colleague and a friend. She is looking out for me, mentoring me about the ways of academia, what's done, what's not done.

I'll tell you a story not often told: as some of you may know, the first women's studies program in the country was started at San Diego State University in 1970. What you may not know is that the original program was created by graduate students and a few women faculty, some of whom were activists, applying in the community what they were teaching in the classroom. For example, while they were teaching about women's lives in the classroom, they were involved in supporting a battered women's shelter. The founding mothers considered the patriarchal values of the academy-hierarchy, objectivity as the only valid means to interpret the world, and a prioritization of value on research to the exclusion of "activism" (meaning community involvement)—to be contrary to feminist principles. The new Women's Studies Program was considered a dangerous program. As a result, the original women's studies program was disbanded. A new program was established, more traditional, objective, where scholars did not do "biased" activism; women's studies came into the university on patriarchal terms.

The academy itself has been co-opted from its original vision. In 1990, historian Page Smith traced the more than 100-year history of silencing of the academy in the U.S. According to Smith, John Hopkins University established the first graduate school in the U.S. in 1870, on the principles that "scholarship in the U.S. might become the great engine of social reform" and that the "world (might be) redeemed from coldness of heart and injustice by a new cadre of scholars dedicated to reform" (Smith, 1990, pp. 56–7). That original vision did not last long. Owners of the new universities, who were also owners of the railroads and sweatshops and coalmines, branded advocacy of social justice reform as "unscientific" and lauded those who opposed these reforms as "objective." Professors who espoused ideas considered "dangerous" to the status quo were fired.

I believed then and still do, that it is time to reclaim this original intent for higher education. As Maseo Miyoshi writes:

> While we (in the Humanities) have no doubt that we ought to have risen in resistance and struggle, not in cool analysis, against the Holocaust, the rape of Nanking, and the destructions in Vietnam, we are overlooking the acts of inhumanity that are taking place right before our eyes. We still insist that scholarly decorum be heeded, that we be not one-sided. What took place in the past can claim our undivided rage; from what is taking place, we avert our gaze, and reflect on its epistemological limitations. We keep arguing about Otherness and its representations—nearly ad nauseum—while ignoring an other being decimated. (1989, p. 201)

I have come to know that maintaining the status quo is in itself a form of activism. That "objectivity" in academia can too often mask support for the status quo.

Finding a home for the vision

By 1996, I have been doing social action writing for 13 years, collaborating with Kira and always keeping what was called my "activism" separate from my teaching. Imagine my surprise when I see an ad in the *Chronicle*, posted by the new California State University, Monterey Bay. They want someone committed to community building and social justice, yes, that's me, someone ready to pitch in and build a new university from scratch. They are looking for a poet who wants to join them in transforming the Fort Ord military base into a university. I interview for the position, do a workshop, challenge the silences, and call in writers' voices. They join me in the classroom, and collaborate with me to assist students to uncloak their silences.

In the workshop, students write, bend their heads over their notepads, their faces flushed. After class, there's Paulo, walking over to me, his eyes shy as lamps. He wants to talk. He is a songwriter, plays the guitar, has been writing songs for years. He has songs he sings for friends, for family, and he has songs he sings for no one. Angry songs. And he wants to show them to me. Would he sing one, I ask? He looks around, motions me to come outside. He leans against a quiet wall and sings his pain, his grandfather's crossing from Mexico, how he is beaten, robbed, left for dead, and he is not dead, he is angry. It is a story his *abuelo* told him so very many years ago; *don't tell your abuela I told you, mijo,* the night air colluding in our secrecy. This is a song he has sung for no one. Audre Lorde is with us between the buildings: "Of what has he ever been afraid?" Why is he singing his song now, I ask. "The will to power is the will to write," he says, passing Gates' voice back to me (1984c).

This experience with Paulo reinforces that this is where I want to be. Then, to my surprise and joy, they ask me to come teach students how to do social action writing. They offer me the job and I grab it. No more explaining to my colleagues about the need for commitment to community involvement, interdisciplinarity, social action, and ethical reflection. I can just hear them saying, to *what*?

So five years ago, I arrive on the shores of this former military base in Monterey Bay. Fort Ord? Not anymore. When I arrive, an online library is being set up, replacing the artillery vault. The survival-training center? Parachutes and cyanide pills gone. It is going to be a child care center.

California State University, Monterey Bay: A creation story

I am in love with a vision that, at last, matches mine. Let me tell you about this place. I am hired in 1996. Thirteen founding faculty have arrived the year before me. The story goes that these founding faculty members are sitting down around a table in a light-filled room at Teatro Campesino in San Juan Bautista, and the president asks them to imagine what the university would look like "if the purpose of the university were learning." Their task is to design such a university. So they lean into each other's lit-up faces and ask themselves another question: "What knowledge, skills, and values do our students need to have in order to lead successful and meaningful lives in the twenty-first century?"

Can you imagine such a blank canvas? I call the founding faculty "inter-disciplinary creators/artists of education." I call them bold, committed to diversity, to our students. They collaborate and come up with 13 skills, values, and funds of knowledge: Students need to be bilingual. They need to know their own and each other's histories, literatures, and cultures. They need to be able to ethically communicate across cultures. They need to know how to read and write critically and creatively. To produce a work of art, to express themselves creatively in the service of transforming culture. To participate democratically in their own government, to be involved citizens in their own communities, and to do service learning. They need to be scientifically sophisticated and value the Earth. They need to know math. They need to be technologically literate. And they need to know how to be vibrantly healthy. These become our university learning requirements to graduate, known at other universities as general education requirements.

With these skills, our students can re-imagine and re-invent their worlds. About 30 percent of our students are Latina/of Chicano/a, from Salinas, Castroville, Watsonville, Hollister, some from farm-working families, and African-American students, some from former Fort Ord military families. Many other students are from working-class families, first in their families to go to college. Many are returning students. My job? To create the Creative Writing and Social Action Program. I tell you, I have been guided to this place.

Establishing the Creative Writing and Social Action Program

I designed the Creative Writing and Social Action Program out of the threads of my own years of experience with collaboration and social action—a program committed to activism and that other taboo word "compassion." The Program is housed within an interdisciplinary new humanities institute, rather than in a traditional English Department. In collaboration with my colleagues in the Program and in the Institute, we define social action writing to be, yes, a form of critical inquiry, and an act of social responsi-bility. It is writing that witnesses, breaks silences, transforms lives. The way we have housed the Program within an integrated humanities context, is, I believe, the first creative writing program of its kind in the country. When Kira Carrillo Corser and I researched homelessness, we had to go across campus to the political science, women's studies, and history departments.

Creative writing faculty help our students to break silences and fine tune the craft of writing poems, stories, memoir, and life stories.

Other Institute faculty assist them to build an integrated humanities foundation for their social action writing. Students learn their own and others' history, how to research it, analyze it, how to make it. They do oral histories, research, and retrieve and write lost family stories. They come to understand and critique the cultural forces that have shaped and formed them. They learn multicultural literary analysis, feed their knowledge of diverse cultures through narratives. They acquire ethical communication skills, crucial to creative writers who write life stories in the form of poetry and fiction. They learn cross-cultural communication skills in which they explore power relations, become aware of their privileges and prejudices, developing keen self-reflection and relational skills. Through service learning, they collaborate with community organizations and develop heightened sensitivity to issues of race, class, and gender. They also learn to visually represent their ideas and images with new media technology, so that they can more effectively invite audiences into their poems and stories.

Social action writing students become involved in the community. To what public issue will the creative writing student respond? What are the ethical issues involved? With what other discipline will the student combine her or his creative writing? Environmental or health issues? Or one of the arts, music, or photography?

When Julie Bliss, one of our first creative writing graduates, wanted to research and retrieve her lost Choctaw heritage in the form of poems and photographs, she studied Native American literature and culture. She learned how to research Choctaw history from our cultural historian. In the National Archives, she met roadblocks, but moved beyond them by doing oral histories of her own family, retrieving lost papers and photographs. Moving across space and time, Julie found a woman in Missouri who knew someone, who knew someone, who knew her lost relatives. She wrote poems, took photographs, and produced an exhibition titled, "Choctaw: Stories of My Heritage Told for the First Time." The images in her poems and in the sepia photographs of her great-great grandmother Mary Garner Cole invoke in the viewer the desire to reach out and touch the rod-iron gate at the cemetery, the imprint of her great-great grandmother's face in ashes in her hands, the palpable braid of hair, a leather thong wrapped around it. Listen to an excerpt from her poem, "Ashes to Life" (1998):

… I see yarn spooled around her finger
she weaves it through itself
into the shawl I have only seen
in decaying photographs
I carry pictures in ashes
Of Mary who is swollen in death
Who is reborn in my palm …

Julie seamlessly integrated the research of her Choctaw history and culture into her poems and photographs, demonstrating the tenacity it takes to grapple with this challenging subject. She built on earlier questions posed by her mother and grandmother, and went on to investigate and find answers to some of these questions. She moved past roadblocks to find some of her lost heritage, and successfully embodied one of her Choctaw ancestors in her poems and photographs.

Adrian Andrade wrote about six generations of his family, from the fields to the classroom. He studied Chicano history and culture, and researched his family's origins as Mexican landowners whose land was taken from them, corning to California as farm workers, generation after generation. Finally, his mother said, "No, you children will go to school, you will not work the fields." When Adrian graduated, second in his family to go to college, the room was filled with four generations of his family, hearing his/their stories, breaking silences, adding their experiences to Chicana/o history.

A central thread at CSUMB is service-learning, where our creative writing students integrate their writing and art with community need. In response to the 1998 welfare reform laws, social action writing students collaborated on an interdisciplinary, cross-cultural project, involving research, creative writing, community involvement, and service-learning. The project, which resulted in a book titled, *Education as Emancipation: Women on Welfare Speak Out,* was a collaboration between our Program and the EOPS/ CARE Program at a local community college, Monterey Peninsula College. A colleague at MPC told me that she wanted "a book that cherishes my students. I'm tired of the way they are being misrepresented in the papers." Her students, single mothers receiving welfare assistance, were seeking college degrees and self-sufficiency. They were being cut off after just two years in college, and would not be able to go on to a four year university and complete their degree, turn their economic lives around.

Our social action writing students researched welfare reform, interviewed the students at MPC, got to know them over several months, took their photographs, wrote stories and poems. For example, Erin Silvas collaborated with Antoinette "Toni" Fernandez, who was studying at the community college to become a nurse. Below is an excerpt from their poem, "Were You There" (1998):

> Were you there mumbling *"welfare bitch"* while I paid for milk and
>   bread and food stamps
> Were you there in the pediatrician's office staring at the corrugated glass
>   reading *We do not serve Medical patients*
>   Are you there now when my sons lie at my sides
>   watching the rain against my bedroom window
>   Or when my oldest son asks, *Mom, why are we on welfare?*
>   Are you there to explain why Michael can't join the soccer team

Are you there at the end of the month when there is
no money for PG&E
or peanut butter ...

No
I am there
   alone with my two sons
   sitting at the pine kitchen table doing homework
I am there doing A.B.C.'s and Arithmetic
I am there on the mauve carpet that covers the tile floor
   studying my medical books
I am there
   a mother, a teacher, a student. (p. 21)

The book focused on lived experiences and perspectives of women on welfare, placing the women most affected by welfare reform at the center of the public discussion. The book was presented by students and faculty at three statewide university conferences on welfare reform, at the Associated Writing Program's national conference, and at conferences in Peru, Hungary, and Russia. Oh. One more story, this one about when we brought the "Matriot's Dream: Health Care for All" exhibition to CSUMB. At the opening, a donor in the community offered us funding to bring the show to Washington, DC. This was 1997 and I was sitting in my office and writing a letter to Hillary Clinton inviting her to attend. You can be sure I called my Dean to ask her what she thought about my putting the letter on department stationery.

"Why are you asking me?" she asked.

"Just wanted to check that it is OK to mix my teaching and my activism."

"Fran," she said, "you are community-building, and on a national level. This is what we hired you to do. If you aren't doing it, you aren't doing your job. Of course, use our letterhead."

Here in the earthquake territory of California, the stories are coming up. We teach students to become aware of their silences, to understand how and in whose interest their silences were constructed, and to break those silences. To research and retrieve their lost family stories, the stories of their communities. To learn the craft to powerfully write these experiences. And when that seismic-something shifts, when they claim their voices, they are transformed, they claim their power, claim social justice for themselves, and that leads, at CSUMB, to engagement in social justice in the community.

To illustrate the process of students moving into voice and claiming power, I am going to include a poem I wrote and dedicated to one of our students:

The Voices Are Coming Up
for Julie Bliss, in search of Mary Garner Cole, 1863–1939

You are a search party traveling back for your great
grandmother, for years you've been studying Choctaw,
you hear faint directions cracking open, you track them back, uncover them
in ditches of history books, the songs the whispers
of family stories, a name, a date, a town inscribed in a bible,
a page in a diary, homestead documents in a thin drawer,
calling you under the canyons the coasts of California to
Iowa to Missouri, and in your face the clocks are clanging
the docks banging together, wind, waves, and fluid fields
of corn hang over hang under you, you pitch the tents of your
questions. *Grandmother, speak to me*, you say, and you can hear
her, calling you back for the voices, for the years she's been
chanting Choctaw, not stripped from your family, not lost
to the conquerors, not lost to marriage nor to gods, she's calling
you, your great grandmother, knowing you've retrieved the eyes
to see her, the ears to hear her, her words, to have them surface
the centuries, the years between you, you will crack the dry earth
of silence, tell the stories she hands you, broken stories no longer,
no longer leeched of her truth, her blood no longer sapped from you.
Adler (2001, p. 9)

Conclusion

We are living in a time when it is no longer sustainable to be silent, and
when a different future *is* possible. It is amazing to me the level of disrespect and violence—a violence of commission and omission—that we
have accepted, and in which we have colluded with our silence. How
many million women, men, and children live on the streets? The homeless
rate in Milwaukee has gone up 30 percent since welfare was repealed in
Wisconsin. Forty-three million people now have no health insurance. Every
three minutes, a woman is diagnosed with breast cancer; every 12 minutes,
a woman dies of breast cancer. Every six minutes, a woman is raped; every
18 seconds, a wife or a child is beaten. One in four of our African American
young men are in prison. We drink toxic water, breathe toxic air, and ingest
poisons on our food. These are just some of the unacceptable facts that are
part of our everyday lives. What part, we are asking more often these days,
does this disrespect play in our policies abroad? If we, as writers, are asking
our creative writing students to ask the tough questions in their poems and
in their stories, to critique our worlds, we had better also be providing them
with the tools to envision and create new ones.

CHAPTER EIGHT

Doing Creative Writing

Right to your life (and your voice)

"A creative writing class may be one of the last places you can go where your life still matters," said the poet and teacher Richard Hugo in his book *The Triggering Town* (1979, p. 65). One of the biggest lessons he learned as a creative writing teacher is "You are someone and you have a right to your life." Many of us come to creative writing wanting to find our "voice." We find our voice through communication, both written and oral. Everyone's life is a story. The participants in your community are looking at a blank piece of paper, and, for the first time, invited to tell their stories.

Why *do* creative writing?

Graeme Harper makes some important distinctions within the field of creative writing. There are the "actions and activities" of creative writing and the "artifact"—the product of what we create when we do creative writing. Throughout his book *On Creative Writing* (2010), Harper tends to avoid the term *process* "when referring to creative writing, in favor of talking about acts and actions and activities" (p. 60). Sometimes, the goal of getting published becomes preferred over the activity of creative writing. The distinction between these activities of creative writing and the final products allows us to separate for ourselves and our participants the value in *doing* creative writing.

A very brief history of creative writing in the academy

Ralph Waldo Emerson is credited with first using the term "creative writing" in 1837 during his famous lecture "The American Scholar" (2009) when he called for creative reading as well as creative writing. Creative writing has not always been an academic discipline in colleges and universities. In his book *The Elephants Teach* (2006), D. G. Myers traces creative writing in the university back to Harvard in the 1870s, when a A. S. Hill began teaching an advanced composition course in which he "permitted each student to turn in two to three creative writing assignments each semester," writes Seth Abramson (2012). These assignments were viewed only by the instructor; no studio workshop where students saw each other's work (Abramson). A decade later Barrett Wendell, a colleague of Hill's, began what eventually would develop into a form of what we know today as the studio method of a creative writing workshop.

Wendell required each student to produce one short "theme" paper each morning—longer pieces weekly. Kathryn Adams, author of *A Group of Their Own: College Writing Courses and American Women Writers 1880–1940* (2001) tells how Wendell described his intent: "What I bid them chiefly try for is that each [theme] shall tell something that makes the day on which it is made different from the day before, with the result that each new bundles of these daily notes that I take up proves a fresh whiff of daily life" (p. 45).

"A fresh whiff of daily life" is exactly what CBL provides to you and your writing. Structured reflection asks you to observe something each time you go to your site that is different from the time you were there before.

"Creative writing was first taught under its own name in the 1920s. It began in junior high school where it was originally conducted as an experiment to replace traditional English [...] with something more appealing to young people" (Myers, 2006, p. 101).

The gradual inclusion of creative writing in the academy as a separate field of study from literature, occurred between those first advanced composition classes at Harvard and the mid-twentieth century. Different universities took on different versions of the "workshop" and types of writing assignments that drew on experiences of students' daily lives.

Seth Abramson contends that "The history of creative writing in the academy is the story of two booms, first in the 1890s and then the 1990s" (2012). Edward Piper, who had attended creative writing classes at University of Nebraska and then returned to Harvard, began teaching a creative writing workshop at the Iowa Writing Workshop in the 1920s, and is often credited with the traditional workshop method; however, Abramson notes, the studio style of workshop evolved from Wendell's classes at Harvard in the 1890s. Mark McGurl in *The Program Era* (2009) asserts that the second wave of institutionalized creative writing occurred after World War II. Whatever the details of its history, creative writing within the academy has flourished since the late 1800s. Currently, the Association for Writers and Writing Programs (AWP, 2012) lists roughly 300 MFA programs in the U.S.

Current issues in creative writing

Each year at the AWP conference, hundreds of creative writers submit a "pedagogy paper"—a one-page description of a teaching approach to enhance student learning. AWP also hosts hundreds of panels, many of which present various ways to teaching creative writing, usually some form of the workshop method whereby students and teachers critique work presented by students. This accepted, and highly defended, method of teaching creative writing is built on the idea that practicing your own writing, critiquing the writing of others is the path toward higher quality creative pieces.

AWP provides guidelines for restricting the size of creative writing classes with introductory courses having no more than 20, intermediate workshops ranging from 12–18, and advanced courses with the optimum size of 12.

In the U.S., with budget pressures and a push to ensure employment within six months of college graduation, class sizes are on the rise. Creative writing teachers are trying to find ways to continue using the workshop method. AWP also suggests rigorous study in literature, in all areas, as well as teachers who are engaged in their communities through "teaching, literature, and the arts."

While researchers and administrators and organizations continue to debate the history and purpose of creative writing as an academic discipline, perhaps the most often discussed question surrounding creative writing is "Can creative writing be taught?" If it can be taught, how do we do it, what are the best practices? "Can creative writing be graded?" How do we evaluate creative writing, not only in the university, but how can you know if the participants in your community based workshops are developing stronger writing skills?

Structured reflection

Personal

1   Why did you select creative writing as a field of study?

Academic

2   What is the purpose of a college-level creative writing workshop and how does it function?

3   Discuss how your college writing workshop is different from the community workshop in which you're participating. What are the discussions like in the college class? What are they like in the community setting? What is the focus in each workshop?

4   Identify several elements of craft that you (and your group) have presented at your site. How did you come up with "lessons" to teach these elements? How does your college workshop teacher teach elements of craft?

5   Discuss what you have learned about the craft of creative writing from teaching it.

6   Write two scenes with dialogue: In the first scene, write a dialogue between you and a person at your sight that actually happened. You may certainly include action and description, but most of the scene should be dialogue. In the second scene, write a dialogue between two people at your site talking about your time with them. You should use some direct dialogue, reported dialogue, and summary dialogue.

7   Describe your ride to your site—how does the scenery change, what types of neighborhoods do you see, what are the most prominent colors you pass?

Reading

Terry Hermsen

Terry Hermsen teaches at Otterbein University. He obtained his MFA from Goddard College in 1988 and his PhD in Art Education from the Ohio State University in 2003. For 25 years he conducted residencies for the Ohio Arts Council and for seven winters he took fifth graders on poetry writing tours of the Columbus Museum of Art in their DepARTures program. His book *Poetry of Place: Helping Students Write Their Worlds* was published by NCTE in 2009. His book of poems *The River's Daughter* (2008) was co-recipient of the Ohio Poet of the Year Award in 2009.

The Assessment Wicket: How Can We Judge the Value of Writers Teaching in the Schools?

1. Remembering Amy

Let me start with a story. The kind of story we tell each other when we've done poetry residencies for many years. We hang on to them, don't we? We remember "that certain kid." Or a moment when we first got a glimpse of what this strange role of being the visitor-from-the-outside is all about. Here is such a moment, for me, from my first residency. It's not exactly a story of success, but one of scrambling toward a brief bit of luck. I think of it often—and wonder how it happened, what strands of events brought me into that classroom at that particular time, with these students and this deeply caring teacher. Every time I try to theorize the value of this grand "living experiment," as Anne Sexton once called it in its early days, I think of Amy Robey, an eighth grader at St. Joseph's School in Springfield, Ohio. The year was 1979, in October, and I was a scraggly-haired poet they chose from the Ohio Arts Council's roster to visit the school for a week.

From the very first day, I felt my whole constitution change. After years of writing and publishing poems in a vacuum, I was now "on the spot." Nothing was assumed. Poetry could be anything, to these students, something to care about or something to ignore. All depending on what happened at *this moment, in this room.* They had no preconceptions. Sure, the traditional question of "does it have to rhyme?" came up from time to time. But if I got them free-associating words down the board, and then building a poem from the connections they saw between the various leaps we made, that too was poetry. If I said it was like a waterfall, or a dancer moving across the page, they had new imagery for this mysterious and ancient human art. My grandmother, educated in Germany in the late nineteenth and early twentieth centuries, might have had 100 or more poems memorized by the time she was 15. They, of course, would have none.

Ah, to be back in school again! I even ate lunch with the students— and on the very first day, I found myself waiting in line beside two African American students (in this primarily white school, there were always two or three black students in each class). They asked me to "say them a poem." Somehow I was not just another adult in line beside them, for the tag "poet" put me in a new category. I could be asked questions like that.

The food in front of us made me think of William Carlos Williams' famous "This Is Just to Say" (1966), which I had fortunately put to memory a few weeks before. So I gave it to them, speaking amidst the swirling trays and clinking spoons:

This Is Just To Say

I have eaten
the plums
that were in
the icebox

and which
you were probably
saving
for breakfast

Forgive me
they were delicious
so sweet
and so cold

We bonded around that moment, around a poem with a fresh breath of humor and connectedness. And for the rest of the week, when we passed in the hall, there was a bit of a smile exchanged between us. Such resonance came in handy, as some events raised some touchy issues in the days ahead.

Walking into their class on Thursday, I could sense a change in mood. Something was edgier. Something was in the air. Apparently racial tensions had emerged—although I never knew the cause of it. Their teacher, I know, was a dynamic force in their lives, teaching them both religion and English, in separate periods. I'd been impressed on the first day when I heard them discussing the song "Eleanor Rigby." "In religion class?" I thought. It made me all the more intrigued by this woman who had been majorly responsible for bringing me to their school. But somehow the question of "prejudice" had come up in religion—and spilled over into English. And the two students from the lunch-line just had to start Thursday's class with asking me to jump in and say, "What is prejudice?" Not knowing the context, I deferred, wanting a bit of wriggle room. "Give me a night to think about," I said to them. "And let's make tomorrow's lesson about that."

What had I gotten myself into? With no educational training in how to approach delicate subject matter, I had to begin with a fully open mind. The answer came from an unexpected source.

Visiting a bookstore that evening, absentmindedly paging through the poetry section, I found a book by Nikki Giovanni entitled *Cotton Candy on a Rainy Day* (1978). She had visited my college years before and I was intrigued to see where her politically charged work had evolved in the time since. Opening up to the middle, I found a poem called "Boxes," part of which reads:[1]

i am in a box
on a tight string.
subject to pop
without notice.

everybody says
how strong. i am.
only black women.
and white men.

are truly free.
they say
it's not difficult to see
how stupid they are

I am not here to extrapolate on Nikki Giovanni's poem—only to say that a spark struck up between me and the page, a kind of answer to my students' question. "Prejudice is putting people in boxes," I thought in a flash. And brought them that answer (and the poem and her book) the next day. Then we proceeded to unpack what that could mean. "Anytime we approach a person or a situation with a preconceived sense of who they are or what they might mean, we are living in boxes," I ventured. And we came up with a range of examples, acknowledging that the "racial box" was probably one of the strongest to overcome.

One could literally feel the tension in the classroom ease up a bit. Not that we'd solved everything in what led up to that moment, which was clearly far beyond my power to unpack. But now we had an image—a bit of common ground. Boxes, huh? What does it feel like to walk around in boxes? To put others in boxes or to be in a box? I came up with a simple format for us:

- First, in a few lines or so, describe an imaginary box you could be in. It could be fanciful, made-up, science-fiction-like, or more personal and something you really feel. (I had wanted to avoid them replicating easy statements about "racial acceptance"—which wouldn't lead toward very interesting poems and would likely drown us in clichéd rhetoric.)

- Then, moving to a new stanza or section, work with what it feels like to be in that box. What happens? Give us a way of experiencing that feeling in as sensory a way as you can.

- And, finally, close with "what next?" How do you get out?

Perhaps the assignment became too lock-step. It was my first residency, after all. I was merely trying to end a good week with something that would speak to the issues at hand. A few lines will suffice to show how little most students were able to do with the assignment:

Here I am in a box
Not knowing how I got here
I just wonder if I'll get out

* *

You're not like everybody else
You don't belong

* *

My box was real strong and
stood me upright
I tried to sleep but
it kept me up all night

Looking back on this writing after all these years, it's hard to face how empty it is. Generalities abound. Not a single line to hang onto or experience. Despite the meaningful discussion that Giovanni's poem and the assignment generated, their writing itself shows me how far off I was from reaching them on a poetic level.

And then there was Amy. Shy but confident, she had her own way about her. Like several girls I was in love with in my own high school days, her beauty didn't seem to get in the way of her being her own person. She had spoken her mind several times earlier in the week, always astutely, with a perceptive aplomb.

Here she wrote the shortest, punchiest poem of the week, with a forceful spirit that still stays with me. Avoiding inventive description (which I had thought would keep the students from purely abstract pieces) she went straight to the heart of the matter:

I am in
a confined space.
Four walls surround
me—shut me in.
For the most part
I am tired.
Tired of scorn, contempt, hate.
I cannot get out.
There is no way out
of the world.

Amy's poem cracked open our contemporary world. Philosophical and perhaps deeply jaded, it asks deeper questions than we'd likely answer in our lifetimes. It did what poems do: it changed language and thought, conceptualizing them into new ways of seeing the world. Notice how she makes use of careful line-breaks, tipping even the first line into the second to suggest confinement. Perhaps she picked this up from Giovanni's use of sharp line breaks. She doesn't need a lot of details beyond the "four walls surround/me" to force us into listening. Like the others, her poem stays pretty generic, but there's an internalization of thought here, shaped by the lineation, that stuns anyway.

Looking back, I have to ask, as I was asking myself then: what makes a poem like this work? And, even more, what does this sort of work—of poets visiting classrooms—mean? And are these two questions connected? I was young, inexperienced, though deeply in love with my time in this school. Is there anything we might learn from those early moments (poetry in the schools was hardly more than a dozen years old at that point) which we might apply to assessing or judging the world of our endeavors now?

Let me venture some thoughts to begin a discussion of those larger points:

- Untrained as I was in the nature of the teaching profession, I believe there was value in my being at St. Joseph's for that week. In the late 1970s, poet Lewis MacAdams claimed, during that same period, "Poets are the wild cards in the school deck." Surely I was such a card, without a clear suit to play.

- Some could no doubt question the legitimacy of such a role, especially now that we have moved into a different age, an age of testing and "accountability." Do we still have room for such wild cards? I would contend yes, that education is or should be deeply about experimentation. Will those experiments be *guaranteed* to "produce results"? Surely not, for that is in the nature of experimentation itself.

- I don't believe we are in the schools to "change society" directly. But we can help students change something equally important: their attitude toward language and thought. Through such change, they may begin to engage the world on their own.

- I see such assignments as *physicalizing the abstract*. Simple as the lesson was, it offered a conceptual metaphor by which to work out a larger social concern. For how can we come to think at our most effective level until we have *tools and images* by which to work our way through a thought? We can offer a framework that is sometimes difficult to create in a classroom: a place where thought meets language meets the body.

- The measure of such movement is not exactly the poems themselves, but the process of creating them.

- Obvious as it sounds, reading was a part of the learning. Nikki Giovanni's poem gave us a way of "entering the conversation" that is literature.

- I see here that Amy "broke the rules." It appears that she felt the issues being raised in that classroom in such intense ways that the hokey framework I had set up no longer fit what she needed to say. One might call her "lazy" in writing such a direct poem. But I would claim that she *embodied* the potential in the assignment, opening it up from the inside.

- Finally, this small residency "worked," to the degree that it did, because the teacher (whose name I deeply wish I could remember) invited me in. She saw value in my visit. She wrote *with* the kids. For those hours, we became a bit of a community, temporary as it was. And I, at least, remember it years later.

2. Framing the assessment wicket

Some 30 years later, what has changed, in terms of judging the worth of writers visiting schools (including undergraduate students involved in creative writing programs across the country)? Not that much, I think. I still believe deeply in the experimental nature of this program. Students need to know what people who love language (aka poets and other writers) do "out there in the world." And teachers, while some have taken or could take on more of the role of a writer in their own ways, can't be expected to go as far as practicing writers in terms of unpacking language in deeply reconstructive ways. There has to be some "division of labor" in this realm, and poets can certainly agree to play the role of "trickster" and inventor, sometimes sparking insights into individual students, situations, and the larger curriculum. As novelist and short story writer Ron Carlson has put it, writing residencies allow teachers to "turn the desk," to step out of the role of director and become a writer with their students again. A healthy break for all! And one we can all learn much from.

But large questions now loom, if we are to make the claim of contributing something valuable beyond language experiments. Let me try and name a few:

- What makes a strong assignment as opposed to a weaker one?

- What "skills" might we propose to teach, if we want to create stronger work and guide students toward creating fresh works of their own?

- What are some conceptual frameworks we could imagine for fostering the above?

- Would we be able to create simple rubrics for weighing individual poems and other pieces of writing without squelching the free-rein that creative writers often need to make their experiments come to life?

- What would be the value of such rubrics—for teachers, for writers, for those of us trying to effectively direct creative writing majors to work productively in classrooms?

- Finally—and perhaps most difficultly—how can we tell if what *we* value as strong poems and writings are valued by the students? In other words, if in our sessions work is created that "knocks us out," as Amy's poem above affected me, does it mean that the students themselves "get it"? We often see the value in spontaneous writing of this kind—often created in 10–15 minutes on the spot in the classroom. Such writing differs greatly from the long-pondered work set up by English teachers in their assignments. Is there any long-range way to create a kind of interchange between the former and the latter?

3. A flexible rubric

Through my 30 years teaching creative writing, 20 or so in the Artists in Education program for the Ohio Arts Council, and ten teaching at the college level, I have found that certain concepts help me create stronger lessons. Others would no doubt have lists of their own, or name what I have found in quite different ways, but I present them here as something to start with. While I have described these elsewhere[2] there may be some worth in articulating them again as questions to ask ourselves as we help our students shape new lessons of their own.

Reflecting back on poems they wrote, I began to see certain patterns, which in turn led to particular questions we could ask of other poems:

1   The best poems seem to grow out of some sort of physical experience, imagined or remembered, or created on the spot.

    So one question might be: *Does the poem use words that evoke a physical sensation or image, or a scene or a story where we can see and feel something happening?*

2   The best poems often make use of original and fresh metaphoric language.

    So we might ask: *Does the poem make use of approaches to thought which are in any way symbolic or inventive?*

3   The best poems are playful even when they are serious, sometimes in their language, sometimes in the way the writer approaches the material.

A question for this could be: *Does the poem surprise us? Does it play with language in more than conventional ways in terms of form or line breaks or imagery?*

4   The best poems reflect the writer in some way—not always in a sense of personal confession, but by offering us a way of seeing that is new and experienced.

Here we might look at: *Does the poem have any "personal investment" or a fresh point of view, taking a slant which steps away from the general and distant into a more immediate engagement with the material at hand, whether that material is observational and direct, inventive and fanciful, or drawn directly from memory and experience?*

I believe one could draw these same principles from nearly any strong poem you chose to analyze. For some quick examples, consider the following fragments from some rather well known poems.

Here are the first two lines of William Butler Yeats' "The Second Coming" (1956):

Turning and turning in the widening gyre
The falcon cannot hear the falconer [...]

Does not some kind of "physical presence" emerge, nearly immediately? We *are* somewhere, albeit somewhere disconcerting and atmospheric. There's a *tension*, as Philip Wheelwright has pointed out, that underlays nearly every piece of art. He says that all art will "bear the traces of the tensions and problematic character of the experience that gave it birth" (1962, p. 46). Yeats' lines draw us in and make us want to hear what the falcon cannot because human experience—and life in general—is so underscored with tension and internal/external pulls.

Consider then the following lines from a poem by a student, a seventh grader taught by a college writer from my English 375 class at Otterbein University. The assignment: to shape two-line stanzas that make a kind of portrait of someone in their family, making use of facts mixed with impossibilities:

My sister:
looks down on me while I look up.

My sister:
loves watching the time go
backwards.

My sister:
lies under a rock when the sun comes up
& walks on water when it's raining.

My sister:
walks to Paris by day
and sleeps in Timbuktu by night.

My sister:
reaches out to me and
waits for my hand.

Isn't there some physical presence here as well? In the first two lines, there's a bit of truth-telling, an establishment of relation. This helps let us know where we are … and then the writer can take us anywhere, as she does with stanza two, where time is shifted. Maybe the writer means that her sister enjoys watching her grow up, reliving things she once did. But that is merely implied. We get the physical sensation or suggestion that time *could* go backwards … and that we could enjoy watching it do so.

Such a "move," so obvious when we name it and yet so easily forgotten in the midst of writing, is worth building on. Let's call it the "metaphoric move," or else the use of surprise, to combine principles #2 and #3 from above. For metaphor and surprise are often hard to untangle. We need the one to create the other. Watching time flow backwards is surely metaphoric here, just as Yeats' widening gyre evokes both a physical and a metaphoric realm.

When Mary Oliver in her poem "Sleeping in the Forest" (1992) says, "I rose and fell, as if in water," we see that same basic move. The physical presence of sleeping in the woods combined with the indelible/unshakable sensation of being water itself. One gets the same, though somewhat lighter, feeling from "In Blackwater Woods" (1983) where "the long tapers/of the cattails" burst and float away "over/the blue shoulders/of the ponds." Poetry, in its metaphoric mode, wants us to believe the world contains shoulders and bodies this way. And why not? The poet shakes up language and perception all at once. Metaphor and playful illusion conspire to make that happen. Cannot we teach students how to do the same?

Consider this poem by a boy name Chad in Savannah, Ohio, whom I later found out was flunking sixth grade. Whatever was causing his problems in school, he was able to write the following poem while gazing out the window on a raining day:

(window to the future)

the wind blows
the trees sway
the field is like an airport
and the last touches of snow
lay on the ground
I can barely see the old house on

the hill
through the mist
the treetops touch the sky
and puddles everywhere I
walk
there's a hole in the trees that
looks like a window in the distance
the view is silent
the ground is wet

(should I go through the window)

Notice how the poem takes its time "getting to the point." Such layering seems essential, to make the "airport" of the parking lot and the puddles from the rain come alive for us. But then there's that hole in the trees and the leap he's made. It's almost like the physical sketching of the earlier part of the poem provides the runway for what he really has to say. He makes a leap—as all good metaphor does. And we want to take it with him.

A comment on the assignment. For such student poems, as we well know, don't usually "just happen." A few minutes earlier, we had read James Wright's "Lying in a Hammock at William Duffy's Farm in Pine Island, Minnesota" (1990) as a model, with its wonderful interweaving of "plain facts" and leaping metaphors. And we'd spent time listing details and potential metaphors of our own, with each student recording both on columns in their notebooks. Simple, crucial tasks for laying down a base for the true inspiration to arrive. When Chad wandered over to me to ask if he could call the circle in the trees a "window to the future," I knew he was testing boundaries, maybe trying to impress. Whatever his motivation, that spark—so unpredictable—became a way for him to imagine reshaping his life. The resulting poem combines surprise and metaphor to go with the physicality of his earlier word-sketching.

Finally, let's consider the fourth principle described above: personal investment or point-of-view. Obviously, each of the samplings here have plenty of that quality, from Yeats and Oliver to the two student poets. Still, separating this quality out to teach and weigh on its own seems valuable, lest we try to teach everything at once.

Consider these famous lines from Robert Frost (Frost and Lathem, 1969):

Whose woods these are I think I know,
His house is in the village though [...]

While these lines mostly just set up the rest, precursors to "the darkest evening of the year" and "miles to go before I sleep," don't they establish a "knowing situation" in and of themselves? To be traveling along a road and know that the speaker is so aware of his surroundings as to guess at whose title is on a particular piece of unoccupied land automatically sets up a personal connection. We are being invited to listen in on his private confession, his noticing of the rich and wintery landscape around him. Frost has not only given us a physical arena for the poem to happen in, he's "crossed the line" into that arena and given us a hand to follow. Maybe we can know that man too. It's a world, after all, where property matters, along with heading down the road to fulfill one's sworn duties.

Consider then this whole poem by Liese Millikin, a fifth grader at St. Peter's Elementary in Mansfield, Ohio. We'll likely see all four factors at play, but in some ways it will be the point of view that carries the day, along with play, metaphor, and physical presence. It might be noted that the assignment was to make some portmanteaus, in the manner of Lewis Carroll's "Jabberwocky," though Liese stretches the word play to include a strong dose of pig latin as well:

Arunning Raway

The dumble fays and drampen bugs all occupy themselves,
While me and the fudwas play in the sun.
And the cooperdops and the riddledoos sing in the grass,
But the world is flippied and damzled about.

I flip down on the crench and the doon is down,
But I haven't gone home.
Dother and Mad come out to lind me,
And I ralk faway to the stream.
Mad has guven ip,
But I reep kunning.

Somewhere, outhere, there's a place for ye and mou,
But I don't wunderstand and I don't even care,
'Cause someone's gonna come lookin',
Someone's gonna see,
That right where I'm astandin',
I'm astayin' here forever.

Like Frost, doesn't Liese here "invite us in"? We become, by implication, the "ye" (or is it the "mou") of her third stanza. We hear her anger in the twisted phrasing of "mad has guven ip but I reep kunning." Along with mystery, word play, metaphor, and surprise, Liese is *situated* within her poem. And that stance is worth noting. Not based in actual memory—or some literal attempt to run away—the writer is *there* and that makes the poem all the more compelling.

Without making some sort of rigid system of these principles, my contention here is that we can construct assignments, in fresh and innovative ways, that address these skills and make them accessible to students, as well as applying those skills for deciding what has been taught. The first claim is material for another essay—and there are many books and resources for shaping such assignments. But the assessment part? How hard is it to weigh what students have taken in?

Simplifying the framework, Stephen Morrow and I constructed a loose rubric for analyzing student poems, based on the questions I have raised above. (See Table 8.1).

Next, we read a sequence of student work from a residency my college undergraduates conducted at a nearby middle school. We scored some of the poems ourselves, but also asked some other undergraduates to make use of the rubric while reading a stack of poems. One could imagine schematizing this even more, scoring a batch of early poems and considering them in the light of poems written after more instruction. I'll leave that for others to compile. For now, my suggestion is to try it yourself, reading the following poem, written by a seventh grader during one of my students' residencies, and seeing what levels you think it achieves:

I remember
Dancing in the
Bathtub then
Opening my eyes
And I was in the hospital
The doctor was sewing
My chin together like
A hole in his favorite
Shirt—carefully—my mom
Standing there looking scared

I remember
My daughter dancing in
The bathtub, closing her
Eyes then opening them. In
The hospital, the doctor was
Sewing her chin together so
Carefully as if her chin was made
Of tissue paper. She was lying there
Looking scared.

I remember,
A week later feeling
My chin and it
Was all healed, no
More thread
I got in the bathtub
And did not
Dance.

Re-reading the poem several years after it was written, I still feel that it ranks very high. Its metaphors are rather finely tuned and specific to the surgeon's careful efforts. Also, there's a nice surprise in the way the point of view shifts from daughter to mother and back again. It's almost like a camera is moving between scenes, zeroing in close to catch the stitchings and then backing up to reveal the two central characters. Of course, a poem this good transcends any numbers we can place beside it, but at the same

Table 8.1 Rubric for analyzing student poems

Category	4	3	2	1	Total
Playful thought: metaphor and surprise	The poem contains metaphoric thinking and the writer utilizes similes that appear to be "grown" from the topic at hand, rather than "plunked down." The poem makes "leaps" that are at once natural and unpredictable	The poem contains some metaphoric thinking and the writer utilizes simple similes and metaphors. The poet is starting to make surprising connections.	The poem contains little metaphoric thinking and the writer utilizes 1 or 2 simple similes and/ or metaphors, often of a generic nature. Mostly the poem stays in the realm of the predictable.	There is no evidence of metaphoric or surprising thinking.	
Strong physical detail in phrasing, sentences, lines and description	The poem contains complex or inventive lines and phrases. Details glow. Sentences vary in length and take on a kind of presence of their own. Strong/ complex details describe a "scene."	The poem contains some creative details and some physical presence. Some sentences are varied in length and utilize strong/ complex details to describe a scene.	The poem contains few creative details. Little evidence of sentence variety. Little sense of a "scene."	There is no use of inventive/ complex sentence or line structure. And no physical description, objects, etc.	

▶

Point of view and personal connection	The writer is able to "enter" the poem by taking an "inside" point of view. Writer uses phrases of insight to show they made a conscious decision as to how to approach their writing.	The writer is able to "enter" the poem by taking an "inside" point of view. Writer uses some phrases of insight to show they made a conscious decision as to how to approach their writing.	The writer is unable to "enter" the poem—and stays on the outside of their subject matter. The approach seems borrowed or unthought-out. May be somewhat insightful but more "flat observations."	Writer is unable to "enter" the poem. Words are just put on the page in an impersonal way, with no insightful phrases, only "flat observations."

time I find the chart helpful in letting me trace out and name my inherent, mostly felt reactions. As a rubric, I'm still hoping that what Steve and I created will help others do the same.

Point made? I believe these categories at least give us something to talk about when we look at what our students have written, or at the poems generated during an undergraduate residency in an area school. Without such data, it might be hard to make claims that much has changed. With it, we can at least begin talking with each other in terms of learning goals and whether our time spent in the school was worthwhile.

4. Joe's question

Let me take all this one step further and ask what's happening on the other side. We as visiting writers or classroom teachers might weigh a poem one way or another—but what about the students themselves? Do they like the same poems we do? The poems created under the auspices of the "poetry assignment" may intrigue us, but will their effects last once we are gone? We become the word-spinners, dancing on the page or in the air before them, and then we invite the students to do the same, oftentimes evoking some rather wonderful poems. But the question remains: once that magic is gone, and students return to their everyday speech activity, what will they value about what we have written—and why?

One measure would be: would the poems *they* chose as their best be the ones we would choose? My guess is: very unlikely. For where we are valuing surprise and energy, they may well want to remain safe and "clear" so that their friends won't think them "weird." Where we want intense engagement with description and physical presence, they often drift over toward abstraction and simplicity. A wild metaphor may move a poet who has lived with too many tame ones. But to a student in a classroom, only temporarily playing the role of poet, the criteria can quickly shift.

This very point emerged in the last residency that my students conducted, in January of 2012 at Grandview High School in a suburb of Columbus, Ohio. At one of the teacher workshops, my good friend Joe Hecker (head of the Grandview English department and a good friend of mine) said this about the student work in a chapter of mine we were discussing, "Well, I don't know about anyone else, but I simply can't read the students' poems, because I know how they were created." In other words, he felt that since they were produced in the "hothouse atmosphere" of a classroom experience set up by a visiting poet—rather than structured over time in an assignment the students shaped on their own initiative—there was something false about the process.

Although I appreciate Joe's objection, I tend to disagree. I see it from my point of view and, knowing the short time allotted for a visiting poet's time with any class, I am aware of the limitations visiting writers face. To take our time, laying out days of groundwork, sending students off to create/invent assignments of their own, is likely only possible in a college atmosphere, or in a special high school creative writing class, where time allows the luxury of much trial and error. Still, how do I answer my friend Joe? Could we allow for more student discovery, for learning through failure, rather than setting up something of a full-proof situation where however students take a prompt they are bound to stumble into something wonderful? Put out a bowl of juicy words and ask the students to juggle them into a pre-arranged format, as many of us are wont to set up, and voila, a poem emerges. Some of these will be more amazing than others—and show up in the final booklet—but what ultimate lesson has been taught? Have we mainly given our students the sense that poems happen via tricks and games? Are they in any way consciously applying the skills poets use?

Part of Joe's question has to do with whether the students even value what they have written. Without a long study, I have to say I don't fully know. Several times over the years I have by chance run into a student from a past residency. And I can report that they DO often say they still have the booklets we created. Once, during intermission at a music concert at Heidelberg College, I met a student I'd taught from New Washington High School five years before and he told me that several days ago he'd coincidentally had been reading the booklet we created, admiring the poems once again. This despite him being now a senior in college, set to graduate in music. That's only circumstantial evidence at best. I want to believe the poems last, but can I be sure?

I do know that frequently, if given the choice, students would choose their "safe" poem for a culminating booklet, which proved to be the case at Grandview. Because of Joe's strong beliefs in student ownership, the teachers wanted the students to work through revisions of their poems and polish one to submit for the booklet, including something from every student in the school. The result was very different than an anthology selected and edited by the visiting poet, as these two examples—chosen completely at random—will attest:

A Child I Know

You arrived defeated,
The victim of circumstance.
The blood in your veins plagued by the actions of those
    before you.
How are you supposed to grow?
How are you supposed to learn?
You don't know my name,
You don't know my language.
But your dark eyes captivate me and draw me closer.
You continue to love,
Despite being betrayed by it in the past.
I hold you in my arms, my memory, my heart.
And I will hold you there forever.

Anna

Summer Time Excitement

Day in and day out
I feel the joy and I want to shout
Little kid memories and little kid times
All grown up, but it's still the same
No worries except for one
That this summer time sun
Will soon end
And until then
I shall have my fun

Rick

What I want to ask, with as little bias as I can muster, is "Why may have the students chosen to submit these poems to the residency book?" Of course, we can't read inside their minds, but since the rest of the book is filled with poems very much like these, there may be some commonality between them.

Here are some elements I notice, in partial reference to the rubric above:

● They both deal with "lost youth" themes in fairly generic ways. No one is mentioned by name, which may be intentional. (Many high school students have told me, "I want to keep my poem general, so that everyone can relate to it.")

● No specific places emerge. Someone "arrives defeated," but to no place in particular.

● All metaphors are what might be called "borrowed" ones. Veins are "plagued by blood." One person, perhaps an immigrant, doesn't know another person's language. (Or maybe, metaphorically, they can't find a way to "relate," as we so often put it.) "Dark eyes captivate" and "draw me closer." Days "go in and out."

● All is very heart-felt—the loss of memories, the struggle to survive after being betrayed by love. But nothing speaks specifically of a particular writer or person. These could be written in Amsterdam or Kansas City, in Alaska or Mexico.

Okay, maybe I'm not so unbiased after all. On my "score sheet," they rank very low, even though the students may have cared for them very much. What to make of that? I would never condemn the poems, only ask: if these are what they want to write and most value, what do we do with the skills we have come to teach? Throw them away? Make the students feel bad because what they want is so much different than what we value? If my good friend Joe wants students to take more ownership of their poetry, is this what we have to settle for? Is this even "settling"?

Before attempting an answer, let's look at two poems with quite different textures. These are from a single class assignment, and in contrast to the "polished" poems above, were dashed off in 10–15 minutes at the end of a period of looking at some contemporary poetry on the theme of "earth, water, fire, and air."

Fire

A pumpkin lays at rest, in the crisp fall air.
Condemned to rot, its toothy grin turns into a scowl.
Until America's youth, in its finest, stumbles upon the pumpkin.
What to do with a rotted pumpkin? Light it on fire of course!
Splash of gasoline, and the strike of a match, light up the old
    Jack-o'lantern once more.
They shout with the joy of a young boy on Christmas day as their
    creation burns.
The pumpkin explodes, as a foot finds its way to its teeth.

Eric

FIRE
I have burned myself

on fire before

AIR
The air always seems
to be fresher right before
a swim

—

I like flying but
not being near the edge
of something

WATER

Once I fell into a
crab pool.

—

Cold water hurts
the delicate lining
of the stomach.

MATH

The Pythagorean Theorem
is easy.
Integrals suck.
Whoever created integrals
sucks too.

Cameron

Neither of these poems were selected by the student to go into the book, for perhaps obvious reasons. The second one is perhaps too raw and honest to be presented to parents, teachers, and administrators as an example of "fine literature." Indeed, it's more like a list of fragments having to do with the four elements (one of those being, of course, the world of "math"!). But look at how gutsy it is. How much each little fragment seems to grow out of the life of a *particular* student at a *particular* time, with particular emotions (about cold water, about the air right before a swim ...). He seems to be trying to name tensions, in Wheelwright's vein: how some kind of math makes sense, while some doesn't; how some types of "flying" excite and other similar experiences (as in being close to an "edge") do not. Abstraction—which is so much a part of the late adolescent mind—is still strongly present here. But it's been *grounded in experience.*

The same can be said for the first poem as well, focused on a single moment of adolescence in a town where everyone is expected to be "good" but where emotions run strong. Such honesty would not be welcomed in a school book either, one supposes. But there may be other reasons for the poem not being valued by the writer enough to take it further. Perhaps it would seem too "minor" of an event to make much of. Clearly this memory occurred to Eric, in the midst of the classroom exercise, but stepping back and weighing it against other of his writing, he may have had second thoughts.

Without claiming brilliance here, it seems clear that where the second set of poems reveal many of the assessment tools addressed earlier, the first show almost none.

To state the dilemma again: does all this mean that the poems in the second batch are all "false" because the students didn't choose to revise and polish them for the anthology? And does it mean that the students who valued the types of poems in the first batch didn't have a positive experience from the residency, or come away appreciating strong poetry? Most of all, does this discrepancy mean that the principles articulated earlier for judging student poems are not helpful?

I think the answer to all these questions is a strong "no." Students from Grandview very much loved their time with the college poets visiting their classrooms. They showed up in droves at the closing coffee house reading and read their work with enthusiasm. Clearly, something powerful happened. And good poems WERE written—even if the booklet didn't quite reflect the best of the lot. And though it would be hard to prove, I believe that under the surface the Grandview students made use of the principles being taught.

Here's what I think did NOT happen: students were not given much experience in weighing what makes a good poem. They no doubt created some—but never were asked to decide *what* they thought was good or bad, or compare they thought to other poems they had read. So they went safe. They chose generality over precision, cliché over surprise, easy emotions and situations over risk, the distant and impersonal over the invested and particular voice.

In the short span of a typical residency, it's hard to tackle that weighing process. We're rushing to get some poems down, to teach new skills with each exercise, to keep the momentum going. There's little time for assessment, or striking a balance between poems that break new ground and poems that please the students' sense of "speaking grand thoughts."

So I don't know. Are the lessons we bring in—and get so excited about—truly genuine? I think they are, though you may conclude otherwise. I believe that one day, if Eric and Cameron were to re-read their earth-water-fire-and-air poems again, they'd see some real spark of their teenage personalities within. That is, if we as teachers and visiting writers can help them to do so.

The principles are there for us to teach, drawing on or extending/reinventing some of these guidelines and assessment tools, and adding new ones. The next step, however, may be trickier: how to find ways to help students in our classes hear the difference themselves.

CHAPTER NINE

Changing Them, Changing You, Changing the World

A deeper understanding

By this time in the semester, you are more familiar with the participants as individuals, with their own personalities, their own set of problems, their own senses of humor, their quirks and preferences in what they want to write. Where you once felt unsure of how to handle the various person-alities of your participants, you now feel comfortable with your task of getting them to write. You've made adjustments in your lesson plans to accommodate the preferences and skill levels of your group.

Working with the homeless, mentally ill, elderly, or at-risk school children you now have a new perspective on the social issues they deal with every day. You may begin to realize that no matter how much you do during these 12–14 weeks you're with them, you're not going to drasti-cally change their lives. Many of us enter a service project knowing that we want to have a strong positive impact on those we serve. Although it may be difficult to see, you are making a big difference. Seeing the difference in a short period of time is sometimes obvious and sometimes not so obvious. You may not ever know the extent of your impact. You may be lucky and have your participants thank you and tell you how much they appreciate being able to write, to be creative. You also face the risk of being told what you're doing is not helpful or that writing is not what a person wants to be doing.

Eric Fershtman, a student who worked with mentally ill adults, posted this reflection after his eighth week (2012):

> There was a thin young man who showed up to my class this week who happened also to be deaf. [...] I sat the young man next to me, and we established a routine: after I explained an exercise to the class, I'd turn

my attention to him, and write the instructions down on his paper. He'd occasionally ask for examples, which I'd provide. Grammatically, his sentences were all over the map, and often, even after the given examples, not quite written to the instructions. Still, when he'd show me what he'd written, I'd give him a smile and a thumb-up, and he'd nod grimly, the way a soldier might, and then mess around with his cellphone until it was time for the next exercise.

Something peculiar happened, though, as we came to the final exercise. After I'd explained it to the class, I turned toward the young man, but he shook his head, and began to write. I thought maybe he'd gleaned the instructions this time from watching me speak; the social worker had mentioned that he was a competent lip reader. After a minute he showed me what he'd written, and here I produce it for you: "I don't really need writing in my life."

Eric does not stop with the easy answers. Teaching creative writing to mentally ill adults has its weekly and particular challenges. This is not the first time I've seen this type of response to CBL projects. The response Eric received from this participant, I've heard from school children, from persons living with dementia, from youth in foster care, from men in prison, from women in domestic violence shelters. But it always takes the teaching artist off his game for a moment. Eric does not, in his reflections, simply *describe* the experience, he explores his personal and civic reactions:

What can you do when somebody tells you, in writing, that they don't really need writing in their life? What I did was this: I smiled, said okay, and felt sorry for him. Because I thought, if anyone needs writing, it was this young man. If not for "therapy," like the rest of us, then at least—at the very least—for communication. It seemed to me by choosing not to write that he was restricting his circle to the privileged few who could read sign language.

Now I'm wondering, though, if he realized that which is taking me an achingly long time to realize and explain to myself, which is this idea that writing mucks things up. That it further complicates things that are already almost hopelessly complex by trying to fit them into neat little formulas we build for ourselves.

What is exciting to me is that Eric, like many teaching artists, is recognizing the layers of complexity in finding a voice, and how not having a voice, not being given the opportunity to communicate one's life story, can make one feel hopeless. The deaf and mentally ill participant has certainly already dealt with feeling hopeless. When I read Eric's reflections each week, I worried that he'd fall into a deep hopelessness for writing and give up his CBL project. But it is precisely this level of reflection that I'm always hoping for in my students.

What you're getting: Transferrable skills

Students who participant in a CBL project of any kind develop skills that cannot be effectively taught in a textbook or classroom. If you are working with a partner or as part of a team, you're learning flexibility and team work. Whether you're working individually or with a team, you're learning how to juggle many aspects of your life. Keeping up with your school schedule and homework and maintaining a job is a challenge. Now that you're also planning and leading creative writing opportunities in your community adds another element to your organizational and management skills. You're learning diversity—and not just at your site. If you're working with other students from your class, your team is also teaching you a bit about diversity. Certainly not everyone is keen on being part of a group. And maybe you've had to deal with conflicts within your team. Perhaps you've been designated the leader, either officially or by default. Perhaps you are the peacekeeper of your team. You're learning how to handle frustration with your fellow teaching artists and your participants. Not to mention all the knowledge you're gaining about social justice, arts in the community, arts administration, nonprofit organizations, and perhaps fundraising.

Review your Project Overview that you designed at the beginning of your CBL project and consider your plans for a celebration and begin locating any donations or supplies you will need. The skills (organization, management, team building, leadership, fundraising) combined with knowledge learned outside the classroom (diversity, social issues, arts in community, arts administration, nonprofit organizations) prepare you for so much more than if you were in a traditional workshop or creative writing course. Having these skills and this knowledge allow you the possibility of discovering what it is you might want to do as a job or career as you develop your writing.

Several of the essays in this book are by writers who once participated in a CBL project, and discovered that it either confirmed what they wanted to do, or changed their life path. Lisa Chatterjee, for example, never imagined herself teaching. After she graduated, she did do a bit of wandering while she tried to figure out what she would be most happy doing, but she now teaches in public schools in New York City, something she would never have considered without the requirement of CBL at an inner-city public school in Orlando. Another student, Ashley, already knew she wanted to join the Peace Corps after graduation. The work she did with her CBL project helped solidify that decision. After the Peace Corps she went on to work for a human rights organization.

Jason wasn't sure what he wanted to do after graduation. He conducted his CBL project at a halfway house for youth, where teens are court-ordered to serve a specific period of time while taking drug rehabilitation classes, life skill classes, and continue their education. I'll never forget the conversation Jason and I had one day after class in which he told me he was worried that we, his creative writing professors, would be disappointed if he wanted to be a high school teacher for high-risk teens. Was he kidding, I asked. I'd be thrilled. He would be perfect, I knew that. He taught locally for a while after graduation and then made a decision to return to Detroit, his hometown, and teaches at one of the most needy schools.

Stephanie was hired by a large publishing company, and during the interview she was told that it was her CBL project at the homeless shelter that set her apart from other applicants. Stephanie had created a small portfolio of her CBL work—pictures of her with the kids, some of their writing, some of her reflection. The interviewer told her that everyone comes in with a degree in English, but not everyone has experience working in a team, organizing four months of activities for people who are different than she, organizing and holding an end-of-project reading/celebration that included community members, parents, fellow students, and administration from the shelter. She got the job.

What they're getting

When you started your project, it was easy to dream of changing lives, and you are. You might not be able to see the many small and big ways you're making a difference, but you are. The great thing for me is that after I've been working with a group for several weeks—the sixth or seventh visit to my site—I've started realizing how very much I'm learning from the participants. My hope then becomes that they are also learning something. Maybe they're learning something about telling stories. Maybe they're learning that they have a right to their lives, and a right to write about it. Maybe they're learning elements of craft. Maybe they're learning that they really are talented, and want to continue writing. Maybe they're learning how to share their stories with others. They are certainly learning that someone cares enough to plan creative activities for them.

Structured reflection

Personal

1   In Chapter 3, I asked you to consider the possible challenges you anticipated having at your site. Look back at your response and

discuss how you either met those challenges or what real challenges you're having.

2   What has been the most satisfying experience so far in your CBL project?

3   What has been the most challenging moment so far? Consider how Eric handled the deaf man at his site. How might you have handled it differently?

4   In this chapter, we talked about transferrable skills. What skills do you think you've developed because of this project?

Academic

5   Find a published poem or story that could have been written by someone at your site. For example, if you're conducting your CBL at a drug rehabilitation facility for adults, you might find Raymond Carver's "Where I'm Calling From" (1986). After you have found the poem or story, read it and discuss how the experiences conveyed in the poem or story are similar or dissimilar to the people at your site.

Civic

6   Brainstorm at least seven "why" and/or "how" questions related to your site and CBL project. For example, "If desegregation ended in 1965, why is the percentage of African American students at this inner-city school 99 percent?" "How does the staff deal with seeing poverty every day?" "Why don't the families of these elderly people visit them regularly?"

Readings

Nathaniel V. Mohatt

Nathaniel Mohatt received an MFA in poetry from Saint Mary's College of California and a PhD in Creative Writing and Community Psychology from the University of Alaska Fairbanks. He is a Research Scientist at the Western Interstate Commission on Higher Education in Boulder, Colorado, and a Clinical Instructor in Psychiatry at the Yale School of Medicine. He conducts research on participatory public art in behavioral health, whereby people in recovery from mental illness and addiction collaborate with their communities to create and/or perform art. This research is concerned with using public arts participation to (1) reduce the social stigma of mental illness and addiction and (2) redress harmful public narratives of historical trauma and anomie and promote community resilience. He is also a poet, educator, and promoter of community art, and lives with his wife and two daughters in Colorado.

Citizens of Words: Service-Learning in Creative Writing Education

Introduction

As a graduate student in creative writing at Saint Mary's College of California, I had the opportunity to teach creative writing in an alternative high school for students at risk of dropping out. My students came from lives very different from mine, unstable and often filled with violence. I would come to class for one hour a week and never know if I would see the same faces. The lessons I prepared were hit or miss. Many times I would see my lessons connecting—there was one quiet girl that would not write at all most days, but a couple times her head would be down, braids falling over her cheeks, pen moving across the page, eyes fixated on her work. Other times the lesson wouldn't seem to reach anyone. I tried a lesson on improvisation in Jazz and Rap, thinking my students, who were predominantly African American living in "inner city" San Francisco, would connect to the musical traditions, but instead they made paper airplanes and laughed at my musical choices. I can't say what worked and didn't in these instances. I don't know what was going on in that girl's life from one week to the next. The improvisation lesson could just as well have been ill conceived on my part as some other external factor could have predestined any lesson to fail. I have always believed in and advocated for the important psychosocial role of the arts in promoting healthy communities and resilient minds. But the major conviction that I took away from the semester was a drive to understand what worked and didn't and how similar programs can best be successful, in terms of creating a positive experience for both creative writing students and the communities we work with.

To begin to answer these questions, I have compiled information from a variety of sources, including interviews, AWP conference presentations, books and articles, and my own research and experience. Bringing it all together paints a rewarding and challenging picture. Creative writing holds a unique position in contemporary society, being both an art form and valuable to enhancing verbal communication skill in the information age. Creative writing in the public sphere, like all public arts, can inspire profound change in people and communities. As Jane Golden, Director of the Philadelphia Mural Arts Program, says, "Art can save and transform lives and change communities" (2011). From the individual experience of insight and skill building, to the power to form bonds and connect people, to the chance to address and redress public narratives of trauma, creative writing has the power to create hope, change, and opportunity.

Why do it?

Benefits to community and community students

Over the course of 2011 and 2012 a unique and power public art project took place in Philadelphia, PA, using creative writing and mural painting to build a community for healing from the all too common tragedy of suicide (Mohatt et al., under review). Within the grand scope of this effort was a storytelling workshop, where people not only shared their personal stories, but also learned the tools to write and tell the story more effectively. The writing workshop truly was as Margot Galt, writer and educator, describes they can be: "It creates its own arena, where we pause to listen and remember. One person speaks, but sparks light up in everyone's private darkness. Soon the place is ablaze with connections" (Galt, 2006, p. 4). Participants in the workshop began to think of each other almost like family and express that these connections have created for them profound healing (Mohatt, under review). Teaching creative writing in this context created a tight knit group of people who through writing and sharing of their writing discovered commonality. Creative writing can create safe places where such powerful sharing and bonding occurs.

The safe place of art and writing not only helps people connect, but also permits and celebrates new and different voices. Writing is inherently caught up in questions of who gets to speak and be listened to, who is given by their community the power to generate knowledge. Both participation in the generation of knowledge and validation of one's contribution to community knowledge can improve the health and well-being of individual people and their communities (Trickett and Ryerson Espino, 2004; Wallerstein and Duran, 2006). Furthermore, divergent and opposing voices are necessary to a healthy, thriving community capable of tackling life's most intractable problems (Rappaport, 1981). In this way, teaching creative writing is an essentially political act that can give expression to people who have been silenced, traumatized, or excluded. Teaching creative writing throughout our communities empowers multiple voices and helps ensure that this power, to speak and be listened to, is available to people from all walks of life.

The value of having voice cannot be underestimated, but writing creatively also provides people the opportunity to participate in the process of creating something beautiful. As Jesse Ross, a writer and teacher in Florida, says "just as people get beauty and enhanced experience of life from seeing a beautiful painting ... I think the same is true for those who get to experience the beauty of creative writing" (2010). Experiencing beauty can be thought to generate a "pact of aliveness" that sustains life—that is, beauty inspires people to preserve it, share it, and create more beauty, creating a cycle of renewal and preservation that sustains culture and creation in the face of the many destructive forces in life (Scarry, 1998). The experiencing and creation of beauty "decenters" the self, turning people towards appreciation and care for some other, other than themselves, thereby providing an education in cultural values, justice, and goodness with social value beyond the economic impact of the arts (Winston, 2006). As Jane Golden says of murals, so too can be extrapolated to the participation in any art form, especially when leading to a public performance, display, or availability: "people understand that what they bring ... will then be a tool of inspiration to many others. They know that they are going to work on something that is beautiful and meaningful, and that they are connecting to a greater good beyond themselves" (Golden, 2012).

Research shows that under the proper guidance creative writing can promote positive health outcomes (Robinson, 2000; Baikie and Whilhelm, 2005; Esterling et al., 1999; Robinson, 2000). Expressive writing, a therapeutic technique focused on having people simply express their feelings in writing without concern for the quality of the writing, can help people process traumatic events and is linked to both positive physical and emotional health outcomes (Pennebaker and Chung, 2011). Research has also demonstrated that after school arts programs for at-risk youth lead to improved life functioning (McCue, 2007, p. 596). Participants in the storytelling workshop from the suicide prevention project in Philadelphia, state that the writing helped them heal by simultaneously promoting new connections and friendships while leading to important and powerful new insights into their experience (Mohatt et al., under review).

Writing is also an important skill and commodity in today's economy. Communication, creative thinking, adaptability, knowledge of words and skill in word usage, and the ability to apply creative writing techniques to others areas of life are all valuable and marketable skills that creative writing education provides. Creative writing skills are "... valued because they're increasingly used as a productive force in the post-industrial knowledge economy ... creativity and 'thinking outside the box' have become primary tools for production in the American theater of the global economy" (Healy, 2009, para. 3). Teaching these skills is an important and highly valuable service that writers can provide.

Douglas Unger, author and professor of English at the University of Nevada Las Vegas, collaborated on a couple of studies to evaluate the economic impact of UNLV's Writer's in the Schools program. In one such study, they targeted youth at risk of dropping out of high school and provided mentorship, SAT test preparation, and writing education. Of the 20 youth that participated, 19 not only graduated from high school but also went on to college. Although the social-emotional benefits of such success may be heart-warming, the economic benefits are staggering. The overall estimated economic benefit of this program with only 20 at-risk high school students neared $1 million due to increased academic outcomes and estimated long-term economic activity and reduction in use of public welfare services (Talarico et al., 2010). The National Endowment for the Arts' report, *To Read or Not to Read: A Question of National Consequences*, from 2007 finds that people are reading less and that "... weak reading skills strongly correlate to lower academic achievement, lack of employment, lower wages, and fewer opportunities for advancement. Deficient readers are more likely to be imprisoned, and they are less likely to be active in the nation's civic and cultural life. Strong readers earn more, vote more, and have more rewarding career opportunities" (Burriesci, 2008).

The significance of the NEA findings for this discussion is that the simple act of teaching writing in our communities can increase literacy and by doing so have deep and lasting benefit. If, through more active engagement in our communities, we as writers can help boost reading and literacy, we also help people find jobs, lead healthy lives, and be engaged citizens. By teaching creative writing across our communities we fulfill a vital role in sustaining vibrant and healthy people, communities, nations and cultures.

Benefits to creative writing students

The most important benefit, in my experience, of community service to creative writing students may be to enhance their awareness of the role of the arts in communities. When Nance Van Winckel, author and professor of creative writing, began Eastern Washington University's (EWU) Writers in the Community program, she quickly learned that more than bestowing some profound gift on their community, "it was 'the people' who were bestowing on EWU's writing students and professors] the jewels of their poems and stories" (Van Winckel, 1997, para. 1). By showing up and listening, writers and writing teachers participate with the broader human community in the creation of art, thought, voice, and expression. At the most basic level, creative writing students should teach creative writing in community settings so that they may participate in the larger world of poems and stories, and see themselves as embedded in communities of readers and writers. Teaching writing and leading workshops in our communities permits us direct access to the active culture of our varied communities, and that is a very profound gift to writers hungry for experience.

Through the experience of teaching creative writing in community settings, aspiring writers learn to be citizens and how the writing profession can serve the greater population. Regarding the benefit of community service, Dr. Chris Sindt, poet and Dean of Graduate and Professional Programs at Saint Mary's College of California (SMC), states, "The best thing was really the almost routine experience of service and in most cases exposure to a population that was unfamiliar to our students. ... The students see how the creative writing experience functions outside of the MFA workshop" (2010). Jesse Jay Ross, a writer, artist, and high school teacher who promotes service-learning, argues that the benefit of service "... is raising social awareness and doing more than just creating a worker with the school system and creating instead a citizen, someone who feels responsibility" (2010). Poet June Jordan emphasizes that school can and should be "... a place where students learned about the world and then resolve, collectively and creatively, to change it!" (1995, p. 7). By having creative writing students teach writing in community settings, we nurture citizen-writers who understand the value of creative writing beyond their own internal practice, writers with personal experience of how their work can promote healing from trauma, lift up and empower new voices to enrich public dialog, and build connections between diverse people.

How to do it?

The following list of recommended practices comes from compiling personal experience with the information I have gathered from interviews, casual conversations with other professionals, and a review of the literature. I offer them as issues for consideration, as creative writing students and programs move down the path of service-learning. They may not be comprehensive, and they may not all be necessary under every circumstance, but their consideration and application should enhance the service-learning experience for creative writing students, university programs (faculty, staff, and administration), and community partners.

- *First, there must be administrative support from the university.* This provides participating faculty, staff, and students with the time and resources needed to build and maintain relationships with community settings. To operate a successful community service program requires administrative support for this time commitment (Sindt, 2010).

- *Relationships based on trust and mutual benefit will lead to long-term success and a sense of value by all.* At the heart of community work is the hard work and commitment to building and maintaining relationships, ensuring that all parties are both contributing to the success of the program and receiving appropriate benefit (Wallerstein and Duran, 2006).

- *Programs must provide their students with some base-level of training.* While some people will be natural teachers, most creative writing students are inexperienced. New teachers need be taught the ropes. Training can take many forms, from classroom education, to providing resource tools, to mentorship and practicum experiences. Training should provide students with basic knowledge of how to prepare a lesson plan, information about their placement, resources to apply and adapt, how to facilitate discussion and creation, what to avoid, realistic discussion of the challenges, and familiarization with basic ground rules.

- While training provides knowledge and tools, *support and feedback nurture the student-teacher.* Peer mentorship and feedback are valuable assets to a service-learning program. Students will get the most from their experience when given the opportunity to get feedback, ask questions, share their experiences and provide support to others. Some examples include regular meetings with an advisor, discussion groups with others conducting similar work and group teaching instead of working individually.

- The support and feedback to students should *include the community setting as a co-partner in the education of the creative writing student.* Students should also be taught, mentored and supported in communicating with their community placement in order to best understand the needs of the community they are serving and to tailor the integration of their lessons into the lives and education of their students.

- *Programs should provide their students with guidelines, rules, and other structural supports designed to maximize positive outcomes.* Rules on how to interact, what to wear and what to say or not to say help contain the learning experience within manageable boundaries and go a long way to ensuring that students don't make inappropriate or foolish mistakes (Thaxton, 2010). The community settings that we work with will know these rules best, and learning from them is essential. For example, when working with mentally ill populations there are basic rules that counselors and other health workers learn. Creative writing students teaching in these environments must know and follow the rules.

- Just as basic rules of operation are important for the student-teacher, so too is it important to *ensure that the learning environment is supportive and contained in order to encourage openness.* According to Angela Wiseman, assistant professor of literacy education at North Carolina State University, trust is "an essential component to encouraging deep involvement, reflection, and interaction through poetry" (Wiseman, 2007, p. 46). Workshop guidelines for writing and critiquing poetry are essential to establishing a comfortable environment, especially in community and alternative settings (Jordan, 1995, pp. 35–54; Hudson, 2010).

● *All such efforts should include the opportunity for community students to publish or read their work, the opportunity to have their work publically recognized.* If we are serious in any way about giving voice to our students, we must provide public reading and/ or publication opportunity. An important element and outcome of having our students teach in non-academic settings is encouraging people from all walks of life to have their words validated, appreciated, and publically recognized.

Conclusion

Writing is for our communities—"for the people" as June Jordan says. Alternately, per Francis McCue, poet and self-proclaimed arts instigator, "Art is inseparable from civic space" (McCue, 2007). A creative writing discipline that exists in and of itself, for itself, isolated within the academy, created and consumed only from within its self-ordained academic boundaries, runs the risk of irrelevance. Schools from day care through high school, prisons, community centers, and other non-academic arenas should be every bit as much the places where poetry thrives as universities. Creative writing programs can teach students not only to write but also how to be artists—artists in the sense of producers and promoters of the role of art in life. Creative writing programs have the opportunity to show their students how to imbue the lives of the people and communities around them with art.

To achieve these goals we must also strive to change the discourse on community and creative writing. Today, when I talk about this subject, I find myself and others discussing our ideas in terms of how to bring writers into communities. Yet we are community members, just as much as anyone else—that is, we are already *in* communities, but we have become accustomed to thinking of our art as separate from our communities. The arts have not suddenly become irrelevant. The arts remain central to cultural expression and change, both embodying contemporary thinking and culture and pushing outwards on cultural norms to encourage change and transformation. Creative writing is not separate from community, but is and always will be embedded in community.

*   *   *

Christopher McIlroy

Christopher "Kit" McIlroy is author of the story collection *All My Relations* (1994), which won the Flannery O'Connor Award, and the non-fiction *Here I Am a Writer* (2011), drawn from his experiences teaching writing in Native American communities. He lives in Tucson, Arizona.

Keeping it Real: Creative Writing Under the Shadow of Standardized Testing

The Dog That Wants To Get Over the Wall

Hello, I am a dog. Will you help me get over this wall? So the dog went to the wall and then he got a stick and jumped up but that wall was so big that the dog crashed into the wall and fell. So the dog got a ladder but it did not work. The ladder was too little and the wall was too big. So the dog was thinking and then he got 4 plungers and he got on the wall with the 4 plungers. The plungers stuck to the wall and he got on top, but when he got up the wall he saw a bigger wall and the dog cried. So the dog said how will I get to my house on time said the dog. So the dog got the 4 plungers and he got on the wall. So he climbed and climbed and then it was night. The dog screamed what will I do said the dog! Then his owner called him and then when he heard his voice the dog jumped up and up so that the dog landed on top of the wall. The dog said hooray but when he opens his eyes he sees a bigger wall. When he saw the wall the dog said no!, no!, no!, and no!

It's tempting to interpret this existential parable (complete with suction cups) in light of the author's background; her parents emigrated from the repressive theocracy of Iran. But Kylie Baher was born in the U.S. and composed this story in second grade. She laughed while writing it; she thought it was funny. Part of what we cherish about creative writing is its defiance of formulaic analysis. It is too much like life, with its infinite complexities, contradictions, and unfathomable scenarios.

In contrast, a standardized writing rubric, e.g. the Six Traits, which until recently formed the basis of most state assessments, including the Arizona's Instrument to Measure Standards (AIMS) in my home state, Arizona, depends exactly on such a formula. The Six Traits—ideas and content, organization, voice, sentence fluency, word choice, and conventions—have been helpless to convey the mythic dimension that Kylie unknowingly opens with her tale. They could commend her for "a thorough, balanced explanation/exploration of the topic" or rue the inconsistency of verb tenses that "do distract the reader" but perhaps "do not block meaning."

Capturing creative writing in a rubric is like trapping a dream with a waffle iron. Which is why AIMS, and most state standardized testing systems, haven't even tried doing it. This is why, along with testing culture's climate of fear, in states like Arizona, creative writing has been marginalized in public schools to the point of vanishing. Arizona's story is that of much of the nation as a whole.

A high school student who must pass AIMS to graduate, and whose failure could contribute to the firing of administration and faculty, and even the takeover of her school by the state, is not invited to write like this:

Is It "I Am" Or "My Name"

My name belongs to a dead white woman. How it got down to me?
I don't know. Josephine. Does not suit me. It has no meaning
But I am a meaning, a meaning for laughter
Like a feather of the eagle being patted over a child's body for blessing
    The child laughs.
I am a meaning, a meaning for strength
Like a feather of the eagle being patted over my grandfather's body
    for blessing. My grandfather who is a warrior.
I am a meaning, a meaning of gentleness
Like a feather of the eagle being patted over my mother's body
    for blessing. My mother a heroine.
I am a meaning, a meaning of a birthmark.
Like a feather of the eagle being patted over my body for
    blessing. My name Spotted Feather.
        Not just my name it's who I am.
(Josie Frye, 11th grade, 1996)

From the time my wife and I, and a poet friend, founded the non-profit ArtsReach in 1986, through the first years of the current millennium, we encouraged Native American students in southern Arizona to find their voices, to uplift their communities, and to stir outsiders with their gifts of expressive writing. The Arizona Commission on the Arts granted me that same freedom, from 1979 to 1987. So did the Tucson Unified School District (TUSD) in the early years of my author-in-residence program.

This past year I taught persuasive writing to high school students in Josie Frye's old district, and to middle school students in Josie's old district, and to fifth graders in Josie's old district. And to second, third, and fourth graders in TUSD.

Many of those teachers, and their administrators, are brave enough to let me sneak in the occasional story or poem, too. But in doing so—in not using every classroom moment to teach to the test—they put their own careers at risk. After all, Josie's poem runs afoul of the Six Traits stricture against "repeated patterns of sentence structure" although the allowance that "figurative language may be used" could award her points for Word Choice.

The severest fault of Josie's poem, though, is that it is not a persuasion. In 2010–11, the last year of record available for this essay, persuasion accounted for over 70 percent of the AIMS writing prompts, grades 5–12. While responsible persuasion hones critical thinking, its dominance of the testing field probably owes more to its relative predictability as a form. The vagaries of assessing writing have bedeviled AIMS since its inception. In 2008, AIMS writing scores overall inexplicably dropped nine percentage points from the previous year, falling at every grade level except eighth. In

2006, while writing scores generally held steady across grade levels, they plunged some 20 percent among third graders. As Arizona's then-Superintendent of Public Instruction admitted, "We're doing everything we can to take something inherently subjective and make it as objective as possible."

Given the pervasiveness of persuasion, particularly among the upper grades, no wonder that students relegate creative writing to the days of fuzzy slippers and recess. Put away childish things. When I was permitted to teach fiction to Baboquivari High School students in 2008, most began with an expository introduction. They had forgotten how to write a story.

Little is more capricious than educational theory. During the late eighties and well into the nineties, Whole Language, which gloried in unbound written expression and exploration—damn the spelling! full speed ahead!—held sway over much classroom pedagogy. Arizona even incorporated poetry into state language arts standards.

But as measured performance continued to decline nationwide, institutional education clamped down on writing, along with reading and math. Arizona's AIMS was implemented in 1999 as a requirement to graduate high school, though that ultimate penalty—denial of a diploma for failure to pass—was postponed for several years, since modified and mitigated. In 2000, AIMS was expanded to include third, fifth, and eighth grades. In 2009 all grades 3–12 were required to take AIMS, except ninth, which administered the national-brand TerraNova. With the economic crash, the extended writing portion of AIMS has been cut back, the grading deemed too expensive. It now (2012) begins in fifth grade.

Despite the inability of standardized tests to reliably assess writing, the hierarchy—No Child Left Behind at the federal level, AIMS at the state—absolutely commandeered the teaching of writing in local venues. School districts structured writing curriculum to reflect institutional pressures.

While I would have assumed that top-down regimentation would at least have produced a higher baseline of competence in expository writing, even if at the expense of expressive forms, my inquiries suggested murkier outcomes.

"Honestly, I cannot say students overall write worse or better than a decade ago," responded Dr. Anne-Marie Hall (2009), who oversees freshman composition at the University of Arizona. She condemns No Child Left Behind as "horrible. The fear of not making AYP [Adequate Yearly Progress] for any school is enough to make some administrators take draconian steps with teachers. If it is the second week of February in sophomore year, you must be teaching 'x.'"

Dr. Donna Rabuck, assistant director of a University of Arizona tutoring program for 30 years, agreed (2009). "I'm sorry to say I don't see a difference. You would think that after all they do, it would show up. Maybe they learn those skills and they don't know how to transfer them to a deeper level, when they've come to college? They don't know how to do critical thinking or analysis? What they've learned is a kind of rote way of attacking?"

Climate of fear. Teaching to the test. These casual phrases have come to govern the practice of writing in so many of our schools.

Power shifts in Washington, DC, may nudge the standardized testing foundation but don't promise to shake it. While the Obama administration has sought to relax the rigidness of NCLB requirements, it shows no signs of questioning testing culture itself; indeed its proposed reforms and incentives pledge allegiance to the authority of test results.

Enter the Common Core State Standards (CCSS). In a push to entrench norms more uniformly across the nation, nearly all states have adopted CCSS for language arts and math. (States may add an additional 15 percent of their own content to the CCSS.) Assessment is following suit. By 2014–15, Arizona will join approximately half the CCSS states in using the Partnership for Assessment of Readiness for College and Careers (PARCC) as its standardized test. Other states have opted for the SMARTER Balanced Assessment Consortium (SBAC).

I can't divine, and probably only time will tell, what this bodes for creative writing. CCSS relies consistently on three strands of writing throughout K–12: persuasion/argument, expository, and narrative. As a third of this triumvirate, stories, after a long retreat, could be poised to storm back into the classroom. (Typical of standardized criteria, CCSS averts its gaze from student-composed poetry entirely. Kindergartners, however, will be required to "compose opinion pieces," that is, persuasions.)

Caution: under CCSS, the fuzzy slipper rule still holds. Fiction, by and large, is for kids. For grades 6–12, the CCSS Introduction states, "Fulfilling the Standards for 6–12 ELA [English Language Arts] requires much greater attention to a specific category of informational text—literary nonfiction—than has been traditional." This to balance that goshdarned fondness of ELA classrooms for literature—"stories, drama, and poetry"—with the "growing emphasis on informational texts in the higher grades … the overwhelming focus of writing throughout high school should be on arguments and informative/explanatory texts."

Even when officially sanctioned, stories still will be circumscribed by a generic rubric. While well-intentioned and carefully thought, the CCSS will not catch much lightning in this bottle:

Write narratives in which they recount a well-elaborated event or short sequence of events, include details to describe actions, thoughts, and feelings, use temporal words to signal event order, and provide a sense of closure. (second grade)

Use dialogue and description to develop experiences and events or show the responses of characters to situations. (fourth grade)

Orient the reader by establishing a situation and introducing a narrator and/or characters; organize an event sequence that unfolds naturally. (fifth grade)

Provide a conclusion that follows from and reflects on the narrated experiences or events. (seventh grade)

Organize an event sequence that unfolds naturally and logically. (eighth grade)

Not all stories require dialogue. Many lack a formal conclusion; inconclusiveness itself can be a virtue in fiction. Logic is anathema to some great fiction. By definition, "creative" writing evades a "rubric."

Ultimately, the fate of creative writing under CCSS will depend on assessment. If narrative takes its turn in a testing rotation, students will write stories, at least. If it ain't tested, it won't happen. What am I asking for? More warping of storytelling via the procrustean bed of standardized testing? Is that better than no storytelling?

Students need creative writing. Most are unaware of this need because they never have the chance to engage with or even conceive of it. But given the opportunity, that need bursts forth.

The Boy and the Eagle

There was a boy about eighteen years old. He got really mad at his parents because they were going to let him do the plans to a new house, but they went ahead and did their own plans.

Then he ran real fast toward a place he had never been. It was very quiet and had plants of yellow and red, and tall strong trees. When he had found a place to sleep, he slept. The place he slept had a lot of leaves on the ground which had fallen from the tree above.

Overnight he changed into an eagle. When he woke up the next morning, he tried to talk, but his voice was just a loud squawk. Then he looked at himself, and he had feathers on his arms and all over his body. He could see his beak by just looking down. He looked at his feet and could see that his nails were as sharp as a knife.

He went in a little cave that was dark, but not so dark after he built a fire. And after a while he came out and started to fly, but he saw he wasn't very good at it. On his first try he couldn't get off the ground. On his second try he ran off a cliff. He fell to the ground but wasn't hurt. That's when he learned to fly better by flapping his wings a little slower. It took him a while before he started flying so swiftly. The next step he learned was to catch his prey and be cautious in case there was danger. While he was hunting, he heard a rabbit in the bushes, and after a while he could spot it from far away.

Then, about a year later, he saw his family was searching for him, and he also missed them. Then the next day his family went over to a ditch where inside was a small river, and they went in the ditch. They saw a person who was far away, and there, sitting on the river bank, was an eagle which was their son.

As they got closer, he changed, and when he turned around he brushed off his arms. Four feathers fell off his arms, and on his head was a feather. And his hair was very straight as if the wind had been blowing against it.

When they took him home, he found out they had a new addition to their family. It was his brother, a nice little baby who soon will be told of the place his brother will never forget.

And when the boy thought about things, he thought about how fun it was to be an eagle, and how good his vision was, and hearing. But he still had it in his heart, and it was almost like he had two hearts. He goes to visit where he stayed and sometimes turns into an eagle.
(Patrick Lewis-Jose, 4th grade)

This story written in 1990 could serve as a blueprint for Patrick's life, in which he has overcome the social ills of his rural Native community and a rag-tag school system to earn degrees at Stanford, help form a tight, dynamic family, and teach against the current, successfully resisting a canned curriculum during his first year in the field. Patrick certainly has learned to fly, and I'd credit him with at least two hearts, minimum.

Looking back, Patrick articulates the importance of that first creative writing experience, in which he was asked to "try to express whatever we were feeling or seeing or wanting. No one had ever asked me that before. It changed my life."

Every student deserves that chance. In the interests of a competitive workforce, let us inundate our schools with "informational texts." But don't exclude creative writing. Don't ignore the whole person. Creative writing is a means for young people to grapple with the challenges of meaning and existence at a crucial time of their lives.

But it also can score well. It can feed the beast.

Forgiving the absence of dialogue in Patrick's story—after all, there was no one for his character to talk to—the CCSS evaluator could be gratified by "concrete words and phrases and sensory details" that "convey experiences and events precisely." The story does "orient the reader by establishing a situation." A Six Traits grader could reward its "balanced and thorough exploration of the topic using relevant details."

Or take student poetry, which officially doesn't exist on the CCSS screen.

Sad as a Bum in Jail

I am sad like
a bum in
jail in a cold
cell with murderers
thieves and killers
mean cops

picking on you
they give you
nasty food
you work in a blazing
hot sun smashing
rock and making
license plates
working in a cafeteria
mopping throwup
I want to puke
I am going to hate
tomorrow lifting
weights and playing
basketball that
is orange like
our suit in hand-
cuffs and rattling
chains.

(Luis Arvizu, 3rd grade)

CCSS doesn't ask for "figurative language" in third grade, but it does in fourth. Luis could be rehearsing, couldn't he? The entire poem technically is an extended simile which unmoors itself from its origin, "I am sad like a bum in jail," to make its extraordinary journey into a palpable fear in Luis's life. At the same time, his poem certainly proves he can "choose words and phrases for effect," if that is what CCSS is looking for. Configuring Luis's poem into prose, however, adding the appropriate punctuation, reveals another strong selling point for poetry, if selling what we must do to ensure its place in students' maturing.

> I am sad like a bum in jail, in a cold cell with murderers, thieves, and killers, mean cops picking on you. They give you nasty food. You work in a blazing hot sun, smashing rock and making license plates, working in a cafeteria, mopping throwup. I want to puke. I am going to hate tomorrow, lifting weights and playing basketball—that is orange like our suit—in handcuffs and rattling chains.

The sentences snake and pop together, the long, cumulative phrasing alternating with the blunt statements, "They give you nasty food" and "I want to puke." In no prose of Luis's that I saw did he remotely approach that level of artistry. It was poetry that informed his ear, lifted his cadences. Thanks to poetry, Luis achieved sentence fluency.

Beyond standardized scoring, creative writing can serve other academic goals. *Classroom Instruction That Works*, a meta-analysis published by

Robert Marzano, Debra Pickering, and Jane Pollock in 2001, culled a host of studies for nine strategies that contributed most to student achievement. Among such broad practices as graphic organizers and cooperative learning, Number One on the list was "identifying similarities and differences," which encompasses both comparison-contrast and metaphorical thinking.

The O'odham War

I was in my room. As I was spacing out on the mirror, thinking of old Indian legends and fights, I fell and suddenly I was sitting on a little hill spaced out on a rock.

I realized I was 100 years back in time, in the middle of a war between the Apaches and the O'odham. I got hit in the head by a rock and passed out.

When I came to, I was lying down in a little adobe. Boy, did my head hurt, like a spear going into a heart of an evil person and all their powers releasing. I opened my eyes. I saw an old woman. It was one of my ancestors. I could tell by the way she was dressed, with her long hair, long dress, and no shoes. I said, "Where am I?"

She looked startled. She got a rock and threw it at me. That's when I knew she didn't know I was an O'odham, 'cause of my jeans, black T-shirt, and Vision shoes. The rock felt weird. It got my arm numb. I said, "Lady, what's up with you?" But then I came to realize that she didn't know English. Once again she threw a rock, and continued to.

After the tenth rock I was in my room looking in the mirror. I guess I'm just thinking too hard. *(Wenona Ortegas, 6th grade)*

Through examples such as this, students understand that comparison-contrast need not be an academic exercise. While Wenona and her ancestor both are members of the Tohono O'odham tribe, the differences in dress and language dramatize the gulf between them. Not only does the warrior woman fail to recognize Wenona as one of her own but stones her for her strangeness, more, the estrangement from traditional ways that Wenona's story painfully acknowledges. And that simile—"Boy, did my head hurt, like a spear going into the heart of an evil person and all their powers releasing." Figurative language, indeed.

Obviously, students drafting and revising their stories and poems are honing their testable skills, too, should we choose to view it that way. Emotionally compelled by their own material, they write better, setting new expectations for themselves, and are more willing to revise, for content as well as stylistic and grammatical considerations. It's through revision that the most dramatic learning takes place.

At its fringes, the standardization of writing can verge on the ridiculous. Five-year-olds do not need to "compose opinion pieces." Their job is to explore senses and imagination like this:

I am at the bottom of the ocean! It is as dark as a black hole. Little bubbles rise from me. The bubbles look like little jellyfish as I talk. I see jellyfish and seaweed and coral reef. I see shells rocks and sand. The shells look like clams. Some are open. Some are closed. *(Leksi Grodzki, kindergarten)*

More gravely, though, in its panic to achieve basic competence, testing culture threatens all classroom writing with sterility and inconsequence. Real writing is not a testable commodity. It is a purpose. It explains, informs, persuades, speculates, reflects, discovers—or catches the heart and spirit—because people need it to do so. We must connect students with those authentic drives, not squeeze them into a rubric grid. They will write better, score better, and we'll all be happy.

Perhaps, someday, the pendulum of the educational industry will make one of its wild periodic swings, back to the intrinsic value of writing as a fundamental human act.

Without intending to—that's the beauty of it—Finland's educational philosophy has thrown down a challenge to the entire standardized testing hegemony. Unlike the annual exercises of AIMS or CCSS, Finland imposes no standardized test "until the end of high school." Teachers are not "judged by their students' test scores" (Ravitch, 2012). Yet over the past decade Finnish students have scored among the highest in the world—often **the** highest—in the Program for International Assessment, a measure of proficiency in reading, math, and science. Finnish educator Pasi Sahlberg, one of Ravitch's sources, credits a range of factors, including the selectivity and rigor of Finland's training of teachers and an emphasis on "learning, rather than on preparing students for tests" (Sahlberg, 2007 p.156).

Perhaps, someday, the assessment ideology will be forced to reassess itself—and find itself wanting.

Perhaps the dog will make it over the wall.

In the meantime, though, we lovers and teachers of writing are not as alone as it may seem. Classroom teachers and even administrators sympathize, not even secretly. "I wish I had more time for creative writing" is a common refrain from the classrooms I visit. Not long after Arizona imposed AIMS, a primary school principal requested a "Six Traits poetry workshop" for his second graders. I don't blame the principal for that mutant monster. He was just trying to jimmy poetry into the system.

We must keep helping him.

CHAPTER TEN

Giving Community Members (a Loud) Voice

Turning words into voices

All of these weeks of preparation and working with participants, and you might begin to wonder what difference it's going to make. Writers grapple with many different responses to CBL projects. Some of us feel burned out by the sixth or seventh time we've worked with homeless children, and that's quite understandable—it can be emotionally difficult to see stark situations that we've not encountered before. Some writers are energized and hope to continue what they've just begun. You are probably quite aware by now that a semester-long connection with your participants is not a long time. Whatever you're thinking about your project at this point, one of the central components of doing creative writing in the community is giving community members a voice, a way to put their stories into words. You have helped validate their world. In *Ways of Worldmaking*, Nelson Goodman reminds us that "We can have words without a world but no world without words or other symbols" (1978, p. 6).

When you started your CBL project—perhaps a new world for you—of offering creative writing activities, you may not have known if what you would do with your participants would make any difference. Perhaps you still feel this way. If there is only one thing you feel you can give yourself credit for in the lives of your participants, it can be this: you have been a consistent presence in their lives. You have returned week after week to share an hour or so with them. Just by the act of returning to them week after week, you tell them their voices matter. Their words are important. Their stories are worth telling. You are letting them know that their lives have meaning.

Brittany, the student who worked at an inner-city school, reflected on how voice gives us history, a common history, and a history that allows us to understand each other. Throughout Brittany Osbourne's (2012) project, she became increasingly interested in how children of African American decent learn to use their voices:

> Without words history is not remembered, only imagined. For me, creative writing serves as a vehicle to transport the ideas, occurrences, and ancestral memory of the past to the present day. The words people place on paper or read should hold significance beyond mere self-gratification. Notwithstanding the genre or audience, teaching creative writing must transcend classroom boundaries. Community Based Learning (CBL) is a method I have come to love and enjoy, which accomplishes this.

Celebrating

Celebrating the voices of your participants is one of the most satisfying aspects of your project. Even if you've encouraged your participants to read their writing aloud each week, planning an official reading or celebration adds an extra dimension to what it means to have a voice. The CBL project allows everyone involved to discover that together our voices are powerful tools in building community.

Publishing the work of participants

There are many different ways to celebrate the work you and your participants have done. Whatever you do, it's important for the participants to see how their voices enter, and therefore, matter in the community. The writing process, as you know, includes prewriting, drafting, revising, editing, and, finally, publishing. For our purposes, there are two aspects of publication:

1   Print publication
2   Reading/celebration

Throughout your CBL project you've been helping participants with reading. Publishing can take many forms. Publishing allows a writer to gain more confidence in his/her writing, and gets at one of the central purposes for creative writing in the community: giving community members a voice. In Chapter 3 I listed several possible ways to print the writings of the participants. In the rest of this chapter I will use "publication" to refer to both printing and reading the work of participants.

Preparing for publication

1 Talk with the community partner (your on-site contact) to determine how to best publish the work of your participants. The community partner is the best resource for helping you decide whether or not you should hold a private or a public reading. With the community partner, determine a specific day and time for the reading. Plan to have the print aspect of publication ready to distribute at the reading.

2 Prepare to print the work. Depending on what you planned at the beginning of the semester, you may be creating chapbooks or anthologies for the group. Here's a review of the list from Chapter 3 of some possibilities. You may come up with some other ways to put words into print.

   a Record each person reading a story or a few poems they've written, and then post the reading online. Maybe add images and music to this recording.

   b Create a private or public blog where and post the stories and poems.

   c Create a newsletter or newspaper of the stories and poems.

   d Create a chapbook for each person or a chapbook anthology that includes a few of each person's writing.

   e Create a broadside or poster of one piece of writing by each participant. Ask each participant to select one piece of writing he/she is most proud of, put it on a large piece of paper, decorate it with clipart or art by the student. Then hang up the broadsides on the walls of the room where you hold the reading.

   f Scan the pictures the participants drew throughout the semester, put them all in a three-prong folder, and give a copy to each participant.

   g If funding is available, you may print a perfect-bound, professional-looking book. Whatever you do, it's important that the participants see how their voice enters, and therefore, matters in the community.

3 Discuss the publications with your participants. This kind of celebration adds a whole other level of self-worth for your participants. This allows their voices to be heard and seen. The celebration is best when held the last week of your classes or during final exam week. This is usually earlier than when public schools will be ending, and thus making this closure aspect even more important. School children might not understand why you're not staying with them the entire semester. Samantha Sanabria worked with sixth–eighth graders in a rural area of central Florida. She had initially planned to create chapbooks herself for the participants, but after discussing it with her participants and their teacher, they decided to create their own books. "The kids really enjoyed putting their stories on construction paper and decorating them according to their own personalities. I can't wait for Friday when they all get to share them."

4   Locate any donations of refreshments, and tell the donors when you will pick these up. Often a local grocery store or café will provide drinks and refreshments.

5   Determine who will be invited to the reading and send out any necessary invitations. Again, include your community partner in these plans. At schools, you might invite other classes, administration, and parents to attend an evening event where the children you've been working with can read one or two pieces they've written. At a shelter, you might invite the board of directors in addition to other residents and staff. If possible, you might hold the reading at a local book store or coffee shop. Work with the manager/owner to arrange a date and time. Consider how you might get community members to attend. Would it be appropriate to invite someone from the local or your college newspaper?

6   If your reading will be off-site, work with your community partner on transporting participants to the reading location.

7   Prepare the program for the reading. You could also plan on reading—perhaps something you wrote based on a prompt you gave to your participants, perhaps a reflection of how much you learned from your participants. In this way, participants hear how their lives have affected you.

8   When you hold the reading, be sure to take pictures.

Listening to their voices and seeing their words in print impact you and the participants in surprising ways. Brittany discovered the joy in listening to the fourth graders read as well as seeing the stories in print.

I learned that listening and allowing students to talk was just as important as getting them to write. During the writing process, many students wanted to tell me their stories before they ever wrote them on paper. During one of my lessons I even had a student wish to share her story (she had just written five minutes earlier) orally rather than read it from her paper. I was awestruck by how natural and fluid the students' stories were told verbally. Consequently, one of my primary jobs as instructor was to show my students how their oral voices could still exists in the stories they wrote.

Structured reflection

Personal

1   Think back to when you first learned that you would be required to spend an hour a week at a community site conducting this project and either your excitement or resistance or your concerns. Has there been a shift in your thoughts about CBL? Describe that shift.

Academic

2   How are you going to publish the work on your participants? What plans have you made so far?

3   Earlier I asked you to list several questions for a reflective or analytical essay. Using one or two of those questions, make some detailed notes that describe your thoughts so far about those questions.

Civic

4   What happened this week that's different from any other week at your site?

5   Now that you've completed several weeks of workshops in the community and you're almost finished with another semester of college workshops, what do you think are the similarities and differences between college and community writing and the workshop settings?

6   How to the participants at your site advocate for themselves?

Readings

Lisa Chatterjee

Lisa Chatterjee graduated from the University of Central Florida with her Bachelor's Degree in English—Creative Writing. She is currently working as an NYC Teaching Fellow, receiving her Master's in English Education 7–12 through Brooklyn College while teaching high school English in Queens, New York.

The Children We Leave Behind

The first few weeks I spend mostly at home, designing idealistic plans, excited by those two new words: field work. Excited but afraid to have to leave my shell, afraid of what new beasts could form from my responsibility to these children, who are not my own, who might not even like me.

On the seventh week, well past the last date to start, I drag myself down near the school for the first time, past the swanky developments flanking the university, past the city center with glass and spires of bank buildings gleaming in the heat. The ride on the 408 is as harrowing as I'd imagined, and my nerves cackle louder in my ears the closer I get to the scraggly bits of asphalt that comprise the area after downtown Orlando.

This is where I used to go when I was on probation, when I'd make the six a.m. drive down to the barbed-wire dream house of Orange County Corrections, where the Ken-dolls wore orange jumpsuits and looked like they could use a shave. For six months I was bound to piss in a cup for the officer with hard eyes but cute dolphin earrings, something grandmotherly moving behind her robo-cop shell (later I found out that I knew her son, a pothead in every sense of the word—oh, sweet irony, you kill me). I'd cultivated a hatred for this city then, and that same blank ink of thought seeps into me as my nervous hands try to locate this school.

I get lost just a street away. I drive for a while, debating if I should try moving farther up the road, but then decide to flee, panicked by the echoes of my former drug counselor's words the last time I got lost around here— "make sure to roll up your windows, that's a bad area"—this coming from a hefty man who spent his youth dodging bullets in the Bronx.

On the eighth week I finally make it: Ivey Lane Elementary stands before me like a bottle of absinthe, slightly eerie and full of possibility. I march into the school before there's time for regrets. The first thing I notice is the woman at the desk. Her nails extend several centimeters past her fingertips; her hair is woven with copper, and around her neck hangs a large, round chunk of what is commonly referred to as "bling bling." What have I gotten myself into?

In the classroom I'm a shaking jellyfish, shapeless and at a loss for what to do. The teacher, Ms. Howze, has a body built for hugs and comfort, but her voice takes the roar of a lion when the children step out of line. All of my thoughts and actions are clouded by the bronchitis that's been infesting my lungs for over two weeks now. I try to keep distance from the children while still getting close enough to learn their names. Each name I am told, I promptly forget. Sometimes I can't even pronounce them, and repeat them over and over, the wrong way, while the poor kid in question stares like I'm not smart enough to be here. I spend most of the hour observing my peers working, and trying in earnest to discern which of the students are boys, which are girls. They have suspicion and pride laced all through their eyes and the curves of their lips. I sit down with Kayla and Toyriel, with Bianca and Josias and try to get them excited. Mostly, they make fun of me for being short and pass on answering my questions.

Over the next few weeks the kids begin to recognize me. They write an extra paragraph when I ask for an extra paragraph. They call me over for my approval before reading to the class. I've learned that my goal here is just to encourage them to write, but even reading their sweet stories about candy waterfalls and great castles in space with explosions, makes me grimace at their language, a rough slang that bears the obvious marks of poverty. I correct some of them, only to have the same language I try to deem for home only repeated back to the kids by their teachers, a fleet of nice-enough ladies who drawl, "you write good." As I begin to know the kids, the situation deflates me even more.

Jameisha's by far the tiniest in stature, a slip of a thing like those miniature ballerinas on music boxes, but she is the most commanding, the biggest punk. She stomps and pushes other kids out of the way, but only to get to you first, to drench up every bit of the spotlight. When upset, she says nothing at all, just bores holes into the paper or the floor with her practiced, indifferent gaze. Sometimes her every movement is so spiteful that a bitter taste will start to fizz on my tongue, but then I soften she seems like a girl who doesn't get much attention. She seems like she's used to fighting for it, but too proud to let it show.

Next to her is Kierra, who wears small round glasses and plays mother hen. She is the silent woman behind the curtains, pulling all the strings. When she and her best friend Kayla have a fight and break up, it is Kierra the other girls side with. The war lasts three weeks and casts a tense net over the whole classroom, palpable, constricting the work we do with childish hatred. Kayla's essays are all about the same malicious antagonist, named, coincidentally, Kierra, each time fated for a cruel new death. For three weeks, no one goes near the miniscule (and only) white girl with the graham-colored hair; fire comes off her in waves.

When peace is restored again to the classroom, the antics of the boys cause the teacher to lose her mind and take away recess, casting that awkward net again. There is Deverias, who is as devious as his name suggests: his grin easy and confident, he spends all class every class leaned back in his chair, cracking jokes but not doing a damn thing. When I ask my peers about this I am told, in a whisper, that he's been given up on. I know Ms. Howze, like me, does not miss the glint of longing to belong in his eyes, but she, like me, has no idea how to let it flourish. I imagine then that a lot of these kids have been given up on, not only by administrators, but by their parents, by the state. I think back to my childhood and how, though I spent most of the time raising and teaching myself, my parents at least tried to have a warm hand against my back should I lose my balance.

Gradually, I begin to work at the newly created Writing Center, in the hopes that I can try to instill in these kids the tools they will need to succeed in the world—even if for now that world is just the fourth grade. Week after week, we get asked at the front desk where or what the writing center is; week after week teachers forget to send their kids, or provide them with assignments, or equip them with paper and pencil. But my classmates and I, with the help of a grad student, do our best with what we've got, mustering the sweetest disposition possible to point out all the errors in the work we receive. The saddest part is that the work is great. These third and fourth graders are stars as much as any child at an upper middle-class school, but their writing is cheapened by the lifestyle they come from—a lifestyle whose crass grammar and language inevitably slip into the writing no matter how many ways we try to weed it out.

As my time at Ivey Lane Elementary begins to run out, the white walls seem to mock me even louder. At night when I can't sleep, I wonder what will happen of the kids who show so much promise, or how I will cut the modest bridges they have built to my heart.

What of Lidea, whose cheeks pull her face into ecstasy every time she sees me in the halls? Who from the very beginning turned out page after page for me, always willing?

What of Yardrick, the future boy genius, who says the least but writes with a passion? Over the weeks his stories have dwindled as he realizes that his talents are going underappreciated, that he does not get special treatment for following the rules.

All I can think of is how I wish to hold each child in my arms for five minutes, and that the heat of my body or the smell of my hair will somehow wash away every bad thing that did or will happen to them. The mother in me writhes and beats at my ribs, wanting out.

On my last day I am numb and careless. It is easier than letting loose the reservoir of feelings this place conjures. I do what I am here to do, I smile at the kids; I try not to be too nice lest they want me to stay. As I walk out of the building, it is more than the Florida heat that burns me up. Ivey Lane, a play on Ivey League. But who will carry these children to the top? Who will prevent others from kicking them off?

*　*　*

Scott Parsons

Scott Parsons is the director of the Osborne Writing Center at Hathaway Brown School, an all-girls independent school in Shaker Heights, Ohio, where he also teaches English and is inspired daily by his students. He previously taught English at a public vocational high school, where his students won numerous state- and national-level awards for their creative writing, including over $120,000 in college scholarship money. He is a past editor of *Ohio Teachers Write,* and his writing has appeared in *English Journal* and *Sow's Ear Poetry Review.*

Writing Out of Grief

School, according to a well-known saying, is the place where creativity goes to die. Although I had never heard that expression until recently, I know that in my own experience it was true. School took away rather than cultivated my creativity and left me with no authentic way to talk about what I genuinely felt or thought. Naturally enough, school had the effect of alienating me from myself: not only did I lack the language to say what mattered to me and what I felt, I was entirely unsure even of what to make of the world inside me. And so I largely drifted anaesthetized through my own life until many years later in college when my first creative writing classes helped me discover the language and the modes to express and to create— those things I did with such grace and ease as a child. In graduate school, when I had my first teaching experience with a freshman composition class, I found that my students, many of them, had suffered similarly. They came to me deadened by the kinds of language demanded by the monolithic five paragraph theme—the dread structure that Robert Atwan aptly refers to as a disingenuous and horribly dull "charade." Perhaps worse, this form promotes an "implicit message that writing should be the end product of thought and not the enactment of its process." As the semester proceeded, my students continued to delight in using fresh language to say thoughtful and authentic things, and I, in turn, took delight in them. And this was one of the great discoveries of my life; to my complete surprise, I was shocked to find myself in love with teaching—so much so that at the end of grad school, I opted not to pursue a PhD but an M.A.T. instead and go teach public high school. I had, I thought, found my true calling.

Eleven years later, I was close to burned out and thought often of the Leonard Cohen song "First We Take Manhattan" and its opening line, "They silenced me to twenty years of boredom / for trying to change the system from within." In many ways, my adult years in school were all too similar to my childhood years in school: testing was a fixation and creativity, at best, a frill if not at times somehow seen as disruptive or even dangerous in that it wasn't in a traditional sense measurable. In my last year of teaching public school, for instance, we had a mandate to give our students a 100-point test every two weeks and were told by one administrator that "writing is not an assessment of what a student has learned in your class." My means of survival through these years was the creative writing opportunities I regularly offered my students, sometimes covertly. I felt, often, swallowed by a system with which I felt no compatibility. What also helped sustain me through these years was the collaboration I had developed with my friend David, a poet who had become a regular figure in my classroom, conducting workshops, residencies, developing student poetry readings. We'd made anthologies and recorded CDs of student work and generally thrived off the give-and-take of a true collaboration. So, dispirited as I in many ways was, I began my eleventh year of teaching high school with my primary goal, as ever, to offer my students chances to be creative, speak truly, use language to heal—and I was excited to see where it would go, knowing that, as always, it would take forms and produce magical moments I could never anticipate. I was fortunate, too, to work with Lori, my wife's sister and a talented guidance counselor who often saved students from abusive homes, nurtured others through crushing personal difficulties, or simply tutored them in math. Often, she did the same for me; her office was my safe spot—the place I could retreat to at the end of a difficult day and feel some sense of home.

Two months into the school year, my wife and I woke up late on a Saturday morning. The answering machine was blinking when we came downstairs. "Cherie, this is Greg. Something's wrong with Lori, she can't move half her body, and she can't really talk. I called the ambulance and they're on their way." While they waited for the ambulance, her children came and sat with her on the bed. The paramedics, when they arrived, wheeled her away while her children said goodbye; she was unable to say goodbye to them.

Sometime during the night while she slept, we learned later, a blood clot had broken free in her leg, traveled through her circulatory system, and entered her heart, from where it should have moved into her lung and caused a pulmonary embolism. But there was a hole in her heart—undetected, always there—and so the clot passed through it and moved on to lodge deep in her brain.

When she woke in the morning, numb and half paralyzed, her two children and husband were in the kitchen, making pancakes. She tried to call out to them but couldn't. Her ability to speak was mostly gone. So she used her working arm to pound on the wall above her head until her husband came in and found her in bed confused and afraid. At the hospital, the doctors gave her an aspirin and advised the family to be patient. This could all clear up in a day, the doctor said, and there was nothing to do right now but wait. Cherie sat with her as Lori tried to explain what her children were supposed to wear that night to a wedding reception and where the outfits were. Still having difficulty speaking, she tried to communicate using a whiteboard but became frustrated and started to cry.

The next day, when she didn't improve and a cause wasn't presenting itself, she was life-flighted to Cleveland's University Hospital and their premier stroke center. This was going to be a matter of weeks, not days, the doctors there advised us. We would have to be patient.

Before the day was over, she went unconscious. Her husband was directed to call her name, which he did louder and louder. Soon he was perched above her chest screaming her name repeatedly. She was unresponsive.

Cherie brought pictures of Lori and her family to the hospital room, so that the medical staff would know something of who her sister was and that there were people who loved and relied on her. She was more than a room number or a bed or a patient. Next, as a precaution, the doctors removed the left half of her skull plate and stored it in refrigeration—as a precaution, they said, in case her brain were to swell and push against her skull. We had to understand that we were in for a long hard time of it—a matter of months not weeks—and Lori was fortunate to have such a supportive family. The next time my wife took me back to her room, Lori's head was visibly swollen on the left side, and her eye was puffy and black. She showed signs of life, though; her body moved in the bed, as it would if she were shifting in her sleep to get more comfortable.

That movement, the team of doctors and nurses were soon explaining to us, was merely reflex. Lori was never coming back. We were shown pictures of where the clot had lodged, deep in the stem of the brain, and told why that made any kind of recovery impossible. Suddenly, the plan for us now was to withdraw care and make her comfortable. Sometime after midnight, we are driven to a hotel room where for three hours Cherie and I sleep, clutching on to each other, mostly unable to speak. We wake at dawn and continue to hold each other. This is the first time in my life that I know what it is to feel desolate. Cherie talks about sharing a room with Lori growing up. For almost 15 years, they had shared a bed. She has no real sense of self outside of being a sister.

While Cherie is in the bathroom, I look out the window over the gray city just beginning to come to life. The curtains are open, and a warm light infuses the whole room. The most beautiful and lurid sunrise I have ever seen glows across the entire sky. The sun is red and swollen. I recognize the beauty of it but can't feel it stir inside me.

Later in the day, Lori's children are brought to the hospital and ushered into a small conference room where Cherie and I sit with Greg while he tells his children that their mother is dead. And that it is OK to cry. Then we shuffle distractedly to the car. Greg sits between his children in the back seat. "Dad," his son says in the back seat as we pull out of the parking deck, "did you get the picture of our family?" Greg lifts his head and says yes. The way he has just said "our family" suggests something that is permanent and not something that now exists in the past tense.

We spend the next week with Cherie's parents and draw comfort from the shared circle of our grief. These are, in fact, the only people I am able to spend time with because nothing outside this grief feels real. But then I have to leave it and return to work. After the morning bell on the first day back, I stand in front of my first class in a kind of shock, moving some papers around on my desk while I try feebly to speak to my students. I hear someone in the second row of tables lean over and say to her tablemate, "Look, his hands are shaking." The second day I don't remember. On the third, three students in my second period class are drawing on a piece of paper when I come into the room. At the top of the paper, I see the words, "We are sorry for your loss." After the bell, one of them comes to my desk and asks if they can all take their card to Mr. Smith. "His goldfish died," they explain, "so we made him a sympathy card." I didn't really see any way for me to continue. The only thing that was real to me was grief, and yet this grief, seemingly, was the only thing I could not express or talk about or reveal. I was supposed somehow to drift through my days, as a teacher, pretending.

For weeks I do it and feel completely detached. I look out at students and feel no connection to them at all. I listen to my colleagues talk and feel a complete alienation. It's all made worse because there are so many students who did not know Lori at all. Our school was a two-year vocational school for juniors and seniors, and because she had died so early in the year, almost none of my students, new to the school, knew Lori.

Some did, though, and, somewhat perversely, I draw solace from their pain because it is a clear mark of the impact she made on students year after year. Like the rest of her friends and family, I think often of the paperweight a student had given to Lori the year before, engraved with the saying "To the world you may be one person. But to one person you may be the world."

In the months that follow and through the bleak winter, I am able to find some comfort through Lori's best friends in the building, especially her guidance partner Dave who has moved into Lori's office rather have it be taken over by her replacement. I continue to go to the office after school has ended and talk with Dave, and he tells me of students I don't know but who knew Lori well and continue to struggle with her loss. More than anything, I take consolation from my friend David, the poet, who lost his own mother as a child and struggled for years to process his grief. One night, over beers at a bar downtown, he suggests we hold a writing workshop to create a space for people to grieve, to record our loss, and to pay tribute to Lori and her place in our lives. When I share the idea with my colleagues and some students to whom I knew Lori was important, they are grateful but afraid. I wonder how and why it is that showing our grief feels inappropriate—especially when all psychologists say that the best thing we could do for Lori's children is not hide our grief and tears from them. The morning of the workshop, the students arrive and everyone sits still in a heavy silence. Lori's best friends among the teaching staff are here—all of them but Terry, who peeks in the door and says he can't do it.

I introduce David, who shares briefly his own story of losing his mother in childhood and many years later finding healing through writing of his loss and through reading the stories others writers had shared of their own loss. And then he reads Maxine Kumin's poem "How It Is," written to her closest friend Anne Sexton after Sexton's suicide. "Shall I say how it is in your clothes?" the poem opens. "A month after your death I wear your blue jacket. / The dog at the center of my life recognizes / you've come to visit, he's ecstatic."

Four years later, when Cherie and I clean out our house preparing to move, Cherie will open a container of Lori's clothes she has kept sealed in our laundry room. She will take them out and run her hands through them and say, "I can't get rid of them; they still smell like her house." By now, Lori's husband has married again, has formed a new family, has a baby turning one and another to be born in months. Their house has a smell of its own.

After David reads the poem, we talk about the comfort of the physical things the dead leave behind, and Lori begins to come into focus inside the classroom. We picture her hoop earrings, her lipstick, her favorite dress. We remember her signature sayings and her enthusiastic laugh and the way she used to slap her knee. Then David invites us to write—and to do so directly to Lori, to speak to her. And so we write, and almost immediately people throughout the room begin quietly to cry as they speak to Lori on their pages. David circles around the room offering tissues and patting people gently on the back. For me, also crying, it feels in some strange way good to be a member of this openly grieving group and not the person in charge masking the only things I feel.

When we finish, we share bits of what we've written. I stand in front of the class and read, "Dear Lori, I have never felt so sad. It's April, and sometimes I still cry when I walk the dog." All the manuals on grief and grieving will tell you that there's a great power in speaking out loud to the dead, but there's a vast difference between intellectual knowing and emotional truth and I am unprepared for the way speaking her name overwhelms me. Then Dave, her friend and guidance counselor partner, shares, "The days continue but will never be the same." He struggles through to his last lines, "I wish I had some special object that reminds me of you. But I don't. Instead I find an occasional strand of hair in our office and, as painful as it is some days, I hope they never vanish." At this point, Terry, who has again drifted back into the room, has to get up and leave, saying "I'm sorry, I can't do it" as he slips out the door. Michelle reads, "I still call your cell phone number just to hear your voice" and immediately starts to cry.

Two days before Lori's blood clot, we had cleared the messages from our answering machine, erasing her voice six different times. "Hey it's Lori, I just wanted to talk about the birthday party …" One was older, from the summer, and was representative of a frequent refrain: "Good morning—it's hot outside, and the pool is nice and cool. We have snacks …"

Terry comes to my room two days after our session of writing and sharing our grief and gives me a handwritten page that begins, "I always looked up to you" and continues "You were a caring, giving person, a great mother, teacher, friend—my best friend." In the coming days, a secretary puts a typed page in my mailbox, and former students whom Lori had counseled through losses of their own begin to email me poems and letters. David takes all these pages and begins to craft them into a multi-voiced piece called, simply, "Dear Lori." When we read this text out loud, Lori feels more present among us—or, at least, somehow less absent.

In April, we plan to read the poem at "Giving Voice," an annual event that features student poetry and song from students and adults from Akron and Cleveland who have participated in writing workshops organized through the outreach programs of the Wick Poetry Center, which my friend David directs. When I tell Terry, who had flitted in and out of the room while we wrote, he shakes his head and tells me there is no way he can take part, and though I want him there because I know how important Lori was to him, I accept his decision. But at the reading, he appears by my side in the aisle 15 minutes before we are to go on stage and says, "I have to do this."

We are almost three hours into a student poetry reading that was supposed to run no more than 90 minutes when we begin the poem. But it's clear very early that each of the nearly 700 members of the audience are deeply tuned in as we begin to read. When Joe, a former student, reads his voice cracks seven lines in as he remembers Lori sitting in the audience five years ago when Joe as a high school senior read for that year's "Giving Voice." When he pauses and gathers himself you can feel something shift in the ballroom. The air feels charged. I have never seen this many people so silent and rapt. To the left of the stage where Lori's friends and family sit, you can hear open weeping. When it is Terry's turn to read he steps to the mic and his throat constricts. He tries twice but cannot squeeze out a word. David puts his arm around him, embracing him while he reads his lines for him. Afterwards, he comes to stand beside me and shakes his head slightly back and forth, still unable to speak but glad, I know, that he tried and grateful to be standing here with the people who loved Lori so intensely.

Near the end of the last stanza of the poem, Hal, the music director of the program, strums his guitar and hums in harmony while all the readers speak out lines from their stanza—a chorus of lines and voices. And then it is over and we stand on a quiet stage. The audience hesitates and then stands and applauds for what feels like a very long time. Afterwards, my students mingle with students from other schools and with senior citizens and veterans of the war in Iraq, fellow writers who have participated in the reading. A student from Akron tells my student Kari, who is now a teacher herself, "I'm sorry for your loss. After hearing your poem I feel like I knew her." Lori's father Lyle meets a group of my students near the stage and thanks them and cries.

I see that we have done is perform an act of mourning, which is something so different from grief. Where grief is private, mourning is public; and where grief cripples, mourning heals. And in the days that follow, I feel the healing and talk a lot about how good it felt to speak out loud to Lori. In time, though, I sink back. Throughout my career I thought I had been searching for a poem that healed; I wanted to take away the often horrible pain my students felt and replace it with beauty and art, present them with writing as an avenue for healing. What I was really doing, though, was searching for a poem that cured. And that's not possible. Four years later, none of us who loved Lori are in any way cured of the pain of losing her, and I don't think we want to be. It would be horrible not to miss her. And there is a comfort in having paid her tribute with that poem and in the vital sense of community that brought it into being: community members, artists, teachers, college and high school students, colleagues, friends—all of us working together to make art and to pay tribute, to make space for our emotions and our pain, to create art and to share it.

The next year, Nikki, who as a college student helped me lead poetry workshops for my students and is now a poet and a teacher herself, visits my class to lead a writing workshop in which we write love letters to Life. In the days after, Nikki and David and I trade emails back and forth, trying to take all the lines generated that day and pare them down in a short, coherent, multi-voiced poem. Weeks later, the poem emerges, a woven blend of seven student voices and my own. Soon it will be handed over to a graphic design graduate student who will develop it into a Traveling Stanza—one of a collection of poem posters that will hang in coffee shops and travel through Akron and Cleveland on the transits. It is hanging now in the school where I teach, and often during the year students will return from a traveling on the RTA in Cleveland and report seeing it. There's comfort in that, too.

"Dear Life," the poem begins, "my heart flips for you." My lines come in the third stanza: "You took away my sister and left a beautiful sunrise, / the whole gray dawn heavy with light." I love that my own lines are embedded in those my students wrote, the way our voices hang together to make a single work. And I love the way the poem concludes: "I want to find light in the cracks of your skin, / feel the wind that soars through your body. / I want to grasp you in my arms again, / say *this is how we love.*"

CHAPTER ELEVEN

Publishing Your CBL Project

Publication at your university

In the last chapter, you prepared the reading and the publication to showcase the writing your participants have done. The reading and whatever kind of print publication you decide on are not only for the benefit of the participants, but also for you to see what your hard work has accomplished.

What about publishing the work *you've* done? How might you publish and celebrate the work you've done each week? Consider the two aspects of publication for your participants: print and presentation (reading). There are numerous ways to present your CBL project and what you've learned about yourself, writing, community, social justice, etc.

The University of Central Florida, where I currently teach, hosts an annual university-wide Student Service-learning Showcase. The showcase provides a way for our students to see what other types of projects are done in other disciplines, allows our students to showcase their own project, and allows our students to win scholarships. The showcase is, essentially, a poster presentation and display along with each project's student or student team talking about their projects to faculty and staff who serve as judges for the prizes.

Our Student Government Association provides over $5,000 in scholarship prizes. Amy Zeh, our Service-learning Program Director secured an additional $5,000 from different colleges and organizations within the university. The grand prize is *The Office of Experiential Learning Scholarship,* given to the best in overall project and presentation. The winning student or winning team of students must receive at least one additional award and/or recognition at the event to be considered for this grand prize (UCF, n.d.).

The second largest awards go to five different poster presentations in each of these five categories which are directly linked to service-learning objectives:

Pedagogical value: Service-learning, as you recall, directly links the service in the community to course objectives. For students to be recognized in this category, the judges look for evidence that the syllabus for the course clearly states the connection between "service" and "learning," as well as evidence that the student(s) understand the link between the academics of the course and the service project. Each student is asked to provide a copy of the course syllabus. Judges ask students to articulate the connection between the SL/CBL project and the course objectives.

Quality of the display: The way you present your work weighs equally in our showcase with the other aspects of your project. Judges expect that the display can succinctly and creatively tell the story of students' projects. Judges look for the impact of the project on the student(s) and how well the project is explained.

Value to agency and community: There are numerous service-learning projects that are valuable to "advancing course objectives," but "have little or no value to the sponsoring agency or to the community at large." Judges want evidence that each the students of each project show evidence of the value of the service-learning project to the community partner. Here's where understanding the demographics and statistics of participants enhances learning and, in turn, the value of the project.

Caliber of reflection: Throughout this book I've harped on structured reflection, but not as much as I harp on about it in my classes. Students in my classes do very well in this category at the showcase, and I believe this is because I require they probe each week examining different aspects of their CBL project. Many of my colleagues require a final reflection paper, but the fact that my students have been reacting, responding, observing, writing each week raises the caliber of their reflection. The judges expect that each display provide an example of or the entire reflection. My students simply print out their online reflections from each week and prominently display it.

Enhancement of civic responsibility: Since the structured reflection prompts I use are based on personal, academic, or civic development, my students are able to articulate the value of the CBL project to their under-standing of civic responsibility. The judges want to see evidence in the display that shows how the project fostered civic responsibility, and how the students describe their understanding of being a citizen.

In addition to these primary awards, we also give awards and recog-nition to the best graduate student project, best undergraduate project, most innovative project, as well as projects that engage the arts, projects that are STEM focused, best literacy project, and many others.

Students who enter the Showcase must present their semester-long CBL project in a way that judges and guests can get a comprehensive idea of what the project entailed and what students learned from the project. Each student, or student group, is given a specific amount of space—a 3' × 5' table. Most students use a tri-fold poster board as well as objects, PowerPoint slide shows, and other materials.

Even if your college or university does not have such a large event, a single class or group of classes can organize an informal "showcase." It can be as simple as just your class presenting to each other the work you've done. The way to do this is to think of your presentation as a narrative, a story, of what you did, why you did it, what you learned from it. Your teacher might invite the department chairperson and colleagues. You might invite other students. Perhaps you hold this in your classroom, or you stage the showcase in the library, the campus bookstore, a coffee shop—either on campus or off.

Since I teach a several online classes in any given semester and because some students live hours away from campus, I encourage my students to create a blog, website, video, or PowerPoint presentation of their work.

Publication beyond the university

If your teacher has asked you to write a final immersion or literary journalism essay based on your service work, this gives you a chance to incorporate the research you did earlier on statistics and information about your specific site with the realities of what you've experienced. You will be able to use your structured reflection responses to write an informed essay, like those in this book.

If you're conducting your CBL project as part of a workshop class, perhaps you're already tinkering with poems, stories, short essays, using your observations and new awareness for people who live differently than you. Note how the writers of the essays in this book describe their experiences through their own personal lenses without exploiting the participants they've worked with. Notice how they address the social injustices and celebrate the work they are doing.

Numerous journals publish articles and essays about community engagement. One fairly new publication specifically for undergraduates is the *Undergraduate Journal of Service Learning and Community-based Research* based at Pennsylvania State University—Berks. Other journals include *The Teaching Artist Journal, College English*, and *Reflections: A Journal of Writing, Service-learning, and Literacy*. Literary journals publish work by undergraduate and graduate students that might be suitable places for an essay you might write based on your work. If you've been reading the essays throughout this book, you can see the types of articles and essays that get published. Several of these essays have appeared in other journals before finding their way into this book. Essays are generally reflective, analytical, or narrative. Some journals also accept visual displays of service-learning projects.

Outreach and the university

One of the missions of most universities includes "outreach" which includes a variety of types of programs and projects. Universities bring in writers, artists, scholars, and activists to campus and invite members of the surrounding community. Outreach includes partnerships with organizations that have goals or missions in common with the university. For example, public schools partner with students getting their degrees in education, allowing them to conduct practice teaching semesters. Or a large defense contractor might partner with the engineering department because they are looking to recruit recently graduated engineers. Outreach includes hosting concerts or high school graduations on campus. Outreach has become as term used to indicate any type of activity that is not strictly academic, activities that bring people from outside the university to campus, and activities that take the university off campus. Outreach also includes experiential learning. In addition to service-learning, there are other types of experiential learning:

Internships generally allow you to earn course credit for working at an organization that hires graduates in your major. Internships are usually contracted for one semester. Most schools have limits on how many credit hours of your academic transcript can be from internships. For English majors, this often means working with a local magazine or newspaper. For political science majors, this usually means working in a law office or a political organization. Sometimes these are paid positions, and sometimes they are not. In my department, we ask students to seek out their own internship site, and then find a faculty member who will serve as their "teacher of record," so that they not only get experience in the world of writing, but also earn course credit and a grade.

Cooperative education refers, most often, to multiple terms (or semesters) of work at the same employer, and alternating a full-time working semester with a full-time academic semester. Thus you would work one semester, full time, at the employer, and then next semester, you would take classes full time.

Undergraduate research (UR) is usually available for interested students for course credit. Sometimes UR is referred to as an Independent Study. You work one-on-one with a faculty member on a specific research project that interests you. In creative writing, you might feel that you'd like to read more poetry from the eighteenth century than you were able to read in one of the literature survey courses. Or you might have a specific writing project that you'd like to focus on more than you could in a workshop course.

Volunteering is community service without the academic aspect that comes with service-learning. Often you can find volunteer opportunities through your student government, student activities board, office of student involvement, or an office of experiential learning. If your university does not have an office designated to help students find volunteer opportunities, you can often find nonprofits in your area on your own. Having a well-rounded education means not only doing service in your area of expertise, but also broadening your understanding of service. For those of us who work primarily in our heads, working at an animal shelter might be just the right activity to balance our lives.

Alternative break programs are most often held during the spring break, allowing students to travel as a group while conducting a service project. For example, some alternative breaks go to storm-ravaged cities and help with cleanup or getting supplies to people in need. Others work with Habitat for Humanity. Others travel to a migrant farm and teach literacy. Again, these programs are usually handled in the office of student involvement, student government, or office of experiential learning.

Study abroad provides another way to gain real world experience while you're in college and allows you, most of the time, to earn college credit.

Each of the programs listed above gives you opportunities to explore possibilities that you may not have considered before. If you come to college with your professional life already planned out and refuse to deviate from that path, you might miss a great number of opportunities. When you select a college major, and do activities related only to that major, you limit not only your professional opportuneness, but also limit your world view. Jeff Brenzel, Dean of Undergraduate Admissions at Yale University says, "The truth is, that for your life, for the rest of your life after college, virtually no one's going to care what you majored in as an undergraduate. The question is almost never going to come up. The question will come up: What did you get out of it? What did you take away from it?" (College Board, 2013).

You can find these types of statements from almost anyone who teaches college, has a college degree, or advises college students in choosing majors. The advice I give most often to my students is to take classes that interest you and a class or two you'd never considered taking. You might be surprised. Volunteering, service-learning, co-ops, alternative breaks—all of these other programs provide a way for you to further explore your interests.

"The important thing in college is have you learned how to learn?" says Brenzel, "Have you become a flexible, adaptable, resilient person who is quick down the learning curve in exploring a new subject?" (College Board, 2013).

Structured reflection

Personal

1   Review your initial reflection entries (from the beginning of the semester) and choose one or two, and respond to yourself as you would in a letter.

Academic

2   In Chapter 9, you created a list of several questions about your CBL project. Choose one of the questions that you could explore yourself or find the answer to online. Then choose two of the questions that would enable you to seek an answer from someone else in order to get the answer. Maybe you need to ask one of the community participants, or a teacher, or staff person. Find the answers.

3   Find a scholarly article or essay about creative writing in community settings. There are numerous journals for possible articles. Here are a few of them: *The Teaching Artist, College English, Reflections: A Journal of Writing, Service-learning, and Literacy*. Read the article and discuss how the experiences of the writer are similar or dissimilar to yours.

Civic

4   Whether or not you have been involved in community service prior to this project, to what extent has your involvement in this CBL project affected your sense of "community," "civic responsibility," "activism"?

5   What have you learned about your co-workers (your peers) that you would not have learned in a college classroom? If you're working alone, what have you learned about the paid staff at your site?

6   What could the college workshop method learn from the community workshops?

Readings

Terry Blackhawk

Terry Blackhawk is the founding director of InsideOut Literary Arts Project, a writers-in-schools program serving over 5,000 K–12 students per year in Detroit classrooms. Her poetry collections include *Body & Field; Escape Artist* (1999), winner of the John Ciardi Prize; *The Dropped Hand* (2007) and *The Light Between* (2012) as well as two chapbooks. Her poems have appeared in journals such as *Michigan Quarterly Review, Florida Review, Borderlands, Artful Dodge,* and *Nimrod,* which awarded her the 2010 Pablo Neruda Prize. She has received grants from the Michigan Council for Arts and Cultural Affairs and the National Endowment for the Humanities as well as the Michigan Governor's Award for Arts Education, Creative Writing Educator of the Year from Michigan Youth Arts Festival and a Detroit Metro Times Progressive Hero Award.

Poetry from the Inside Out

As the founder and director of an arts nonprofit serving young people in Detroit classrooms, I am often asked, why poetry? Isn't it just a frill? A time-waster? Don't urban youth need something more rigorous? As a poet, I try not to stumble too personally over this argument. I believe that the inner world and work of the poet represent a challenge to mind and soul that our students deserve. As an educator, I understand that rigor has its place, but so often the "R" word suggests a top-down system of extrinsic rewards, as if a military model of education is the only approach to take with youth from beleaguered communities. The notion of "boot camp" as panacea is grounded in some heavy negative stereotypes, and Detroit youth, almost by virtue of the name, are set up for these stereotypes.

One of my main motivations in founding InsideOut Literary Arts Project was to give the lie to the prevailing narrative about urban youth. As a classroom teacher, I had come to know firsthand the spirit, joy, talent, quirkiness, hope, humor, dreams, intellect—you name it—of our city's young people. Encouraging them to "think boldly, create bravely," as InsideOut's mission instructs, and then sharing their voices with the wider world could surely dispel toxic mindsets perpetuated by the media and society at large.

I believe in intrinsic rewards. For years I have held as a motto William Butler Yeats's definition of education as "not the filling of a pail, but the lighting of a fire." Recently I came across this from bell hooks (1994) that, for educators:

... our work is not merely to share information but to share in the intel-lectual and spiritual growth of our students. To teach in a manner that respects and cares for the souls of our students is essential if we are to provide the necessary conditions where learning can most deeply and intimately begin. (p. 13)

I like to think that spirit was what set the InsideOut Literary Arts Project (iO) underway from the beginning in 1994 when, on an otherwise unremarkable summer afternoon, I received a letter from Hollywood filmmaker Bob Shaye, a letter than changed my life. Shaye, a Detroit native and supporter of my poetry activism with youth, suggested that going citywide with my work would be a "supremely valuable cultural goal." Since he was kind and insistent enough to put his vision in writing, I couldn't help wondering: What if?

From that question, an amazing answer was born: InsideOut Literary Arts Project, today Detroit's largest literary arts nonprofit. I presented Mr. Shaye with a proposal, which he kindly accepted. Soon thereafter, several classrooms of Detroit teens chose "InsideOut" from a list of possible names that we, the adults who got the project going, had set our minds to. I can still see Monique, a tenth grader, raising her hand after my class had voted to say, "This means we are bringing what is inside of us out into the world through our writing."

I wish I had that original ballot now, a missing piece of the archive of this experiment based on the notion that poetry could have a remarkable impact on young people—on their souls, their skills, their sense of themselves. It all started on wings of whimsy and imagination—a general sense of gee—what if?—fueled by the energy of Detroit's youth and lit by the generosity of a benefactor who saw in the creative ferment that emanated from my classroom a spark, something small that had the potential to grow.

Duly named and armed with a generous seed grant, InsideOut began in 1995 in a handful of classrooms in five Detroit high schools. We have grown steadily, adding schools, imagining new programs, deepening relationships with principals and teachers, and evaluating the work to show that we are not "just another feel good program," as a bureaucratic bean counter once sniffed. We are now in over 30 Detroit K–12 schools, with combined service to 5,000 students per year. Our primary work takes place in classrooms where an extraordinary cadre of teaching writers combines their love of language and their love of teaching children. Evaluations show statistical significance in improving students' achievement, attendance, self-confidence, creative use of language, narrative structure, voice, willingness to revise and other key skills. Just one creative hour per week can work tremendous transformations, or, as one teacher put it: "We couldn't wait for the weekly visit from our InsideOut poet. The children were so excited, and I could literally see their writing skills and enthusiasm for writing grow every week."

At InsideOut we go also beyond the classroom to "take the student's work outside" of school walls through publication and performance. Each year we publish a beautifully produced literary journal for each school (28 in 2012), and cap off each year with an in-school gala where students gain pride of authorship as they see their work and their names in print, often for the first time. These books, these talismans, become treasured keepsakes. They complete the circle of writer/reader and give students a real sense of audience and a purpose for their writing.

One of the happiest times of the year for me is to visit schools for these unveilings, and I never fail to be buoyed by the joy of the children and the enthusiasm of the teachers and parents for the program. There's a mesmerizing attraction between the writer and her words in print, but there's also the magnetism of the audience, the readers, and the whole community of teachers, parents, principals, staff members, and friends that, as hooks says, "respect and care for the children's souls" (1994, p. 13). As this excerpt from a fifth grader's poem shows, poetry is the perfect vehicle for this expression, and we are, at year's end, awash in the beauty and affirmation of poems such as fifth grade Amber's.

… Walk through the gold / surface of the meadow / that consists of God / watching me. The cloud of happiness / gives me candy through my heart. // When I talk softly to the flowers, / my soul relies on / what lies behind me. In my world / I am Amber, a beautiful girl.

Or Kori's, grade four:

LET THIS POEM

Let this poem fly like it's never been grounded.
Let each word be like a cane you can walk on.
Let it catch the bouquet at my mom's wedding.
Let this poem be like a mouse walking around looking for cheese.
Let this poem yell like it's never been told to shut up.

Recently Adam, an intern from Wayne State University where iO's offices are located, read through many of the literary journals in our archives, getting acquainted with Detroit through the voices of its young scribes, thousands of whom can be found in the over 350 journals we have published since 1995. I have long felt that our students have a somewhat different relationship to their city than children in other parts of the country, that they take Detroit as their muse and that the city actually becomes a character, a persona in their work. I was pleasantly surprised when, in addition to praising the quality of the writing, Adam confirmed my suspicion, characterizing a Detroit voice expressed by our youth as equal parts honesty, frustration and hope. Detroit youth do not have the luxury of being coy. Images of environmental degradation and personal experiences of abandonment confront them at every turn, but through poetry they write a better world. As alumnus Justin Rogers put it in his slam poem: "This is not just a slam. These are words for a better Detroit."

Justin was a member of the iO team that came home from the 2011 Youth Speaks Brave New Voices National Youth Poetry Slam having captured fourth place in nation from over 50 teams 750 youth participants. The team's wrenching, heart-stopping performances in front of 3,000 at the San Francisco Opera House confronted gender bias, domestic abuse, absentee fathers, working at Walmart and a host of other matters, with courage, honesty and wit. Their success culminated over a decade of iO's community based poetry work with youth.

Since 1998, iO's poetry performance program, Citywide Poets (CWP), let hundreds of youth know that their words and their lives matter. With the mentorship of dynamic stage and page poets who lead weekly after school workshops and organize performances for the youth, CWP empowers young writers socially, academically and emotionally and puts their creative, personal representations of pressing social issues forward to audiences of thousands in the wider community. CWP frequently performs across Detroit at local churches, Detroit City Council meetings, Violence Prevention summits, Martin Luther King Day observances and elsewhere. From San Francisco to Washington DC, Flint, Chicago and around Detroit, Citywide Poets youth reach audiences in the thousands, gaining poise and self-confidence along the way.

Citywide Poets was recognized in 2009 when we received the nation's highest honor in youth programming, the NAHYPA National Arts and Humanities Youth Program Award (formerly "Coming Up Taller") presented in a White House ceremony by First Lady Michelle Obama. In a reception at the Kennedy Center the evening before the ceremony, Lena Cintron performed the following exquisite poem.

TENTH FLOOR, LEFT CORNER
(poetry class)

Bare shaven camera heads
like film exposed. Green nails
on small hands. From the deep
crevices of cold sparkly purses,
wasted bits of paper full
of words too powerful to fit
their allotted space kiss
tiny notebooks (moleskins)
that cost more
than the expensive cup
of coffee needed to fill them.

Discarded gloves left
by the tableside to make
room for anxious finger
that grip pens like oars
in a boat rushing to shore.

This is poetry's womb.

Another iO student captured an audience in our nation's capital, when in May 2012 Ariana Washington, one of Justin's BNV teammates, shared a program with Cyndi Lauper—headliner for the National Youth Mental Health Awareness Day's "Heroes of Hope" program. Ariana's poem honored her aunt Asura who helped Ariana to grow and thrive despite losing her mother to a brutal murder at the hands of her father when she was very young. Thanks to Citywide Poets, Ariana experienced the personal safety and commitment to craft to help her frame her life story through breathtaking poetry.

As iO alumna Shawntai Brown wrote recently that, through Citywide Poets, she "learned about cultures, resources for writers and youth, diversity, art, and developed a pride for my city that has brought me back to work professionally in Detroit." By traveling to other cities, she "realized the demographics of Detroit were not what the rest of the world looked like. As I mingled with youth from other cultures, I struggled. My black, female, church-raised, urban identity seemed threatened by the larger white culture once I left Detroit. That exposure and struggle, however excruciating it seemed then, was a safe, mentor-guided and realistic taste of what I would come to experience in college." In addition to becoming a stronger writer and critical thinker, comfortable reading and analyzing literature and providing critiques to others, Shawntai credits poetry slams and public readings for improving her performance ability and unveiling a knack for theater that had been hidden in quiet classrooms.

"Writers-in-residence," she goes on, "the people iO assigned to work with youth were inspiring. They were going to school, touting degrees accomplished, carrying their work with them and finding new places to share. Most important, I felt like they respected me and believed in me, even if they weren't the same race as me, or from the same side of town … I began writing, not to be successful, but to be honest, ask questions and create art I could understand myself better through" (Private correspondence, March 2013).

Collaborations with Detroit cultural organizations have been crucial in bringing young people like Shawntai to the community, and many new partnerships have developed on the heels of winning the NAHYP Award from the White House. Our move to Wayne State University has placed us in the heart of the Detroit Cultural Center. The newly restored Virgil H. Carr Center, our city's home for African American visual art and jazz, and the Museum of Contemporary Art Detroit have both opened their doors to iO's youth workshops. They have hosted a multi-arts poetry-infused youth camp conducted in 2011 as part of "Big Read" programming on the work of Emily Dickinson; our Brave New Voices slam tryouts; and "Scratch the Page"—iO's guest poets series which recently brought poets such as Gregory Pardlo, John Murillo and Rachel McKibbons to model the life of a professional poet and to work and present with our youth.

Our partnership with the Detroit Institute of Arts has been especially rewarding. I first started teaching creative writing in 1988, the same year that the Detroit Institute of Arts launched a ten-year Writing About Art project, and my students and I enjoyed beginning each year's creative writing course by exploring, discussing and "entering" the imagery in the year's 10 slides selected by the museum. (Please see my essay: "Ekphrastic Poetry: Entering and Giving Voice to Works of Art" in *THIRD MIND: Creative Writing through Visual Art*, for more on this wonderful method of teaching.) The project brought us into the museum to see the works of art live and in person after we had written and talked about them in class, and the year culminated with a beautiful publication that published the students' writings alongside the images that had inspired them.

In 1995, tenth grader Shysuaune Taylor's poem, inspired by Reginald Marsh's painting *Savoy Ballroom* (1931), gave the 1995 DIA *Student Writing About Art* publication its title—"Blues Remedy." Marsh's masterwork is a gem of the Harlem Renaissance, a painting chock full of dancers whose reds and blues twirl and twist, filling the frame with exuberance. One can almost hear the music, tap a foot to the beat and feel the heat of those exultant bodies, and Shysuaune created a poem that captures that Harlem energy with a decidedly Detroit flavor.

BLUES REMEDY

we dance
red
to the blues
we're boombastic
yellows
and delicious
browns
we entwine
ourselves
in the dark riches of
Marvin Gaye's voice
aggressions leave
with the incoming rhythms
of soul,
black soul

we smell the inner city
in a ring of cigar smoke
hear it in a bell
of cognac
the gray sign
of a time
when worried black clouds
got lost in Motown
and depression
became platinum
pleasures passed
in the embrace of a slow dance.

Along with Monique, Shysuaune was in InsideOut's pilot class. Much of what I learned about teaching poetry came through students like him, and seeing how they could take fire and grow was much of the inspiration for InsideOut.

Shysuaune took many awards for writing, and he was not afraid to confront difficult personal topics in poems such as "Baby Black Boy Blues" that was published in *You Hear Me?: Poems and Writings by Teenage Boys* (Franco, 2000). In another example of "Taking it Outside," Shysuaune was one of two iO editorial consultants retained by the book's editor Betsy Franco. He was also one of my student editors and always made sure to have his locker next to my classroom door; sometimes, it seemed, for protection.

Shysuaune died suddenly in 2002. But I'm ever grateful that iO helped him develop and share his talent. Shysuaune loved poetry. He won many awards and was one of the first students whom we trusted to serve as an iO poet-in-residence himself, earning rave reviews, even as a young teaching artist, first with sixth graders and later with youth at an alternative high school. The title he gave to Crosman High School's literary journal, *Above, Not Beneath*, capsulizes iO's expectations and understandings about the potential and struggles of Detroit's young people. Shysuaune lives in my mind as a youth who was unafraid, the epitome of why iO carries on its mission of helping every child to "think broadly and create boldly." Their creative voices today ensure a better future for us all.

*   *   *

Sharlene Gilman

Sharlene (S. E.) Gilman has worked in social services, publishing, and academia. After many years of writing, she ended up teaching writing and literacy in a variety of contexts—in colleges and universities, at a correctional institution, reservations, and as a tutor and tutor trainer. After moving to Pennsylvania, she recently completed a PhD in Curriculum and Instruction, Language, Culture, and Society from Pennsylvania State University. Her interests include the serious art of play and the play of art in constructing identity and activism, classroom climate, and equity in education.

Who is the Self that Performs? Teaching and Learning Creative Identities and Creative Writing at a Youth Shelter[1]

The shelter kitchen is crammed along every wall with refrigerator, stove, sink, washer, and dryer. In the middle of that noisy, crowded cross-road is a picnic table that accommodates eight if they wedge themselves in. Three of us meet with as few as one to as many as four or five young people at the shelter, although there is no predicting who will show, or how long they'll stay. We enter as guests at their kitchen table.

Ashley, Will, and I expected to engage in creative generation, but we also entered thinking of ourselves as "teachers." We intended to examine texts as models. And although we expected to inspire and affirm, we thought we were out to "teach" craft. Clearly from the first, other things mattered more to our participants: homelessness, self-mutilation, abandonment, acting out, survival. These young people were *participants*, *not* "students." All were here unable to enjoy safety in their families. We were not pedagogical missionaries and we were not therapists. In terms of starting a youth shelter writing group, we found that our young women—and occasional young men—used writing for different purposes, and engaged at varied levels of invention and resistance.

At one position in this spectrum, we were offered revelation and rage, in rhythm and rhyme. In faltering middle ground, the most inexperienced was just beginning to put her feelings into sentences she could declare. At the end of the spectrum of freest invention, one woman wrote with remarkable imagination but often avoided the personal or deeply coded it. How could we accommodate *all* their interests and their purposes for writing, and *not* ours? After our first session, we realized that we had entered the shelter with colonizing "teaching," or "fixing" intentions, possibly the last thing any of the participants here needed.

One thing we did was to address our participants as "writers." To contrast, some other discourses of identity to which these teens may have been subjected might have been "troubled," "abused," "unwanted," "homeless," "uncontrollable," "deviant," "emotionally disturbed," "victims," or more. Employing *"writer"* as a transitional identity—within this transitional community—could temporarily interrupt other labels, and offer an alternative to adolescents who shared an experience of displacement and trauma.

Useable transitional identities and their discourses can serve as crucibles of growth, and did so—both for the participants and us, the facilitators.

Because sessions were voluntary, we never knew who would be attending; we quickly conceded any objective that connected one session to the next. We had to let go of outcomes. The randomness reminded me of Ellsworth's commentary on Massumi: no teaching experience is fully intentional; no matter how much we try to engineer learning, the unintended brings something new. Ellsworth defines pedagogy as "sensation construction," not pre-packaged, ready-made, and delivered. All teaching and learning is an experiment in thought. Experiences are like bodies—not things we "have" but what we "are": "[The] 'I' of an experience does not precede the experience, but emerges from it" (2005, p. 26).

Ellsworth draws from D. W. Winnicott (1986) the psychologist who wrote of "good enough" nurture: good enough safety, good-enough growth, and who wrote of transitional objects and transitional space: "a time and place out of which experience and learning emerge" (quoted in Ellsworth, 2005, p. 17). He meant space in which the self engages in exploration and is held so that growth is possible—psychic space opening between self and world, self and other. Ellsworth extends psychic transitional space to actual sites where opportunities provide for experience and learning, a third space of interactivity. The shelter was such a place, just as adolescence is such a space. Temporary shelter and a time of displacement is very much "transitional living" in a holding environment, just as adolescence is that temporary bridge between childhood and adulthood.

A few young men attended a few sessions sporadically, but three young women stayed with us consistently over 14 meetings. The eldest perplexed us. This young woman spun her imagination the furthest yet coded the most from outsiders. Two younger women challenged us, were the most resistant, and their experiences may have temporarily held open the most crucial interactive space for growth, as our own discomfort provoked awakening for the facilitators as well.

M. J. on her poems: "I memorize them in case I might need them."

M. J. self-identifies as a reader and writer. She is African American, but like other identities that could have emerged and did not, reference to race or racism never appears, perhaps because self-disclosure may be uncomfortable, or that three Caucasian facilitators in a mixed group increased her discomfort with particular disclosures. She shared plans to go to college, and fought back tears the day she told us that she was losing a young aunt to cancer. M. J. freely imagined other voices, inventing with language. M. J.'s associations are loose and she eagerly engages in "assignments" and recipes, going far beyond them.

M. J. Poem

Is it 'cause I don't ice the cubes
and freeze the ice, or cook the pan and
dump the trash, or write the pen and not
the world, or love the him but don't love you.
It's 'cause he sees me just like I do, 'cause
you see me and have no clue.

"This doesn't even make sense," M. J. says, reading the poem aloud. "I don't know what this means," M. J. will often say about her writing; "It just came to me." M. J. steps outside of a self-held at a distance, a distance that our experiments suggest. At the beginning of one session, M. J. reads a love poem from a woman to beloved Charlie, possibly her husband, and the poem's persona describes how she and Charlie are both growing older. M. J. describes the speaker's wrinkles and speculates dreamily, "I can imagine what she looks like [...] Maybe this is a true story going on out there." During a session exploring color poems, M. J. imagines the owner of the house in Tess Gallagher's poem "Perspectives in White" (1976) as "a lonely person." Her children are leaving because she is so controlling. I see her as educated but lonely and distanced from herself.' M. J.'s building of character and situation extends from those mute pieces of furniture described in the poem to a fully peopled world. Do her speculations reflect what M. J. is experiencing, living apart from home and family? Isn't projection or displacement in imagining what writers do, whether distancing from "real" matters or not?

In some ways, we see her too, but don't have a clue. She draws eyes on her notepad and in her journals. She is shy about saying the word "sex" aloud, and at one point indicates, reading a line from one of her poems, that the word should be *screamed*, but she herself declines to do so. For all of the seeing eyes that reoccur in her poems, M. J. asks us frequently to look away when she reads aloud. She begins to joke with us as it comes her time to read. "Assume your positions," she teases, and we look down and away.

Sight is a lingering, a pause to carefully notice, a space to look that holds us, and a translation because, writes Greene (1995), an art world is a constructed world. With encouragement to explore a plurality mediums, people may come to feel what they feel, see what they see and imagine, and transmute it into form, to "discover all sorts of new perspectives as the curtains of inattentiveness pull apart" (p. 137). Art as invention shows us how to see more closely, to perceive and to wonder more, and set up a connection between that eye's sight and my own mind, an invitation to an encounter with otherness and dialogue with it. Greene compares this kind of encounter with Wallace Stevens' insistence on imaginative sight and subjectivity, keeping open the imagination.

T.'s Terrible knowledge

T., 15, joins us that first day but does not read. "I write poems about death," she says, wary. She later brings in thick folders of typed work. Her reds are about cutting, blood, razors, and revenge written in rhyming couplets. Some imagery is powerful and most uncomfortable to hear. We "instructors" are shocked about what to do with the difficult knowledge of T.'s lyrics of self-mutilation and rage. "That was good," says Ashley. "In a painful sort of way." We give her praise, we suppress our discomfort, and when we make reference to it, it is with a light, humorous touch. Sharing T.'s difficult knowledge first changes our view of our role and strategy as facilitators at the house. In that discomfort, we begin our own learning.

T. had begun by testing us. In subsequent sessions, she speaks often and more assertively. Proud of her spurting poems, she subverts norms even while fitting into a discourse of Goth: dark eyeliner, dark clothes, long sleeves. Shock is her arsenal. She tells us she writes lyrics for local bands. She is prolific, and her sanguinary works are meant to be shared by an audience.

T. most actively resists our notions of "teaching." She only uses the suggestions and experiments that suit her and completely ignores others. In discussing creativity that comes from destruction, Winnicott asserts that first an individual needs to recognize internal aggression. "Toleration of one's destructive impulses results in a new [...] capacity to enjoy ideas, even with destruction in them, and the bodily excitements that belong to them" (quoted in Britzman, 1998, p. 53). T.'s relish of cutting and vengeance is expressed by the growing audibility of voice as she reads lyric after lyric, often ignoring our writing prompts. Her enjoyment of the destructive act is unconcealed. It challenges our norms, and our shiver is resistance to her pleasure. Our reaction causes us to acknowledge what confounds, troubles, or repels us.

Anderson and MacCurdy (2000) explain in *Writing and Healing*, that one may engage in writing to "change from a singular self, frozen in time [...] to a more fluid more narratively able, more socially integrated self" (p. 7). To use some art, make meaning or healing, one need not have experienced a particular trauma; to live is trauma enough. As Flannery O'Connor said, "The fact is that anybody who has survived his childhood has enough information about life to last him the rest of his days" (cited in Fitzgerald and Fitzgerald, 1969, p. 89). For me to make sense of my life as a teen, identifying as "writer" helped me to negotiate situations that frustrated and threatened me: family arguments, verbal abuse, the house-arrest of childhood, the constant monitoring of my movements. Reading and writing, I could fantasize escape or pretend revenge, turn intense attention to noticing my feelings, my surroundings, and keepers, to make use of their characters and voices. Likewise T. can escape her limitations, transform her disappointment, anger, or disgust by writing, the best revenge. It is no coincidence that the most successful of Koch's work (1970) in writing poetry with children were using prompts of wishes, lies, and dreams. The Ego dreams for fulfillment, Freud (1968) writes in "The Relation of the Poet to Daydreaming," and the ego "is the hero in every daydream and in all novels" (p. 129). Phillip Reiff's introduction to Freud's *Delusion and Dream* (1968) delineates between the expressive dream and expressive art by its communicative intent: expressive arts invite participation with and identification with others. Reiff writes, "the step from soliloquy to public address is therefore the step from neurosis to art" 1968, (p. 13). But this step is a side-step and easily a back-step as well; both serve the imaginative concealment of aggression and wish-fulfillment, not a grasp at some Romantic ideal of Beauty or Truth. Goth, of course, includes romanticizing death, passionate aggression, mourning, as well as shock value, yet these only take hold by contrast with the goody-goody, "Up-With-People"-pro-social discourses to which T. is subjected, ones she actively resists. At a later session, when one of the occasional boys reads *his* suicide poem which ends in redemption, T. sneers, "That was pretty good—until it got all positive."

In terms of creating a holding environment for T. and her terrible knowledge, we learn that we are there to hold open toleration of her destructive impulses while she holds open our conceptualization of our role, both our "writerly" and our "teaching" identity, the most prosocial role she resists.

B.: Mourning in the smallest voice

B. joins us by the third session. B. is also 15 but seems younger, with the least experience working with words or hearing herself. She resonates least with assuming an identity of "writer." Yet she is actively mourning, exiled from both her mother's and father's homes. B. hides her mouth when she talks; her voice, a rushed whisper. But when she writes her flat, brief sentences, she is doing the hard work of working through. We support B.'s honesty. We tell her that we feel her words. We hold her tentative speech as much as we hold T.'s rhyming moving violations.

Grief is hard work. In the *Problem of Anxiety*, Freud (1963) writes that mourning demands that "one must part from the object because the object no longer exists [...] the tie to the object has to be dissolved" (p. 97). There is no point in longing and wishing for it to be otherwise, and the profundity of real loss distinguishes melancholy from mourning. On working through, Deborah Britzman (1998) discusses Bettleheim's work with traumatized children and asks how we can tolerate the difficulties of learning and loss while making insight from one's "conflictive experiments in learning" (p. 43). She explicates from Anna Freud's "About Losing and Being Lost," that hope is connected to toleration, with mourning's work as a desire to detach from the dead and reattach to the world, including its struggles with ambivalences both without and within, tolerating "the self's relation to its own otherness and the self's relation to the other's otherness" (p. 134). Learning takes place from the emotions, writes Britzman, including learning from the emotions of those who teach us, learning from students' seeking approval, or evading anxiety. Britzman confirms that learning also takes place from how we, as those who teach, bear our own ambivalence and otherness.

As facilitators of creative writing at the shelter, we had to wake up: we were not teachers there although we were better read and better practiced; the stance of "teacher" as expert is unstable and often maladaptive as well. We were guests at their table. Adopting "writer" as our own transitional identity, we were and they were mutually engaged in processes but from divergent needs, uses, and standpoints, and resistance to inequalities and discrepancies are meaningful, inevitable, and probably even necessary.

Pedagogical ruse: Loosening from emanations of self

Yet we were there to focus ourselves all as writers, to learn to guide and hold open the space for all of us. The first pedagogical issue that concerned us is trying to insert "otherness" as openings in a creative conversation, encouraging our writers to take up masks, to use sounds, and other voices in our weekly experiments. We begin using recipes, throwing in the literal kitchen sink or the sounds of the appliances that hum and whir and thump around us, inviting in randomness, trying to encourage alternatives to what we see as fixedness in their writing ideas, to extend the self in imagined other's stories, other lives. However, B.'s reaction to "otherness" experiments is telling: B. protests, "What's the point? I write about my experiences, not some random thing."

When art pushes us into discomfort, writes Green, it facilitates a vision of other ways of being. Discomforts resist normalizing and acquiescence. Our workshops' discomforts frequently cut both ways: over fourteen weeks, our primary goal became holding open that space for safety and expressiveness, including our students' refusals.

The holding environment we are constructing at the shelter is intended to create a community to hold otherness. Greene writes extensively of this relation that returns time and again to some binary of self and other (or as Winnicott called "self and non-self") and thus to questions of identity, emphasizing the importance of breaking down barriers and embracing incompleteness. Greene addresses identities of teachers and students in this way: she writes of the flexibility and imagination on the part of teachers, "to break with ordinary classifications and come in touch with actual young people in their various lived situations. [And on the part of students] It takes imagination on the part of young people to perceive openings through which they can move" (1995, p. 14).

When we support B., hear her pain and naked mourning, and tell her we hear those emotions, we hold a space open for what she is living now. As facilitators, simultaneously, we attempt to insert "otherness" as openings in the conversation, encouraging taking up voices and personas, in our poem-recipes, so alternatives can be considered as a place for freedom of movement, insisting nothing of our participants, need be compromised or lost.

The second difficult issue was revision: revision is tricky stuff. Revision requires a level of one's own discomfort. Creating or exploiting dissatisfaction within these young writers with what they offered would be threatening. How could we develop satisfaction in artful making yet ask them for self-critique without making them ditch group like they would school English class? We were able to note and promote some short-term looking-over, but revision never gained traction.

To be a learner one must defend oneself against the demands of learning, writes Britzman. Our participants taught us this by insisting on writing in the voices they had and knew. Resistance demands respect. We feared they were reinforcing or fixing perpetrator or victim stances, but over time, what became available to our writers *did* show gradual change. As sessions went on, T. was teased to "read something without blood in it," and volunteered a love poem. B. wrote a circus poem, experimented with inverting clichés and metaphor, then wrote a haiku, more willing in the spirit than at the beginning-to-middle sessions to write about "some random thing".

In the community of "Soul Vomit"

The teen writing group at the youth center in neighboring Bellefonte invited our writers to participate in a coffeehouse reading that the youth center teens voted to call "Soul Vomit." After 14 sessions, going public would be an ideal activity. We made a pact with the girls to drive them to and back from the reading, to bribe them with coffees and pastry into coming. The younger girls are to meet us at the coed shelter but when we arrive, only M. J. is there and asks to speak to me on the porch, alone. Too many obligations, she says: too many chores to be done, applications to write; she doesn't have her caseworker's permission to go. She has an extensive list of reasons for not going to the reading and can't be persuaded. We suspect she has a case of stage fright, of being the object of too many eyes. But although the younger girls are late, they are eager to come with us. Even made up in eyeliner, dressed with earrings and in denim sparkled with rhinestones, in the car, T seems younger, subdued and more vulnerable like she did at our first meeting than the jaded persona she enjoys when she reads. B takes one poem with her, folded into a secret square.

At the "Soul Vomit" reading, we listen to the youth group read their poems first. T could hear another teen, one with a live-in family, make use of cutting imagery. She and we hear more poems of teen suicide, angst, and anger. T. reads two cutting poems, and here she is not alone.

Those who write from crisis or trauma, claims MacCurdy, may discover even the "painful awareness of being utterly different [...] can be shared. Differences can [...] bring people together and give them permission to speak" (2000, p. 177). At the reading, we took part in a larger communality, affirming an identity of "writer *in the community*"—*of other writers*. A public reading opens another third space, a shared discourse. It shifts what makes up the poem and the writer's meaning of it, sharing in the presence of others

After everyone else has read, we are down to B., who brings a lone poem. She had been uncertain if she wanted to read in public, but we start to clap and repeat her name in syllables, like calls for "Jer-ry, Jer-ry!" on the Springer Show. "Read so we can hear you," shouts Ashley. B. reads "Home," a list poem of what home is. The gist of it is—"Home is good, / Home is pain; / Home is just a place / I can't be for a while."

After reading, B. heaves an out-loud sigh we all hear. In that sigh, a breath taken and released, we hear a gap where self and its discourses are a little transformed. In the moment of making public, the space for self and world is held open again. We shout and clap, *even louder*. Ashley gives B. a hug. Everyone claps for a complicated life young but already made difficult—difficult to live and to say, now opened by standing up to declare, plaintively spoken for community to hear.

CHAPTER TWELVE

The Value of Creative Writing in the World

When you come to the end of your CBL project, it's surprising how quickly the time has passed. You may wish to continue your community creative writing workshops. I encourage you to step away for at least a couple of weeks to rejuvenate, evaluate, and reflect on what you have accomplished. Reflect—let the experience sink in. Stepping away also gives your participants a chance to reflect on their time with you, even if they don't do this in the same structured way that you have been doing. You've built a relationship with your participants, and saying goodbye can be difficult, especially because many of the participants you worked are too often accustomed to being abandoned. Rather than thinking of your CBL project ending as a abandoning them, help them to understand what you have learned and how important your CBL project has been to you.

Derek Miller signed up for one of my service-learning workshop classes. We would be holding a traditional workshop, and in addition, each student was required to conduct a CBL (field work) project. Derek almost dropped the course, and was initially afraid of the project because he did not have the confidence to speak in front of people. He chose to work with a few other students at an inner-city school. Here is an excerpt from his final reflection essay. As you can see, Derek got over his fear. And in the first part of this excerpt he talks about going back the following semester. Derek went back each semester until he graduated.

> I truly had a great experience with the field work at Ivey Lane. In fact, I enjoyed it enough to sign up again next semester. My greatest satisfaction about Ivey Lane was making the kids smile, which sounds corny but is the truth. I enjoyed seeing their faces light up when I entered the classroom, the immediate questions they asked: "Derek, what are we going to do today?" and "Did you bring candy in?" I could tell that they

appreciated me being there. Ms. Geer's class was very accepting of my entire group.

One of the things I learned is how to connect with elementary students. Talking to each student individually helped immensely. By asking questions about their lives, dreams and families they felt more comfortable with me. Once I earned their trust they wanted to write the best story/poem, in hopes it would impress me. I also received great joy from the students' hard work, as for the most part they gave the writing prompts their all. After the students had finished, a lot of them would raise their hand and immediately want me to read their work. If anything I hope I taught the class the importance of being creative. (Miller, 2007)

You might be considering continuing your work beyond the semester. The teacher in the classroom where you've worked with school children may be asking you to return. The participants at the shelter may ask you to continue with them. It is important, though, to have a set period of time for your residency, or at least a time period that says, "We're going to work together for this many weeks, and then we're going to celebrate." Once you complete this residency, this CBL project, you could arrange to create a second residency for the following semester either through another class or as a volunteer at the site. Or you may want to consider designing a CBL project at a different site, with a different population.

After the fall semester, Derek took December off; after going back to Ivey Lane for the spring semester, he took the summer off. Although Derek returned, these breaks between each of his writing residencies allowed him time to reflect and to return with new enthusiasm for the next group of children he worked with. Each semester Derek and the children needed closure.

The publications and readings help with this closure. But it's also important to be honest with your participants, to let them know where you are in your journey of learning. Consider writing a note to each one of the participants.

You and your participants have been changed. Learning is a type of change. We tend to resist change, and since learning is changing perspective it's only natural to resist that change. Learning adds to previous knowledge. Learning means changing your perspective. At some point, we learn to embrace resistance. Sometimes, the greater your resistance, the more you learn.

Civic responsibility

Whether your CBL project lasted four weeks or 12 or 14, you've witnessed how the statistics of the group you're working with look like on a weekly basis. You've seen social problems and challenges. If you worked at a shelter, you dealt with transitional groups—some weeks there may have been two participants; other weeks there might have been ten. In foster care facilities, although a few participants may have remained constant, you probably had a few come and go. This type of inconsistency made it difficult to create lessons that built on one another. In schools, you probably ended the CBL project with most of the same children you started with, though in high poverty areas, you might also have experienced a tremendous turnover. These challenges or others like them make you more aware of the complexities of the social issues in our society.

Lindsay Cohen created a very personal CBL project, worked with breast cancer survivors, one of whom was her own mother. With the help of her mother, she formed a small group of women and created writing prompts and lessons that would benefit them. After her work with this small group of women, Lindsay's career path shifted:

> My sense of civic responsibility has increased since creating my service-learning project. I want to empower those who are losing hope, and help them realize their full potential. No one should feel alone, as we all need to come together and create a stronger sense of community. Ignoring problems does not make them vanish. This project means so much to me, as I truly believe I want to make a career out of teaching theatre and creative writing as therapy. (Cohen, 2008)

Imagine

Imagine if everyone provided some kind of service for one hour a week. Imagine the poverty we could overcome. Imagine the illiteracy we could correct. Imagine the poor health we could change. Imagine the way a community could function if everyone did a small part. One central purpose of service-learning—of any type of experiential learning—is to allow college students understand that the purpose of an education is not just to make you academically smarter, but to also teach you what it means to be a citizen of a community. It may have taken several weeks before you were actually able to begin your project because of all the hoops you had to jump through: background checks, orientations, trainings, etc. I hope by now you see these challenges as waits and hurdles that were worth it. Shaun Ward conducted his CBL project at Boys Town, a foster care facility near our campus.

> My time at Boys Town was more than just for class credit. It was more than just an assignment once a week. It served a purpose beyond helping kids write and find new hope in an old form of self-amusement. It's about understanding where we are today and where

we once were as a society. I have understood the great privileges that come with being able to read and write efficiently. The children at Boys Town were great vibrant minds that took to reading like oil does to water. I made it my quest while there to ensure that I could influence just one child to take an interest in something so powerful as the use of language. I may have gotten Tyler and Kumario to want to write and stretch their minds, but they gave to me much more than I have imparted to them. Through my research and watching first hand their development, I have experienced what literacy can do through fresh eyes. I have always been empowered to write and create my voice, to read more, and learn as much as I can so I may one day bestow it upon others. However, through this study I have come to see that I want to be an educator and do my part to help other teachers eliminate illiteracy. To see these children develop confidence and enjoy writing outside of the classroom requirements has been a blessing. I am proud to say that with the help of my group we have possibly changed the lives of two young minds.

I'm certain that Shaun started the semester with what Coles calls "young idealism," anticipating that he and the other students who went with him to Boys Town would dramatically change the lives of all of the kids at their site. Yet here he is at the end of his CBL project, thrilled that he impacted two of them. This is "mature idealism"—a realistic understanding of what can be accomplished, and how valuable it is to have an impact on two lives.

Structured reflection

Personal

1 Write a thank you note to the participants and/or the staff at your site, thanking them for the opportunity to learn from them. Be as specific as you can in this note. Your teacher might want a copy of the letter(s) you send.

Academic

2 Write a poem or short story or essay that draws upon your experience at your site.

3 What do you think you taught the participants?

4 What is the value of creative writing in the community?

Civic

5   Describe the reading/celebration that you (and your group) had for the participants. What have you learn about the daily lives of participants at the reading that you didn't realize before?

6   Think of one participant from your site who have had some kind of effect on you and describe how being part of that place defines who they are.

Readings

F. Daniel Rzicznek

F. Daniel Rzicznek's collections and chapbooks of poetry include *Vine River Hermitage* (2011), *Divination Machine* (2009), *Neck of the World* (2007), and *Cloud Tablets* (2006). His individual poems have appeared in *Boston Review*, *The New Republic*, *Orion*, *Mississippi Review*, *Hotel Amerika*, *Shenandoah*, and *Notre Dame Review*. Also coeditor of *The Rose Metal Press Field Guide to Prose Poetry: Contemporary Poets in Discussion and Practice* (2010), Rzicznek teaches writing at Bowling Green State University in Bowling Green, Ohio.

Poetry-in-the-World: Where Service-Learning Goes Beyond the Classroom

When someone asks me "What do you do?" I sometimes forget to say "teacher" and, blowing my cover, reply "poet." Even in the college town where I live and teach, many people I discuss poetry with seem amazed that poets still exist, without betraying the slightest inkling that they themselves might be capable of composing a meaning-full poem. In contrast, I have encountered several lines of thought on poetry-in-the-schools within the academic creative writing community. Either viewed as a vital link between the academy and the public, providing both student-teacher and student the benefits from learning about and practicing poetry, or met with a cock of the head and a statement such as "we used to do that, but the interest simply wasn't there" or "we don't have the budget for outreach" or, worst of all, "you can't expect children to really *understand* poetry." This last statement implies that poetry is a matter of "great seriousness" that only a select, formally educated few can fully enjoy. The potential result of such unfortunately loud, but not very widespread attitudes, is that poetry is not as widely appreciated as it could be in American culture. Poets, according to mass culture, must occupy either one side or the other of what has been deemed a worthless coin: either the tortured, manic-depressive artist or the pretentious, tweed-clad blowhard, but never an ordinary individual engaged in one of the oldest human practices: the transference of experience and feeling via language. The masses, like it or not, gravitate to what's available, immediately accessible, and advertised as such to them.

Yet there remain occasions for poetry to be included, as in the 2008 inauguration of President Barack Obama and Elizabeth Alexander's recitation of her poem "Praise Song for the Day" written for the occasion. Maybe CNN had a poor camera angle at the moment, but when Alexander was announced to the audience, it looked as if roughly a third of those assembled turned and went about other business—heading for the concession stands, the port-a-johns, the exits. A central and consistently frustrating question for lovers and supporters of poetry is how can it be rejuvenated as a more-widely appreciated and more-widely accepted art form in the United States. Despite its relegation to the status of either a "lost art" or a pile of Hallmark-infused rubbish, poetry is still popular, still attractive. How else can one account for the ever-widening array of literary magazines available both in print and on the web? What other explanation for the rise in popularity of MFA programs for poets? Poetry (and all fine arts) hang by temperamental threads in academic communities, facing reduced funding and tighter budgets, but hundreds, maybe at this point *thousands*, of aspiring poets still arrive in university towns and metropolitan centers every year to begin masters' programs promising to make them better poets, better teachers, and better business people (i.e. publishers and promoters of their own work, what many in the field have come to refer to as "po-biz"). But once the dust of workshop settles and the thesis receives the necessary signatures, where do these "certified" poets go once they've been handed their degrees? How do they spend their lives, their time? Do they continue to write and study? Do they strive to publish? *Poets & Writers* estimates on their website that over 300 writing programs presently exist in the U.S. What good is it all, really?

In the spring of 2002, my next-to-last semester as an undergraduate at Kent State University I enrolled in a class dubbed Teaching Poetry in the Schools with the naïve but noble idea that somewhere a career as a poet, or at very least as a teacher of poetry, awaited me. I had been writing poems since I was very young, but never with much dedication and certainly no sense of poetic tradition. A handful of creative writing workshops introduced me to revision but until 2002, my poetic "process" consisted of a few drinks, an entire pack of cigarettes, and a knack for imitation. The tail-end of a hard winter found me as an unlikely candidate to bring poems and writing prompts into local third grade classrooms, but there I was: already convinced of my own superiority as a writer, unbreakable in my shyness, and so lonely that I was no longer aware of it.

When David Hassler breezed into his Teaching Poetry in the Schools classroom on a January evening, he knew half the class members by name. Many of them were established student-poets: editors of campus publications, winners of competitive poetry scholarships, and regular participants in local open mics and readings. My guard went up and my always misplaced sense of outsider pride kicked in. That first night of class, I heard more unfamiliar poems and poets mentioned than familiar, and realized it was time to go back and tinker with my poetic radar, to widen my scope as much as possible. As a class, we would be heading into area classrooms of all grades as representatives of poetry, *as poets*. The immediate sense of responsibility overwhelmed me and, after that first night, I considered dropping the course. We had a lot of work in store, the first goal being to learn how to teach, the second to actually go to the schools and test our prompts and activities on students from third grade through high school.

The good news for everyone in the class was that we had David as our guide. He remains, for me, the standard by which all forms of enthusiasm are to be judged. I had met a few poets before, but never one who insisted constantly and directly that poetry can and will change your life if you let it; that it's worth reading, worth writing, worth teaching, worth sharing, and that with a little coaxing and a measure of practice, it can find an important place in anyone's life.

What I remember the most about those three-hour evening classes is the writing. I had never before been asked to produce creative work in the classroom setting. We spent several weeks trying out our ideas for prompts and jumping-off-points on one another. This feeling was new: no booze, no cigarettes, no wee-hours-solitude. Just an idea, a blank page in a notebook, the sound of a dozen breaths being drawn simultaneously and, from David, the word "Okay." I can't admit to remembering much of what I wrote in class that spring, but the feeling is easy to call up: excitement, stress and concentration shaken roughly and garnished with uncertainty. A year and a half later while pursuing my MFA in poetry at Bowling Green State University, my soon-to-be-mentor Larissa Szporluk asked a very similar thing of her graduate workshop, and while a few of my peers found themselves consistently unsatisfied with the results of these in-class writing exercises, the practice lit an encouraging fire under my work. This type of writing-under-pressure-amongst-your-peers remains a favorite exercise that I use with consistently dynamic results in undergraduate and graduate writing courses that I teach. The idea itself has been around for a while. Kenneth Koch's two seminal texts about teaching poetry writing to schoolchildren (*Rose, Where Did You Get That Red?*, 1973, and *Wishes, Lies, and Dreams*, 1970) show how tangle-free and productive the process can be. The basic formula, upon which there are as many variations as there are teachers who employ it, is reading a poem or piece of writing aloud, instigating a quick but potent discussion of what happens in the poem as well as *how* "it" happens, and then giving the students time to write. Sharing at the end of the experiment is generally encouraged (this is where an overwhelming sense of community and belonging can sometimes emerge) but not a requirement.

For my first day as a poet-in-the-schools (my first day of formally teaching anything to anyone), I decided to take in a poem by Charles Simic entitled "Stone" The poem describes, in language that is both accessible and surreal, the speaker's journey into the interior of a common stone. I had found Simic's poem in Jack Collum and Sheryl Noethe's *Poetry Everywhere* (1994), a text that David had required for our course and that I would soon consider indispensable. But that was not my first brush with Simic's poetry. In 1999, my mother happened across Simic's slender *Unending Blues* (1986) in a discount bookstore and, based just on the title alone, purchased it as a gift for her music-obsessed, slightly bookish son. Aside from the Beats (my early love of rock and jazz lead me naturally to the work of Allen Ginsberg and Jack Kerouac), *Unending Blues* was, at that point, my sole encounter with the work of a contemporary poet, in this case a living, practicing poet. It was unlike anything I had read before: surreal, a bit dark, but somehow light-hearted and playful about its own darkness. Every threatening moment was balanced by something so outlandish or unexpected as to be hilarious. This was a model I followed unsuccessfully for some time, cranking out failure after failure during my first two years of college. So finding a Simic poem in *Poetry Everywhere* gave me great hope while serving as a clear sign that I was, in fact, on some sort of "right" path with poetry. I probably would have chosen to teach "Stone" to the third graders of Holden Elementary even if it hadn't been the perfect choice, but it turned out to be just that: unintimidating, full of both fact and mystery, and chockfull of that anything-can-happen sense that makes poetry continuously attractive.

That morning, my expectations were low. I had hot-wired my nerves with too much coffee, and wandered the halls of the elementary school in a caffeinated flurry of nerves and sweat. I should mention that I also had a two-man camera crew following me, as I had agreed to participate in a documentary that another student in the course was directing. Throw in a PA interruption in the middle of my recitation of "Stone," and on paper, you have a recipe for chaos. Just as Koch suggests in his introduction to *Rose, Where Did You Get That Red?* (reprinted as "Teaching Great Poetry to Children" in Koch's *The Art of Poetry* [1996], part of the University of Michigan Press's Poets on Poetry series) I read Simic's short poem two or three times to the class, and then asked the students which parts they liked, which words and images stood out for them. We filled the blackboard with words and images, and when I asked them what other "things" they could imagine venturing inside of, every hand in the room shot up. In his introduction, Koch insists that *this* is the moment to have students begin writing, when their ideas are at the surface and just beginning to bubble over. The sense of quiet struck me right away: a roomful of third graders all with heads bowed and pencils beginning to move back and forth, down the page. I stood back a moment or two, afraid that any movement or noise from me could shatter the silence, the very oxygen that these poems and poets in-the-becoming were thriving on. Later, as some students shared their examples with their classmates, oohs and ahhs erupted from various corners of the room. I think every student in the room was smiling. I know the teacher and her aides smiled. Maybe the film crew, too. Years later, what sticks with me more than any of the poems written that day is the sense that anything was possible during the hour I had with the students, and that we all went "somewhere" together. But one line does stand out in my memory: a young boy wrote about journeying to the center of a snowflake, ending his short poem with the question: "Will you reincarnate or suffer?"—a line that left all who heard it quite speechless.

What this all comes down to is that poetry has saved my life, and I think, idealistically, that it has taught me compassion, patience, and self-worth. What I'm looking for, what I know that many other poets and teachers are looking for, is the middle ground between the ivory tower of academia and the torpor of the greeting card aisle. Language, as it accelerates and takes on more and more new connotations and denotations, is in constant danger of being taken for granted, little more than a means from point A to B, a way for us to get what we want when we want it, but less and less about meaning and knowing. Poetry is a basic human practice—not a "softer side" of expression and certainly not "something cute for kids." I'd like to see poetry find its way more deeply into the mainstream consumer culture, but not, of course, at the cost of quality and complexity. The routes along this treacherous and confounding middle way are as various as the travelers found there: nationally and stated funded programs exist across the country to bring poetry into schools, libraries, hospitals, nursing homes, and prisons. Technology, for all the aimless naval-gazing it encourages, has allowed poetry to take on a vital and accessible existence on the web, with organizations such as One Pause Poetry (based in Michigan) providing multimedia resources for readers and writers of all ages.

Poetry may be seen as problematic or scary because reading it leaves one vulnerable to new ideas, challenging concepts, and it may even invite uncomfortable personal memories on the part of the reader. Writing poetry multiplies these characteristics, to the point of uneasiness. Poetry makes us ask ourselves the slippery question: who am I?—a question that many ignore in favor of the autonomy and security the culture provides. When one considers the most troubling aspects of so-called civilization (social injustice, remorseless violence, environmental degradation) it's clear that poetry can do very little to directly solve such problems. What reading and writing poetry *can* do is remind us of our individuality, of our own day-to-day choices, and what the world can (or can't) mean. Poetry enlarges and enriches my personal universe. It points me toward joy and it sobers me regarding loss. It holds up unanswerable questions that remain worth seeking answers for. The practice of poetry requires care, honesty, and concentration: a sort of meditation mediated through language, leading to a simultaneous confirmation and questioning of identity. In ancient times, in times of spiritual need, one had to seek out the oracle. Now it seems the oracles need to venture into their communities and not wait to be sought after.

*   *   *

Carly Gates O'Neal

Carly Gates O'Neal teaches English, creative writing, and literary magazine at a public high school in Palm Beach County, Florida. She holds a bachelor's degree in creative writing from the University of Central Florida and is currently pursuing a Master of Fine Arts from the Sewanee School of Letters at the University of the South. Her poetry has been published in *Flint Hills Review*, *Steam Ticket*, and *Hawai'i Review*.

How Service-Learning Cultivates Empathy and Social Responsibility

The need for empathy

I passed the quiz out to my class as if it were something humdrum and compulsory, like many of the end-of-the-year school climate surveys passed along by administration. After instructing them to answer honestly and not share their answers, I allowed them to begin. As they read the first question a few students began to noticeably shift in their seats, stealing glimpses at other classmates in hopes their choices might buoy to the surface of their expressions. Most finished the questions begrudgingly, some protested by shaking their heads and cursing inaudibly, and a handful refused to either take the quiz or finish it. By the time we were ready to discuss the results they had all silently formed one consensus: I was mean for having given them the quiz.

"The Morality Quiz" is a three-scenario quiz that supplements the *Time* magazine (2008) article "What Makes Us Moral" I had given them to read for homework. Each scenario puts the reader in a different hypothetical situation that divides the heart and mind between what feels right and what is known to be logical. As we discussed our answers, the patterns that emerged were what I had expected: my students found it easier to push the mortally wounded man off the sinking raft (to save their own lives and the lives of the other passengers) when the man was a stranger, but when asked whether they could do it if that mortally wounded person were a parent, the room grew silent. Similarly, when they discussed the trolley scenario emotional distance made the difference. Several students found it relatively easy to pull a lever and switch the track to save three people at the loss of one or, conversely, stand by and do nothing while three people died and one friend was spared.

My students had been reading the novel *Ender's Game* (Card, 1991), in which humanity allows "xenocide"—the act of purposefully exterminating an entire species. My intention was to use this quiz as a platform for the discussion of "other": to make a connection between the dehumanizing of an enemy and the acceptance of segregation and genocide in our world. My students—lovers of gangster stories like *The Sopranos* and *Scarface*—had no difficulty understanding the sense of "tribe" found innately in us all, but they did not generally include in that tribe those outside their small circle of family and friends. In fact, when I brought up the notion of Good Samaritan laws which, in some nations, require one to provide reasonable assistance to someone in need of help, many were appalled at being held accountable for not calling 911. I was surprised to think that one of my students might shrug off the responsibility to report a witnessed accident or robbery (Kluger, 2007).

I shouldn't have been that surprised. Over the past few years I have heard about schools teaching character development and social skills directly because what teachers were already integrating into their classrooms (and what may or may not have been taught at home) wasn't enough. Indeed, my high school implemented a leadership program to help students who had potential but lacked emotional control, and my former principal worked diligently to establish a Junior Reserve Officers' Training Corps (JROTC) program. Yet, despite those programs, the next school year contained just as many (if not more) instances of violence, verbal abuse, theft, and disrespect for other persons and property. In Linda Perlstein's *Tested* (2007), with its inside look at how No Child Left Behind has affected an elementary school, I found my thoughts resonating with hers: "The problem wasn't that these children didn't realize that it was bad to litter or trip [others]. It was that too often they didn't seem to care" (Perlstein, 2007, p. 67). These students were only practicing moral behavior with those they viewed as part of their tribe, which obviously did not extend to classmates or the school as a whole. My classroom nemesis is student apathy, and what scares me most is that their apathy extends beyond school to life. Many of my students share my dread of extinction when they talk about energy, climate change, and future crises, but for the most part they do not seem to hold my hope for human ingenuity and perseverance—they don't trust the global community to pull together for a common cause because they don't see the global community as part of their tribe.

These students are of course capable of empathy; some scientists believe the discovery of mirror neurons in both humans and primates has shown that we are hard-wired to share the experiences of others as if we had experienced them ourselves (Slack, 2007). But feeling empathy isn't the same as acting on it—human morality is much more complex, as Kluger observed in "What Makes Us Moral": "The rules we know, even the ones we intuitively feel, are by no means the ones we always follow."

Then I remembered that even the protagonist of our novel, Ender, was ready to give up on saving the world until they brought him back down from his school in space to Earth so he could experience what life on it was like again. What I felt my students needed was an experience that would not only help them to realize all they shared with others, but one that would also show them the reward of taking a leap of faith to help those in need. Something that would put them on the path to what Jeremy Rifkin, activist and writer of *The Empathic Civilization*, believes is what we need to do to save our planet: extend our empathy to the entire human race. That feeling brought me to service-learning.

The power of service

Long before *Ender's Game* brought my students to the issue of morality, I was asked as an undergraduate to participate in the University of Central Florida's first service-learning project in the spring of 2003. I no longer remember the circumstances in which I was asked to be part of the program, but I do remember the moment I began to realize the impact that experience would make.

In our first gathering before the project began, we met the English teacher whose class we would take over once a week, and received instruction and advice from Joann Gardner, a professor from Florida State University whose program—Runaway with Words—we would implement at PACE center for at-risk girls. We had pulled student desks into the typical workshop circle, when Joann asked us to start by introducing ourselves and revealing what had prompted us to join in on this endeavor. I flushed with panic: I hadn't really thought about why I volunteered to help at-risk girls. I was a junior in college, majoring in English with an emphasis in creative writing because that's what I loved. I had no career path in mind and never would have dreamed of becoming a teacher—I felt too shy and insecure to be capable of such a career. I had signed up because I loved writing, and as I listened to the responses around the room I thought back to Mr. Kinney, the high school English teacher who was responsible for keeping me in school and giving me confidence in my own writing. I realized now I wanted to do those things for someone else; what I didn't realize was how profoundly my experiences at PACE, and later at the Coalition for the Homeless, would change everything.

I signed up to volunteer at PACE with the expectation that I was going to teach teenage girls to use creative writing as a therapeutic outlet for their fears and frustrations, to help them find their voice. As we stood outside the building waiting to be buzzed in on the first day, what I imagined was straight out of Hollywood: I thought the girls would be hardened and tough and I feared they would not warm up to me; I thought I was going to be the expert, teaching them how to recognize the personal and societal ills to which they had been oblivious or indifferent. I didn't expect the giggles and the smiles—even on the first day. I didn't expect how easily many would open up, detailing more hardship than most of us will experience in an entire lifetime. But what I really didn't expect was how world-wise they already were. They saw through the veil of material culture into the heart of what makes us human in a way I had never been cognizant of at their age, and they were perhaps more true to themselves than I was to myself even then, as a college student sent to instruct them.

I began to truly appreciate the fact that everyone has a story, and that understanding made me look deeper at what was behind the teenager acting out, the homeless child being so quiet and responsible. Behind them all were the basic threads holding us all together, and I found it terrifying to think how easily I could have been one of those children. Sheer luck landed me with the parents and family I know and love—a family who has been fortunate enough to be prosperous. I have been cognizant ever since I began to volunteer that my family, on more than one occasion, has kept me in my apartment and off the street.

Feeling humbled by these experiences, however, was not in any way unusual or unique. Each week my classmates and I would write passionate reflections about our experiences at our service-learning sites. After returning from our first week at the Coalition for the Homeless, another student in my group, Maria, filled pages about how deeply these experiences had affected her. I remember in particular how moved she was by how close the children were with each other, and how quickly they would offer up anything they had in gratitude despite how little they actually possessed. She ended her piece by proclaiming that she wanted to drive to the Coalition every weekend, pile our workshop kids in her car, and take them all to McDonald's as a reward for their selflessness. I spoke with Lindsay Hunter (2009), another classmate involved in these projects, who remarked that the experience definitely affected the way she now sees other people, and homeless people in particular: "It makes you look deeper, deeper even than you would look anyway as a writer, you know?"

My desire to continue my service after the conclusion of the class was also not unique. Several students expressed an interest in finding a way to teach creative writing to the community for a living—so many that our instructor posted numerous links to organizations where we might have the opportunity to do just that. I don't know how many of those students went on to pursue careers in teaching or community outreach, but the desire, and the sense of responsibility to our communities, was there. We were no longer momentarily bemoaning impersonal statistics—we were driven to help individuals now that we had experienced the beautiful faces and personalities attached to them. Trisha Rezende (2009), a friend who taught at PACE alongside me, also felt the experience had a lasting impression on her, prompting her involvement in more community programs, particularly in the aftermath of Katrina, while attending the University of New Orleans.

These reactions seem to be fairly widespread. A study published by the Higher Education Research Institute of UCLA in 2000 reveals that of 22,236 college undergraduates interviewed, "better than four service-learning students in five felt that their service 'made a difference' and that they were learning from their service experience" (Astin et al., p. iii), and of 2,635 freshmen students who had not decided upon a major, "41.3 percent of those who engaged in service-learning during college planned to pursue a service-related career on the follow-up, compared to only 18.5 percent of undecided students who didn't participate in service" (Astin et al., pp. 21–22).

My desire to involve my own students in service-learning was realized in the fall of 2008 when I discovered Books of Hope, now called E-luminate, a service-learning program which pairs U.S. schools with sister schools in Uganda, serving their needs by writing and binding informational books and donating school supplies. The program provides for Acholi children who, according to the Books of Hope website (2010), are "refugees, orphans, former child soldiers, and former slaves." The program is directed by Abha Thakhar (a former grass-roots organizer with an academic background) based on her husband's concept of reaching out to these children, who at the time were night commuters, traveling vast distances each evening from Internally Displaced Person (IDP) camps into larger villages for safety. The concept sent hopeful and human rights messages as "constructive diversions" for Acholi children whose lives have been torn apart by civil war. When Thakhar took over the program in 2006, the war was over and the children were no longer night commuting, but the schools at the IDP camps were ill-equipped—the kids were, in her words, "lucky to have ceilings" let alone books and supplies.

When the members of my after school writing club and our National English Honor Society (NEHS) chapter saw the DVD highlighting the conditions of these Ugandan schools and the enthusiasm of students and teachers about Thakhar's delivery of the handmade books, they were sold. They were eager to pick their book topics and begin writing, though the difficulties of writing for a multicultural audience quickly surfaced. Suddenly my students became hyper-aware of their own lives of privilege: cell phones and iPods, McDonald's and shopping malls. Book topics that had seemed simple became complicated when they began to realize the amount of explanation that would be necessary. "Do they even have apples in Uganda?" asked a student making an alphabet book. "Everything I try to write makes Americans look like gluttonous pigs," lamented another.

The desire to understand the world of these Ugandan children drove my students to host a Ugandan-themed party, each student researching and reporting on a different aspect of Ugandan culture: we listened to royal court music from Uganda while dining on coconut candy and curried potatoes. My students poured themselves into every detail of the project, their books bright with pictures and scrap-booking supplies, and at the end of each book wrote a personal message to those children across the globe, imploring them to stay strong and never give up. We held a school supply drive to send supplies along with our handmade books, and we received more supplies than would fit in our limit of five twenty-pound boxes. When the picture arrived of a Ugandan child holding the first book we sent, several of my students cried.

After the last book was bound and the last box was packed, I asked my students to write a paper reflecting on how this experience had impacted them. While some were honest enough to admit they had originally signed up out of a need for community service hours, most of them felt they had made a difference—one they not only *wanted* to continue to make in the future, but one they had a *responsibility* to continue. One student, Sarah Grunder (2009), wrote:

> I feel an increased sense of responsibility to give back to my community because of my participation in community service. I feel that despite our differences in race, religion, age, or sexual orientation we are one family, and that we are accountable to how we treat other people, especially for those needy people in our own area.

Forward, not back

But what about the impact on those we have served? Herein lies the leap of faith. We knew the children and teens we served at the PACE Center for Girls and Coalition for the Homeless on a first name basis only. With the exception of a picture of a child holding a book, my students and I have no contact with the Ugandan children—for their safety as well as ours—and that single photograph provides no evidence of any long-term positive effects. Or negative, for that matter. After hearing about the role of American evangelicals in Uganda's anti-homosexuality bill, one of my students, who had written a book on sexuality and the importance of accepting everyone regardless of sexual preference, was crushed. He had worked hard to respect different cultural values and ideologies while maintaining ideas that he felt were important to basic human rights, and now he was imagining a potential book-burning at the arrival of our delivery. Fortunately, Thakhar didn't believe his book was inappropriate. "Cultural relativism is cowardice," she assured. "Bad things happen, and just because we respect them doesn't mean we should accept it."

She was able to tell me the initial reaction to the books made by American students at participating schools around the nation: the Ugandan teachers and students love them. When 7,000 books arrive for a school with 900 students, the children are able to take books home and actually own them. They also love all the pictures because the schools don't have visual aids. Students learn by reciting the material presented by their teachers. "Literacy is a challenge when everything is so oral," Thakhar explained. She is beginning to chart long-term effects on student achievement. The 2009 shipment of books was the largest yet, and she hopes to find a way to objectively look at the real evidence of students using and reading the books.

Despite the lack of hard evidence, there are glimmers. Thakhar (2010) told me a story of several Ugandan women who, upon hearing of the devastation of Katrina, decided they wanted to help. For two weeks they labored, breaking stones to sell for construction projects. Their contribution may have been small, as each woman earned less than a dollar per day, but the message behind their generosity is everything we hope to see as a result of our service. One of my NEHS students, Meghan Miller, said this in her reflection of that hope:

> Everyone in the world has the responsibility to participate in community service to help make the world a happier and easier place to be. If people are helped, they are more likely to help others, exhibiting the ripple effect. If the children in Uganda grow up to have the opportunity to help others, they would most likely do so because they would remember how happy they had been when others helped them.

Hope for the future

While society is too complex to subscribe to one philosophy, I do think writers and activists such as Jeremy Rifkin are correct in believing we must move toward an "empathic civilization," being socially and environmentally conscious and taking responsibility to care for other humans, animals, and the planet. Our survival may depend on that. Rifkin writes:

> If we can harness our empathic sensibility to establish a new global ethic that recognizes and acts to harmonize the many relationships that make up the life-sustaining forces of the planet, we will have moved beyond the detached, self-interested and utilitarian philosophical assumptions that accompanied national markets and nation state governance and into a new era of biosphere consciousness.

We have seen the potential for this empathy in the wake of disasters such as Katrina and Haiti, and the power of the individual to act in such disasters with the aid of modern technology, like Twitter's impact on the Iranian protests. Through service-learning we can help our students to realize their connection and responsibility to the world around them. After all, like the protagonist in our novel, *Ender's Game*, sometimes you have to be reminded what you love about the world in order to want to save it.

APPENDIX A: RESOURCES FOR STUDENTS

Semester-long CBL projects

I've included three full semester-long CBL projects. One from Danielle Merola who worked with fourth graders. Another from Eric Fershtman who worked with mentally ill adults, and another designed by a group of students in two separate creative writing classes who worked at a shelter for the homeless with adults.

Community-based learning project

Student: Danielle Merola
Project Title: The Sense Journals
Community Partner Details:
    Mr. Bearden
    (Winegard Elementary, fourth grade)

Project Overview: To incorporate the five sense lessons (sight, smell, sound, taste, touch) into element lessons (earth, wind, fire water) at the end of our time together. I would like to have a showcase and possibly split the class up into four groups based on the elements, and have each one do some sort of performance art piece that has to do with their assigned element.

Project Goals: I would ideally like these students to come out of the class with not only a deeper understanding of creative writing but a love for it. I want them to know that a poem does not always have to rhyme and that a couple sentences can constitute a story—anything to keep them writing and wanting more.

Preparation for the Project:

1   How is your project going to assist the teacher's curriculum? What additional curriculum areas would he/she like you to address in the classroom? What goals does the teacher have for integrating the creative writing with other subjects? How can creative writing address those goals?

Mr. Bearden is readying his classroom to take the Florida Writes in February. My project will help him in this task. His class is a sheltered ELL class but will take the same Florida Writes test as all other students at the school. For this task, I am going to give a vocabulary lesson at the beginning of each lesson. This could be easily incorporated into the five sense lessons. For example, during the taste week, I could give the words sweet, sour, munch, chew, etc. Or the sight week, stare, gaze, look, eyes, etc. The vocabulary lesson will be the springboard for the rest of the hour. I will use these words throughout the lesson and encourage the students to do the same in each exercise. Mr. Bearden suggested I encourage the students to write everything down. For this task, I am going to provide them with "sense journals," and each week, give them a simple journaling assignment, such as, after the week we discuss the sense of sound, having them write down the loudest sound they heard.

2   What *skills and knowledge* will students be able to demonstrate at the end of the residency in terms of art forms and their basic subjects (math, English, social studies, science)?

They will be able to use simile and metaphor while writing. They will be able to identify their senses and the elements of the earth, how their senses work with everything around them. They will improve their vocabulary. They will feel confident sharing their work with others.

3   What will the culminating products be? Will there be a culminating performance or exhibition? Will it be seen by others? How can you link this project to the community? (Ideas: performance that is open to the public; try to get a local gallery involved that will display your classroom's artwork, etc.).

I'd like them to perform in an elements show at the end of the year. I'd like to break the kids up into four groups: earth, wind, fire, water—with each group using the senses to write about each element and doing a performance art piece.

4   How will you know when you have accomplished your project goals? In what ways will the children be able to show evidence of their understanding of what you've taught them? What evidence will you have and how will you measure their progress?

They will have the journals, and I will assign a topic for every week that I am there. The children will hopefully use their journals in the future. I will measure their progress by the test at the end and by doing mini vocabulary tests every week.

Weekly Lesson Plans

Week One: Introducing the five senses

Overall Objectives: This week will be an introduction week. I don't think I am going to focus on any particular sense but rather just get them involved and engaged in the writing and journaling process. I want to get to know the students and demonstrate to them how easy it can be to journal all the time. I would like to introduce each sense and give them an idea of what we will be doing. A couple exercises will be involved in doing this.

Specific Goals:

- Teach the class the importance of journaling
  - Goal: using the senses, journal about something that will come easy (what's the best meal you ever ate, best day you ever had, your favorite song, etc.).
- Concrete vs. abstract language
  - Goal: show examples of both and the way concrete images can be used effectively.

Sequence of Instruction:

- Introducing myself and the program: 5 minutes
- Ice breaker: 10–15 minutes
- Introducing the five senses: 15 minutes
- Concrete vs. Abstract language: 10 minutes
- One day, I will be a _____ (use a concrete noun): 5–10 minutes
- Give journal assignment for next week

Anticipated Challenges: I hope the students will not struggle to learn concrete vs. abstract language but that is the area I am most worried about this week. I plan on having many examples to keep this struggle to a minimum.

Week Two: Taste

Overall Objectives: The sense this week is taste. I'm hoping to incorporate some treats for the class and ask them to write about what they taste. I will start the lesson with a little ice breaker. I am thinking of having the students form a circle to foster intimacy. I want to build on their vocabulary so I am going to be handing out a vocabulary sheet with exercises for them to work on.

Specific Goals:

- Vocabulary having to do with taste.
- Have them talk about what they taste by journaling.
- Teach them to explain more about what they are eating then just "it's good" or "it's bad." Rather, say things like sweet, spicy, salty, etc. Goes back to concrete vs. abstract language.

Sequence of Instruction:

- Icebreaker having to do with taste: 5–10 minutes
- Share journals: 5–10 minutes
- Vocabulary worksheet: 10 minutes
- Treats with journaling: 20 minutes
- Group story exercise: 10 minutes

Anticipated Challenges: Last week, the only difficulty they had was letting go of the abstract words they're used to and replacing them with concrete language. I'm thinking it will be the same this week but I'm hoping to find other ways to explain abstract vs. concrete to the students.

Week Three: Smell

Overall Objectives: This week, the lesson is about smell. The overall objective of this week is to get students thinking about how the sense of smell helps them in all aspects of their life (i.e. warns them about fire, gas leaks, helps them perceive tasted, etc.). I want to address the fact that students should use their sense of smell when they are writing too because it helps the reader understand the piece better. Also, the sense of smell is often the greatest memory invoker, so we will talk about that as well.

Specific Goals:

- Vocabulary words and completing sentences with them.

- Writing contest: see who can use all the vocabulary words.

- Small writing activity: choose an animal to be. If I were a
  _____, I'd like to smell a _____.

- Mystery scent activity: bags filled with different smells, write about
  each one, guess what it is, where they've smelled it.

- Scent chart: bring home to complete if not enough time. Asking
  questions about what smell the student thinks of when they think of
  school, home, holidays, etc.

Sequence of Instruction:

- Go over last week and read journals aloud: 10 minutes

- Vocabulary worksheet: 15 minutes

- Writing contest: 5–10 minutes

- If I were a ___ activity: 5 minutes

- Smell activity: 20 minutes

Anticipated Challenges: I hope I won't have a hard time sharing the smell
bags with everyone. I am only making six, but think it will be OK passing
them around. They might have a hard time with the vocabulary this week
because the words are all very similar, but I think reading them aloud will
help with that.

Week Four: Valentine's Day poetry

Overall Objectives: This week, I'm going off the path. We're going to review
the last two weeks, and then write some poetry. I'm going to introduce the
students to a simplified form of the diamante poem and ask them to write
about something to do with Valentine's Day, or any holiday that they love.
Then, I'm going to talk about the blog we'll be creating to display some of
our work.

Specific Goals:

- Read the assignment from last week.

- Go over charts with students from last week.

- Pass out prize to contest winner (maybe wait until next week for
  this depending on time).

- Get blog posts set up.

- Pass out Valentine's day treats.

- Construct a diamante poem about a holiday.

Sequence of Instruction:

- Read last week's assignment aloud: 5–10 minutes

- Collect paragraphs for contest: 5 minutes

- Go over the diamante form of poetry and construct one with the class: 15 minutes

- Independent writing activity: 15–20 minutes

- Discuss blog: 5 minutes

Diamante Poem
Line 1 – Subject, use only one word.
Line 2 – Two adjectives describing or two nouns applying to the subject.
Line 3 – Three verbs that apply to the subject.
Line 4 – Two more adjectives describing or two nouns applying to the subject.
Line 5 – Another word for the subject, a synonym.

Example:
Turkey
Moist, juicy
Eating, stuffing, cooking
White, crispy
Bird

Anticipated Challenges: The students may at first be wary of writing a formal poem like this, but I think the structure will give them the ability to think of concrete words that they can use to describe holidays. I hope that demonstrating it before they try it will help them understand it better.

Week Five: Sound

Overall Objectives: First, I'd like to ask the students to share the poems they've been working on from last week. Following this, we are going to develop our sense of hearing by going on a "listening walk." Basically, I'm going to ask the students to be completely silent and go for a short walk around the portable. We are going to listen for sounds. When we come back inside, we are going to write on the board what we heard, what might make the sound, and other words we could use to describe the sound. Then, I'll pass out the vocabulary sheet and read the words aloud but ask them to finish the sentences on their own. Finally, I want to use the vocabulary building and apply it to writing a short poem only using nouns and verbs. For example,

Dogs bark
Bees buzz
Cats purr, etc.

This is to get them thinking about all the different sounds that different animals, objects, people, and places make. I might do a short fill in the blank exercise like I've been doing in the past to get them reading aloud.

Specific Goals: Have students share their diamante poems from last week, stand up, and be loud!

- Build vocabulary using the listening walk and the vocabulary worksheet.

- Ask students if they have any questions that may help them on the test.

- Blog posts!

Sequence of Instruction:

- Go over what we did last week: 2–3minutes

- Give out prizes!!

- Read poems: 5–10 minutes

- Listening walk: 5–10 minutes

- Writing on board from walk: 5 minutes

- Vocabulary: 5 minutes

- Poem building: 10–15 minutes

- Blog posts if time

Anticipated Challenges: I hope that the students cooperate with the listening walk. The only difficulty I see happening is them misbehaving outside of the classroom while we are on the walk. Other than that, I hope for a fairly smooth, structured lesson.

Week Six: Review

Overall Objectives: This week, I want to do a review of the last couple of weeks. I am going to ask the students to share the poems from last week. Then, I want to do a quick oral quiz on some of the vocabulary words we used in the past weeks. After that, I want to ask the students to do a free write for about 10 minutes. I am also going to give back their diamante poems so we can rework them. I've written comments on their poems and want them to make some changes.

Specific Goals:

- Share the poems from last week.
- Oral quiz.
- Give diamante poems back to rework.
- Free write (if we have time); I might give them a topic about spring break.

Sequence of Instruction:

- Come back in and recap what we did a few weeks ago: 2 minutes
- Hand out prize to student who won contest; ask the class to check their work for spelling errors, if they want to hand it back in: 2 minutes
- Ask students to share their sense of sound poems: 10 minutes
- Oral quiz: 5–10 minutes
- Hand back diamante poems to rework: 10 minutes or more
- Free write: 10 minutes

Anticipated Challenges: I am a little apprehensive about handing back the poems, because I don't want them to feel discouraged by my corrections and suggestions.

Week Seven: Sight

Overall Objectives: The first thing I want to accomplish this week is to have the students read aloud the corrected poems that we work-shopped last week. I think that the individual sessions with the students worked really well, and am excited to hear their poems. Then, I am going to hand out a vocabulary sheet. We will work through it together as we usually do. The activity this week will be a game. I am going to hand out slips of paper with animals, things around the classroom, places, etc. on it and the students are going to have to get the rest of the class to guess what they are, using only what they look like. For example, if a student had an eagle, they would say, I have long wings, a white head, large talons, a long beak, etc.

Specific Goals:

- Share corrected poems.
- Work through vocabulary sheet.
- Play guessing game.

Sequence of Instruction:

- Read poems aloud: 5–10 minutes
- Vocabulary worksheet: 15 minutes
- Guessing game: the rest of the class time

Anticipated Challenges: I am hoping that the ideas I give them for the game will go over well and that they will understand the instructions.

Week Eight: Touch

Overall Objectives: My overall objective this week is to finish up the five senses with the sense of touch and to finally add some posts to the blog. First, I'll ask the students if they did anything fun over spring break and take a couple of minutes to see if they used their journals over their vacation time. After that, we'll do the standard vocabulary sheet. I'm going to hand out a few props that have a distinctive texture and ask the students to write about what they feel. I'll have a chart like I've had in the past to ask the students to describe what they feel in a couple of different words and then where they could have felt this before or what it reminds them of. For example, if I give them sand, they could say the beach or the playground. After that, I want to meet with the students one-on-one and have them show me some of their work to include in the blog.

Specific Goals:

- Share spring break stories.
- Vocabulary sheet.
- Touch activity.
- One-on-one conferences.

Sequence of Instruction:

- Share spring break stories: 5 minutes
- Vocabulary sheet: 10 minutes
- Touch activity: 20–30 minutes
- One-on-one conferences as the students are completing the activity.

Anticipated Challenges: Last time I had the conferences, the students got a little unruly at first when I was meeting with the individuals. After a couple of minutes, I finally said they had to be quiet so I could give each student my full attention and they seemed to listen. I hope this problem does not arise this time. I also hope that the touch activity will stay organized because I know passing around objects can get a little unorganized in a fourth grade class.

Week Nine: Free write

Overall Objectives: To have a free-writing period and allow the students to contribute more to the blog while others are working on their writing exercise.

Specific Goals:

- Read sentences from last week.
- Use the same beginning and write different stories using our senses.
- Have students come up one at a time to contribute to our blog..p

Sequence of Instruction:

- Read sentences from last week: 5 minutes
- Introduce activity: 3 minutes
- Finish blog and complete activity: rest of the class time

Anticipated Challenges: I don't think the students will have a difficult time understanding the concepts because it's a review of stuff we've already gone over.

*   *   *

Lakeside writing workshop

Student Teacher: Eric Fershtman
Community Partner: Lakeside Alternatives, Adult Day Program (Mental Health Facility)

A Summary of the experience

Facilitating a creative writing workshop in a mental health facility posed certain challenges that may not be immediately apparent in the following lesson plans. The largest and most pressing of which was, simply, consistency. The turnout for the weekly workshops ranged from three to 14 people, and would often contain new faces that more often than not did not appear again the following week. Occasionally, the turnover, from one week to the next, was dramatic and/or complete. It became clear that the goals of the workshop needed to change: the experience would need to be less like a classroom, in which teachers build on lesson plans as their students work toward an ultimate goal, and more along the lines of an informal writing club, in which participants could feel free to share or not share their work, which may or may not be written according to the guidelines set down by the facilitator. One resident with a particularly nasty case of post-traumatic stress disorder could, during an exercise in which he'd been instructed to write about a childhood memory, instead write about an experience he had in Vietnam. Another resident with clinical depression could, when asked to write about a time she helped someone, write instead about her memory of being placed on suicide lockdown for a night. It became, mainly, about offering an opportunity for the residents of the facility *to be heard*, to be given a voice, with no strings attached. Sometimes, this meant lingering on a particular exercise longer than scheduled. Other times, it meant changing exercises that were too complicated or hard-to-understand. Often, it meant scrapping structure altogether, and letting the participants talk about certain issues they had with each other, and/or with Lakeside.—EF

Weekly Lesson Plans

Week One: Why We Write

Teacher: Eric Fershtman
Location: Lakeside Behavioral Healthcare, Orlando, FL

Introduction: (5 minutes)
I'll reintroduce myself to the class, explain that my workshops will be a bit different (excluding today, because I figure a little continuity will help ease the transition) from Marcia's workshops: they'll be longer (an hour, as opposed to 45 minutes), and they will be genre-specific (we'll have fiction workshops, non-fiction workshops, and poetry workshops, as opposed to the free-for-all that's been going on).

Writing Exercise: (10–15 minutes)
We'll work from the prompt: "I write because …" The purpose of this is to get the participants to think a little more consciously about why they write, why they come to the workshops, etc. I'll suggest they take a minute or two before following the prompt, and if they're up for it, I'll explain that what we're trying to do, is to bring something they've been doing more or less on a subconscious level, up to the level of conscious, where we can learn strategies to help improve our writing, before sinking it back down again. A muscle memory sort of thing. I'll offer the following quotes:

> George Orwell, in the essay *Why I Write* (n.d.): "I had the lonely child's habit of making up stories and holding conversations with imaginary persons, and I think from the very start my literary ambitions were mixed up with the feeling of being isolated and undervalued."

> Joan Didion (author of *The Year of Magical Thinking* (2005), among other things), in her essay also titled *Why I Write* (1976): "Had I been blessed with even limited access to my own mind there would have been no reason to write. I write entirely to find out what I'm thinking, what I'm looking at, what I see and what it means. What I want and what I fear."

Writing Exercise: (10–15 minutes)
Write a paragraph/poem in the present tense about a recent moment of great frustration. Write as though you're still in that moment: let your anger, your impatience, your frustration, shine through on the page. Be honest without resorting to foul language.

> Didion, in that same lecture: "In many ways writing is the act of saying I, of imposing oneself upon other people, of saying *listen to me, see it my way, change your mind*. It's an aggressive, even a hostile act."

Week Two: The building blocks of creative writing #1: Simile and metaphor

Teacher: Eric Fershtman
Location: Lakeside Behavioral Healthcare, Orlando, FL

Warm-up Exercise: (7–8 minutes)
Write a short scene (a couple of paragraphs) about observing a solar eclipse. Short discussion following.

Short Lesson: (5 minutes)
I'll talk about metaphor, giving a short definition: a figure of speech in

which a word or a phrase is applied to something else, and offering a couple of examples (first clichés: "Life is a journey," "Time is a thief," and then something more original: "Memory is a crazy woman that hoards colored rags and throws away food," from Austin O'Malley, 1915, p. 10).

Writing Exercise: (7–10 minutes)
Write a few metaphors for the sun. We'll discuss these.

Short Lesson: (5 minutes)
I'll introduce the concept of simile. Give a short definition: a figure of speech comparing one thing with another, and offer a couple of examples ("Under Midwestern clouds like great grey brains ..." from "Car Crash While Hitchhiking" by Denis Johnson (1992b, p. 4); "When he climbed behind those drums, he looked like a mad king beating his throne ..." from "Blight" by Stuart Dybek (1990, p. 62); "The moon comes up like a fat man withdrawing himself from a lake ..." from *CivilWarLand in Bad Decline* by George Saunders (1996, p. 43). I'll warn against clichés, and we'll make a quick list of clichés we've heard recently, that we aren't to use for the duration of the workshop.

Writing Exercise: (7–10 minutes)
Write a few similes about a solar eclipse. We'll discuss these.

Writing Exercise: (10–15 minutes)
Write a short scene (a couple of paragraphs) about observing a solar eclipse, incorporating the elements of simile and metaphor. Let's be specific: What does the sky look like? Is there anyone standing next to you? Is there a smell to the air? Where are you standing? Are street noises distracting you? (Thinking through these details will prepare us for next week's workshop on sensory detail.)

Week Three: The building blocks of creative writing #2: Sensory detail

Teacher: Eric Fershtman
Location: Lakeside Behavioral Healthcare, Orlando, FL

Warm-up Exercise: (5 minutes)
At the top of our pages we'll write: "Three places I've been..." Short discussion following.

Writing Exercise: (10 minutes)

I'll divide the class into three groups. Each of these groups will receive a scented candle that they're to share and pass around to each other. A couple of sentences on the scent of the candle—with explicit instructions NOT to describe anything visually.

Short Lesson: (2–3 minutes)
I'll explain that the olfactory senses (smell and taste) are very powerful memory inducers, i.e. when you recognize a certain scent or taste, that recognition carries you back, in a way visual recognition cannot, to the original moment you first smelled or tasted it. Useful to remember in writing, as a transition for flashbacks, for example.

Writing Exercise: (10 minutes)
We'll each think of our favorite musician, and describe the way their voice sounds. (Is it deep? Chirpy? Melodious? Raspy?) Again, with instructions to ignore visual description.

Short Lesson: (2–3 minutes)
I'll explain that the sound of something, especially music, can be a powerful trigger for deep emotional states, like love, anger, melancholy, and is probably itself the most *abstract* of senses, meaning the sound of things, more than other senses, leads us to think in abstractions.

Writing Exercise: (10 minutes)
I will again divide the class into three groups. Each of these groups will receive a prop (silly putty, a seashell, and one prop yet to be determined— going to the store on Tuesday to find something wild) that they'll share and pass around. A couple of sentences on the feel of the item.

Writing Exercise: (10 minutes)
We'll describe what we had for lunch, and how it tasted.

Writing Exercise: (10 minutes)
If there's time, we'll do an exercise on visual detail, using one of the props. Next week, we'll put this all together, and begin to talk about character.

Week Four: The makings of character #1: Deciding what they want

Teacher: Eric Fershtman
Location: Lakeside Behavioral Healthcare, Orlando, FL

Warm-up Exercise: (5 minutes)

At the top of our pages we'll complete the prompt: "Three places I'd like to go ..."

Exercise: (5 minutes)
From *What If? Writing Exercises for Fiction Writers* (Bernays and Painter, 1990.) We'll create names for each of the following characters:

- A petty, white-collar thief who robs his boss over several years.

- An envious, bitter middle-aged woman who makes her sister miserable by systematically trying to undercut her pleasure and self-confidence.

- A sweet young man too shy to speak to an attractive woman he sees every day at work.

- The owner of a fast-food restaurant who comes on to his young female employees.

- A resentful mother-in-law.

Exercise: (10 minutes)
Working with those characters (depending on the size of the group, each person will be assigned one character—if the group is larger, we'll double up on characters, but continue to work individually), we'll complete the sentence: "More than anything, my character wants ..."

Short Lesson: (5 minutes)
I'll explain that to create convincing characters, we need to imbue them with a certain amount of ambiguity, i.e. that they need to have a mixture of both good and bad (not necessarily evil) components.

Exercise: (10 minutes)
Sticking with those same characters, we'll imagine in a couple of sentences a good or noble thing that character did recently.

Exercise: (10 minutes)
Here, we'll imagine in a couple of sentences a bad/naughty/mischievous/evil thing that character did recently.

Week Five: The makings of character #2: Inserting characters into scenes

Teacher: Eric Fershtman
Location: Lakeside Behavioral Healthcare, Orlando, FL

Warm-up Exercise: (5 minutes)
At the top of our pages we'll complete the prompt: "Someday I will …"

Exercise: (10 minutes)
Describe the room that we're in: what does it look like? What does it smell like? What does it feel like? What does it sound like?

Exercise: (5 minutes)
Name and provide a deepest desire/need for the following characters:

- A newly married war veteran
- A college student who's just flunked a class
- A young woman who's recently been widowed
- A mother who's just learned her son has cancer
- A business owner who can't think of a way to save his business
- An employee who's been promoted for ratting another employee out

Exercise: (15 minutes)
In a couple of paragraphs, write a scene in which a character (using the characters we've just created) is ANGRILY completing a household task (we're not allowed to explain why the character is angry); this exercise is designed to help us portray emotional states through actions. First we'll create the character: age, gender, name, greatest desire, etc. Then we'll begin to build the scene around the character. The scene needs to contain details in at least three of the five senses.

Exercise: (10 minutes)
In a couple of paragraphs, write a scene in which a character (using the characters we've just created) is SADLY completing a household task. What changes about the scene?

Week Six: The makings of character #3: Talk to me— character dialogue

Teacher: Eric Fershtman
Location: Lakeside Behavioral Healthcare, Orlando, FL

Warm-up Exercise: (5 minutes)
At the top of our pages we'll complete the prompt: "If I could meet anyone in this world, it would be …"

Exercise: (10 minutes)
We will create characters from scratch: we'll give them a gender, an age, a name, a profession, and a deepest desire (along with any other features the participants think to add).

Short Lesson: (5 minutes)
I'll explain that we'll be working on dialogue today, defining just what that is, and giving an example or two from a book—I'm thinking *Jesus' Son,* by Denis Johnson (1992a)—he has some great and hilarious dialogue. I'll offer a tip: that often it's a good idea to read the dialogue out loud or mouth it, to get a better feel for it.

Exercise: (10 minutes)
Write a scene in dialogue in which our protagonists (the characters we created) are arguing with the person they love the most, about something ordinary. For this exercise, it will be necessary to think about the person on the other side of the dialogue—who they are, what they want, etc.

Exercise: (10 minutes)
Write a scene in dialogue in which our protagonists are talking to the person they like the least, about a recently discovered shared interest.

ALTERNATIVE EXERCISE: (10 minutes)
Depending on our energy level, we might do a group exercise, in which we go around the room, each of us adding a line of dialogue to a scene between two characters.

Week Seven: Narrative nonfiction #1: Memoir

Teacher: Eric Fershtman
Location: Lakeside Behavioral Healthcare, Orlando, FL

Warm-up Exercise: (5 minutes)
At the top of our pages we'll complete the prompt: "The best part about me is …"

Short Introduction: (2–3 minutes)
Today will be less structured than most days, because I'm curious to see how the participants do when we "take the training wheels off," so to speak. There won't be any lectures or explanations; I'll just be giving the introduction to each exercise, and then letting them write.

Exercise: (10 minutes)

Work on a scene/recount a memory about a formative adolescent/teenage experience.

Exercise: (10 minutes)
Work on a scene/recount a memory in which you aren't the main character: think about the point of view; think about where you are in the memory; think about the motives and personality of the person who is at the center of the memory.

Exercise: (10 minutes)
Work on a scene/recount a memory of something you did or participated in here at Lakeside, but write it from the second person point of view.

Exercise: (10 minutes)
Free write on a memory of your choosing.

Week Eight: Narrative nonfiction #2

Teacher: Eric Fershtman
Location: Lakeside Behavioral Healthcare, Orlando, FL

Warm-up Exercise: (5 minutes)
Free write on a memory of your choosing.

Short Introduction: (2–3 minutes)
I'll explain that we're going to be trying a few things differently today. Most significantly, we'll be doing a couple of group exercises that will demand we *listen* to each other. A lot of times, we're so concerned with making sure that we're heard, that we forget or neglect to hear others.

Exercise: (25–30 minutes)
We're going to pair up for this exercise. For 8–10 minutes, we'll trade memories orally on something that we've done at Lakeside. The partner who's not speaking will take notes on the memory being recounted to them. Once everyone has swapped stories, then we'll take another 8–10 minutes reconstructing the memory, on paper, from the notes we've taken. This exercise is meant to encourage bonding and listening skills.

Exercise: (10 minutes)
Write a paragraph on something you did today, but from the viewpoint of somebody else.

Week Nine: Narrative nonfiction #4: Empathy, or listening to each other

Teacher: Eric Fershtman
Location: Lakeside Behavioral Healthcare, Orlando, FL

Warm-up Exercise: (5 minutes)
Free write.

Short Introduction: (2 minutes)
Because empathy is such an important topic, I wanted to spend at least another week focusing on it, and then begin to incorporate it into future lessons in some way.

Exercise: (7–8 minutes)
Write about the last time you helped someone.

Exercise: (10 minutes)
Write a paragraph on something you did today, but from the viewpoint of somebody else.

Exercise: (7–8 minutes)
Write about your biggest regret.

ALTERNATIVE EXERCISE: (15 minutes)
Working in pairs, we're going to be writing stories. We'll begin with the prompt: "Suzie's biggest problem was the dog," and trade off with each sentence (minimum eight sentences each). This exercise encourages us to think about where the person ahead of us was trying to take the story.

Week Ten: Conclusion

Teacher: Eric Fershtman
Location: Lakeside Behavioral Healthcare, Orlando, FL

Warm-up Exercise: (5 minutes)
Free write.

Exercise: (5 minutes)
Write a sentence or two on something specific that you've learned this year, preferably not in this workshop.

Exercise: (15–20 minutes)
From *What If? Writing Exercises for Fiction Writers*: "Write a short piece of fiction (or non-fiction) about a page long. It may be a complete short story and it may be the beginning of a longer piece. But it starts as follows: The first time I (or Name) heard SPECIFIC SONG TITLE by SPECIFIC ARTIST OR GROUP, I (or Name) was down/up/over at PLACE and we were doing ACTION."

Exercise: (15–20 minutes)
(From *What If? Writing Exercises for Fiction Writers*) Begin a story from random elements (that we'll decide on together, and I'll write on the board) such as two characters, a place, two objects, an adjective, and an abstract word.

*   *   *

Coalition for the homeless of central Florida, adult workshop

Student Teachers: Students in Advanced Poetry Workshop and Advanced Fiction Workshop at the University of Central Florida

Community Partner Details: Coalition for the Homeless of Central Florida

Overview and Goals: We aim to provide informative and fun writing exercises to adults. We will rotate leading our lessons among us—students in a poetry workshop and others in a fiction workshop. We will all attend each session, assisting the workshop leaders/facilitators for that week by being participants ourselves. In this way, we hope to minimize any uneasiness that participants might have with a group of college students coming into their space to "teach" them creative writing. Those of us in poetry workshop will prepare lessons based on elements of poetry, and those of us in fiction workshop will prepare lessons based on elements of fiction. Our goal is to provide a safe place for participants to safely share their stories and experiences without pressuring them into revealing any more details than they wish. We also believe that creative writing will increase their sense of self, and develop self-confidence. We will organize a reading and create chapbooks for each person.

Reflection/Summary of Experience: At the end of our CBL Project, we made a chapbook for each of our participants who ended the semester with us. Because we worked at a homeless shelter, the participants were often transient. However, there were five adults who were with us throughout the entire semester. We also made an anthology that included four pages of each participant's writing. Additionally, we arranged with the administration at CFH and with the willingness of the participants to hold a public reading. Rather than holding the reading at the shelter, the participants preferred a local coffee shop. They asked us to invite other college students, the public, and other residents.

Weekly Lesson Plans

Week One: Setting and conflict

Teachers: Neil and Erin

Introduction: (10 minutes)
Erin and Neil will briefly introduce themselves and welcome the class, and Neil will discuss how setting can affect (or be affected by) the story's main conflict.

Writing Exercise: (10 minutes)
Neil will present the visual aid (a drawing of three settings and three cut-out "characters"). He will put one character in one setting and ask participants to write one or two lines about that character's conflict.

Sensory Details: (5 minutes)
Erin will discuss adding sensory details to a setting, explaining that sensory details add depth and interest to our writing, and offering examples of what effective details look like, including a short paragraph that gives an example of strong, concrete details in a setting.

Writing Exercise: (30 minutes)

Part I (5 minutes):
Participants will write down a setting and a character. Example: a park with tall oak trees, a fountain in the middle, and plenty of squirrels and birds.

Part II (5 minutes):
Participants will write down one detail and add it to a box of details. Then they will choose three "details" from the box.

Part III (20 minutes):
Participants will write a scene that incorporates the chosen detail and the already-determined setting. (They may exchange their detail/s if they want.)

Reading of Work: (15 minutes)

Week Two: Point of view

Teachers: Beth and Suzy

Introduction: (5 minutes)

Writing Exercise: (15 minutes)
Suzy will ask the class to write about an argument they once had, from their own point of view.

Explanation of Point of View: (15 minutes)
Beth and Suzy will explain to the class that the point of view is the perspective of the story. You can think of it as answering the question "Who is standing where to watch the scene?" It's the character through whose eyes we see the story from. There are three basic types of point of view, and they each affect the story in different ways. In first person point of view (POV), the story is told directly through the eyes of the narrator, who refers to him/herself as "I". Second person POV is the least common of the POVs, and here the character speaking is referred to as "you," the effect being the reader is assigned a role as a character. In the third person POV, the author is telling the story and the characters are referred to as he/she/they. There are two different types of third person: third person limited, and third person omniscient. Suzy will read examples that illustrate all of the different types of point of view.

Writing Exercise: (15 minutes)
Suzy will ask the class to go back to the argument they wrote about earlier, but this time to write it from a different POV.

Optional: (15 minutes)
Beth will ask the class to now expand on what they wrote about the argument. This time add to it and give it a different setting—in a park, a mall, a school, or some other public place. Tell the story from the POV of someone other than yourself: an old man, a young child, a high school teacher, etc.

Reading of Work: (15 minutes)

Week Three: Scene

Teachers: Beth and Suzy

Introduction: (20 minutes)

Suzy and Beth will explain that stories are made up of scenes, and that scenes can be thought of as being similar to scenes in movies. They both work to reveal plot, character, and conflict. Scenes are comprised of dialogue, gestures, actions, setting description, and internal character thoughts. To better understand scenes we will go over the difference between scene and summary, and also how dialogue functions and how to write it.

Suzy and Beth will go over the guidelines for dialogue:

- Make it feel natural.

- Make it feel real.

- Make it brief.

- Make sure it creates tension.

- Make it direct or indirect.

- Make sure tags are doing their job.

Writing Exercise: (25 minutes)
Suzy and Beth will lead the class through the writing exercise prompts.

Reading of Work: (15 minutes)

Week Four: Imagery (poetry)

Teachers: Matt and Cindy

Introduction: (5 minutes)
Matt and Cindy will introduce themselves. Cindy will talk about what we'll be doing with poetry and images. Matt will then discuss how imagery works in poetry.

- Imagery has the same function as description does in fiction.

- Imagery is practically a necessity to poetry.

- It broadens the experience; poetry should be more than the sound and abstract emotion.

- When imagination is sparked while reading it makes the poem more personal.

Ice-Breaker: (25 minutes)

Cindy will ask each participant to make a list of the following. Each list should have five or six items.

- Things I have lost.

- Signs of winter.

- What to take on a journey.

- Things I've forgotten.

- Things I saw when I went outside this week.

Matt will then ask the participants to choose one of the lists and write a short paragraph about that list, using concrete images.

Short Lesson: (10 minutes)
Matt and Cindy pass out samples of poems that show imagery. Together, the class will read the poems. Class discussion following about lines that really stood out to them.

Writing Exercise: (15 minutes)
Using the information from the paragraph they have written, the participants will rewrite the paragraph into a poem. Remind the participants to focus on using concrete details.

Reading of Work: (15 minutes)

Week Five: Description

Teachers: Ashley Rae, Deborah, and Matt

Introduction: (5 minutes)
Ashley, Debbie, and Matt will introduce themselves using three adjectives, and ask each participant to do the same.

Ice-Breaker: (10 minutes)
Ashley or Debbie will explain to the class that we will play a story game. Ashley will give the first sentence of the story. Debbie will give the second. Matt the third, then each participant will continue until the last person ends the story.

Writing Exercise: (45 minutes total)

Part I (10–15 minutes)
Ashley will list five abstract concepts on the board. Ask each participant to list three descriptive phrases or words to illustrate each abstraction. After

everyone has a couple, ask them to read out loud from their lists. Then, they'll write a paragraph description of the abstract they chose using the concrete details from their lists.

Part II (15 minutes)
Rewrite the paragraph into poetic form.

Part III (15 minutes)
Rewrite the poem into a narrative using the guidelines below:
Start the narrative with 'Yesterday I was confronted by (insert abstraction).
Somewhere in the narrative indicate your reaction to the confrontation.
End the narrative with a sound, taste, or smell.

Reading of Work: (15 minutes)

Week Six: Persona

Teachers: Marcia and Mandi

Introduction: (10 minutes)

Short Lesson: (20–25 minutes)
Marcia will define and explain "persona" as it's used in poetry, using material from the book *Imaginative Writing* by Janet Burroway (2007), as well as other material that she can find, if necessary. Also, concrete examples of persona will be given, such as how role playing and using the five senses can be a stepping stone to writing a poem in a particular persona. Then Mandi will hand out four poems that demonstrate how persona is used in poetry. (Marcia will bring copies of two of Kim Addonizio's poems and Mandi will bring copies of Philip Levine's "Animals are Passing from Our Lives" (1969) and "Nostalgia" by Billy Collins (1999), or something similar if she can't find those.) Discuss persona in each of the poems.

Writing Exercise: (45 minutes total)

Part I (20 minutes)
Bring supermarket tabloid headlines, read or briefly explain the stories, and give the assignment to write a short-short from the persona of the person in the headline of their choosing. (They seem to feel more comfortable writing poetry from their prose, rather than jumping right into a poem.)

Part II (10 minutes)
Have volunteers read their prose if they'd like.

Part III (15 minutes)
Have the class start writing their poems from their stories. Let them finish the assignment for homework, and they can read their poems next week if possible.

Note: We plan to have some visual aids, probably posters, to reinforce the concept of persona and to make it easier for the class members to take notes. Also, as stated above, we'll have copies of the poems we'll be using, to pass out to the class. (After each class, Terry and Suzy collect the residents' work to be typed and handed back to them next week.)

Week Seven: Voice/tone

Teachers: Mike and Tere

Introduction: (5 minutes)
Give participants a chance to read his/her work from their fiction workshop last week.

Short Lesson: (10 minutes)
We'll review the concept of persona, and afterwards, we'll take the next step of creating voice, using points found in Mary Oliver's *A Poetry Handbook* (1994). We'll go over some examples of strong voice: Anne Sexton, Sylvia Plath, Dean Young, and Mark Halliday.

Writing Exercise: (40–45 minutes total)

Part I (15–20 minutes)
Participants will write a paragraph, ranting at someone they cannot normally rant to. Then, they'll write a second paragraph, consoling someone who has just suffered a tragedy. And finally, they'll write a paragraph thinking of something they want, and trying to convince someone who has the power to give it to them.

Part II (5–10 minutes)
After all the free-writing is done, we will ask each participant to look over and read their work and give us the most commonly used words for each paragraph. We hope this will let them see the words most used for each emotion.

Part III (15 minutes)
We will then have each participant construct a poem out of their favorite paragraph.

Reading of Work: (15 minutes)

Week Eight: Scene in poetry

Teachers: Lily and Matt

Introduction: (15 minutes)
We'll open the class by allowing the students to read their homework from the previous week.

Short Lesson: (5 minutes)
Explain to the students what scene means and how it is used in a poem.

Writing Exercise: (65 minutes total)

Part I (15 minutes)
The students will make lists of places where they gave someone a kiss, lost something, and lost hope.

Part II (15 minutes)
After they have composed their lists they will need to choose one of these places, and make a list, using all five senses, of things in that place. For example:

Place: Haunted House
I see a cat.
I hear a cackle.
I touch a spider.
I smell a pumpkin.
I taste a candy corn.

Part III (20 minutes)
After the students have done this they will then cross off the two beginning words and add two adjectives before each word.

Ex: A black scary cat.
A gruff, witch's cackle.
A creepy, old spider.
A rotten, orange pumpkin.
A stale, hard candy corn.

Part IV (20 minutes)
Now the students have something to work with. We'll give them time to work on their poem, expanding it with conjunctions and phrases of their choice.

Reading of Work: (15 minutes)

Week Nine: Creating conflict in stories

Teachers: Debbie and Neil

Introduction: (10–15 minutes)
We'll define the words "conflict," "complication," "change," and "climax," and then make the following points:

- Conflict is a fundamental element of fiction. (Do short-short example of story without conflict and the same story with conflict.)

- In life conflict may be seen as a negative, but in literature, only trouble is interesting. This will be evident from the example just read.

- In story writing, we want to reveal what the conflict is and who it involves as quickly as possible. We don't want to wait until the fourth page of a story to start finding out what it is about.

- In our conflict, is something pushing back? It doesn't have to be violence. We don't want to insert violence in a story unless the story calls for it. Use violence sparingly or our conflict will be too easy.

- We may read pieces that are well written, have interesting characters, good description, but if they have no conflict, crisis or resolution, we say,' Where is the Story?' (Another example of short-story without conflict, Margaret Atwood selection.)

- D's of Conflict: Drama = Desire + Danger

- Character must want something and want it intensely. It doesn't necessarily have to be violent or spectacular. It is the intensity of the desire that creates the danger.

- A story focused only on conflict will be shallow, there needs to be a deepening understanding of the characters.

- Have diagram of the conflict triangle—conflict, crisis, resolution. Neil will draw diagram and explain using a short story as an example.

- Discussion and examples of internal and external conflict: ask class members to give one of each, write on easel.

Writing Exercise: (30 minutes total)

Part I (10 minutes)
Have each person write down an occupation on a note card. On a second note card, have them write down an unusual characteristic that a person might have. Example: a piano teacher as occupation that has dragon tattoos on his arms.

Part II (20 minutes)

Have them write a short-short story involving some conflict that this person has. Remember, our goal is to have them reveal the conflict as quickly as possible. Introduce the problem in the first sentence. The character must make a decision about this problem and have them resolve it soon afterward. This will show the plot triangle that we are working toward. Some conflicts may be taken from the list of external and internal conflicts the class has listed above.

Reading of Work: (15 minutes)

ALTERNATIVE ASSIGNMENT: (if times permits)

Plot skeleton: Each story has a "skeleton" consisting of five bones. Every story does not go by this structure, but it is an efficient model for conflict resolution:

1 A believable and sympathetic central character.
2 The character has an urgent and difficult problem.
3 The character attempts to solve the problem and fails, making the situation more desperate, raising the stakes.
4 Crisis situation, the last chance to win.
5 Successful resolution brought about by the central character's own courage or ingenuity.

ALTERNATIVE EXERCISE:

Write a short-short using the plot skeleton as a framework. No more than two or three lines per "bone."

* * *

Forms

Sample letter requesting donations from community businesses for supplies for the writing residency and reading/celebration

To Whom It May Concern:

The Literary Arts Partnership is a service-learning program in which junior and senior English majors are leading creative writing workshops at various locations in our community. One group of students is leading workshops once a week at the Center for Drug-free Living, another group at the

Coalition for the Homeless and several groups are leading workshops in middle and high schools in both Seminole and Orange counties.

Service-learning is a teaching method that combines classroom knowledge with real-world interaction: students put to use what they learn in a course. These students are working in groups of five, designing and leading workshops for the under-served of our community.

Last fall, students taught a ten-week long workshop at the Coalition for the Homeless. At the end of the workshop, the students organized a public reading and made booklets for each of the workshop participants. We're hoping to provide the same for our new workshop participants.

If a student is showing you this letter, it is because he/she is seeking your support for the workshops at community sites or for the public reading. For example, the participants need among other things:

- paper and pens/pencils
- card stock paper for booklets
- help with printing
- locations for public readings
- food, drinks, etc. for final celebration.

If you're able to help, please know that we greatly appreciate it. If you have any questions, please feel free to contact me. If you need UCF's tax exempt form, I'm happy to fax it to you.

*   *   *

Other forms and materials

The forms listed below can be found at the University of Central Florida's Office of Experiential Learning's website: www.explearning.ucf.edu/categories/For percent20Students/Service-Learning/159_143.aspx [accessed April 2013].

Service-learning agreement for agency

This form allows the student and the community partner to clearly understand the commitment between student and agency.

Safety manual

It is important that you be aware of remaining safe in unfamiliar environments. The University of Central Florida provides a safety manual for students who participate in CBL projects. "While serving in the community, there may be some degree of uncertainty and potential risk. Therefore, there is concern on the part of the faculty and staff regarding student safety."

On the job conduct

This information is an overview of professional behavior while on site.

Media Release

Documenting the work you do in the community with video and/or pictures is important, allowing you to create a portfolio of the work you do. Be sure to attain permission to photograph and use participant writing so that you may keep them for future use and pleasure.

*   *   *

Resources for teaching creative writing

Websites

The following websites provide a bounty of creative writing ideas and prompts. Often you can build an entire lesson or even an entire semester project around several prompts. These will certainly generate ideas.

ABC Teach
    www.abcteach.com/
    Lesson plans in several areas.

American Academy of Poets
    www.poets.org
    The site for literary American poets.

Creative Writing Prompts
    www.creativewritingprompts.com
    Hundreds of prompts that would need to be adapted to suit your grade level.

Fun Poetry for Children
    www.gigglepoetry.com/index.aspx
    Lesson plans for poetry and poems appropriate for children.

National Counsel for Teachers of English
www.readwritethink.org/
NCTE provides lesson plans for every grade level.

Teachers & Writers Collaborative
http://twcresources.org/
TWC not only has a new digital resource for teaching creative writing in the community, but also has a long list of books it publishes that focus on this type of work.

Teaching Creative Writing in Elementary
www.ericdigests.org/1996–3/writing.htm
by Christopher Essex. An overview of the value of creative writing as a teaching method.

A few books with ideas for lessons

There are hundreds of books with creative writing prompts that you can use to help as you design lesson plans. Here are a few to get you started.

Behn, Robin and Twichell, Chase (1992) *The Practice of Poetry: Writing Exercises from Poets Who Teach*. New York, NY: HarperPerennial.
Bernays, Anne and Painter, Pamela (1990) *What If?: Exercises for Fiction Writers*. New York, NY: HarperCollins.
Ferra, Lorraine (1994) *A Crow Doesn't Need a Shadow: A Guide to Writing Poetry From Nature*. Layton, UT: Gibbs Smith.
Koch, Kenneth (1990) *Rose, Where Did You Get That Red?: Teaching Great Poetry to Children*. Urbana, IL: Vintage.
—(1999) *Wishes, Lies, and Dreams: Teaching Children to Write Poetry*. New York, NY: Harper Perennial.

APPENDIX B: RESOURCES FOR TEACHERS

Syllabus Sample 1

The Writer in the Community*
Spring 2008
ENGL 597B
47 Burrowes, M 12:20–3:20

Julia Kasdorf
Burrowes 113A
Office: M 3:30–5:30, F 10–11
jmk28{at}psu(.)edu

Goals
This course involves graduate students in the teaching and learning of writing in non-university settings with the aim of increasing your understandings of and appreciation for the practice of writing among diverse groups of people. In particular, we will study and discuss the uses of Teaching Creative Writing in Elementary—poetry, fiction, creative non-fiction—as a means of developing literacy and promoting human growth and healing within the context of organizations that have these purposes.

Methods
All students enrolled in the course will:

- study the theory and practice of pedagogy for creative writing
- study the uses of literacy in diverse settings and for various purposes
- *teach writing* at least one hour per week in a community-based program, with a sensitivity to the specific goals and populations of that program
- *visit* at least one other teaching site and observe the work in practice
- write and reflect on your experiences by keeping a *teaching journal* make a *presentation* as a group introducing your teaching practice

and involving the class in a writing exercise or assignment that will
further our inquiry in this course,

● write a *final paper* that reports and reflects on your experiences
and learning; papers may be personal-narrative or more discursive
in nature, but they should include references to experience as
well as reading. They may examine the processes of "outreach,"
"collaboration," "mentoring," "service learning" or the role of the
writer in culture.

Required texts

Anderson, Charles and MacCurdy, Marian (eds). (2000) *Writing & Healing.*
Urbana, IL: NCTE.
Galt, Margot Fortunato (2006) *The Circuit Writer: Writing with Schools and
Communities.* New York: Teachers & Writers Collaborative.
Jordan, June (1995) *June Jordan's Poetry for the People: A Revolutionary
Blueprint.* Lauren Muller ed. New York: Routledge.
McCormick, Jennifer (2004) *Writing in the Asylum: Student Poets in City Schools.*
New York: Teacher's College.
Swope, Sam (2004) *I am a Pencil: A Teacher, His Kids, and Their World of
Stories.* New York: Holt.

Evaluation and grading

To fully satisfy the course requirements students must fulfill the teaching
component, complete weekly reading and writing assignments, and write
an excellent (finished and appropriate to submit for publication) final
paper. I will observe each student's teaching practice and offer an evaluation
through an informal, individual conference.

*This course was developed in conversation with Nick Coles of the Western
Pennsylvania Writing Project who with Catherine Gammon taught a similar
class for graduate students at the University of Pittsburgh in 2000. It
evolved further at Penn State in 2000 and 2005.

Teaching journal guidelines

The Teaching Journal may be kept as a log on the computer or in a
notebook; the aim is that it will become a space for you to record questions
and stories from your teaching and reading, and it will also inform our class
conversations and provide evidence and ideas for your final paper. Think
of the Teaching Journal as a "teacher's log" or a set of ethnographer's field
notes in which you document detailed narratives regularly—as soon as

possible after a class or session—and in which you also take time to reflect on your work and evolving ideas about teaching and learning creative writing. Some kinds of notes that would be appropriate for the journal are:

- observations of people and settings where you teach

- stories about happenings in the workshop

- conversations or interviews, including meaningful and direct quotations related to your work reflections about activities or lessons that went well or failed and thoughts about how you might improve in the future,

- reflections on readings and on work that you observe at other sites

- connections to your own writing process, including your own literacy and healing

- interpretations and theory-building: What to you make of what you have seen and experienced? What do you care about or remember? What is at stake in this work?

All students will bring four copies of some part of all of the Teaching Journal to class each week; these will be regularly read and discussed by your classmates and myself.

In-class presentation and writing assignment

Each team of teachers will present an in-class writing assignment or exercise that draws directly on the work you have been doing at your teaching site, or it may be directly related to some issue that we have been discussing in class. Presenters may provide as much background information from their teaching sites as they wish. You may present the assignment in writing or orally. You must decide how much time to give to writing relative to how much time you wish to spend with reading aloud and discussion, and whether to do discussion in small groups or large. Planning should be precise but flexible, and the presentation should take about one hour. Even when the exercise is presented orally, you should prepare a written version of it, with a rationale and time-frame, to be distributed in class as a teaching resource for your colleagues.

Final paper

For a final project, you will write a text that both reports and reflects on your experiences with teaching in the community. Include context—nature of the organization and its structures—as well as your efforts at helping to advance their purposes through the teaching of writing. These papers can be created individually or collaboratively with your teaching partners, so that a co-authored paper could be presented. (In the case of collaborative projects, a brief description of your drafting process should also be submitted.) The aim is to both present what happened during your work with vivid and specific details, and to interpret the experience and place it in the context of broader conversations and concerns about literacy, healing, and the development of human beings and their communities. The final papers will likely include: some citations of student work, along with your commentary; connections between your work and texts we have been reading; and plans for future work in this area or changes in your thinking or practice.

A length of about 2,500–5,000 words is appropriate, and prepare the paper in standard format: double-spaced, 12-point type, with MLA-style citations. Papers will be due on April 28, and at this class, you will have the opportunity to present your work in the form of a brief, oral report. Students may also consider proposing panel presentations of these projects at conferences, such as AWP. (Some funding is available for graduate student participation in such conferences.)

*   *   *

Syllabus sample 2

INTERMEDIATE POETRY WORKSHOP
Terry Thaxton
CRW 3310.0W59
Fall 2009

Class information

- Professor: Terry Thaxton
- Course and Section: CRW 3310.0W59
- 3 credit hours

Goals: Our primary goals are to aim toward the discovery of craft and to understand the role of art, particularly literary art, in the world around us. This is an intermediate workshop course for committed writers of poetry that integrates service-learning, in which you will use poetry to enhance lives of persons in your community.

Objectives

- Explore how contemporary literary poetry defined, written, read, and critiqued.

- Discover new ways of approaching the origination of poems.
- Write four–six new poems.
- Identify techniques of poetry in published poets, peers' works, and your own work.
- Provide critical and analytical commentary on poetry.
- Deepen your appreciation for literary poetry.
- Describe how field research in the literary arts contributes to community building.
- Create and participate in an extended writing community.
- Understand and articulate the value of poetry in the community.

Evaluation:

- 30% Begin 5 poems, polish and present 3 poems for workshop (for each poem, you are required to submit a 1-page Discussion of Process)
- 20% Workshop Critiques and Discussions
- 10% Assignments 1–5
- 15% Portfolio
- 25% Field Work Project, Participation in the UCF Student Service-learning Showcase, Thursday April 16, 2009, and Field Work Notebook

Required Text: *The Poet's Companion: A Guide to the Pleasures of Writing Poetry,* by Kim Addonizio and Dorianne Laux (1997)

Course Goals and Objectives

ASSIGNMENTS
Your grade in this course is based on several assignments. Please see the Schedule of Assignments for the structure of the class and for when assignments are due. Three of your five poems will be turned in at workshops, which will be divided into "rounds." *You are required to participate in workshops.*

FIELD WORK ASSIGNMENT
Outside of the classroom, the field work (or service-learning) activities will allow you to further your understanding of craft by leading people in the community in writing activities. This will allow you to explore the writing

process not only in your own lives and in the classroom, but as an empowerment tool for marginalized and underserved persons in our community. The process will invariably reveal to you the value of literary poetry as a powerful tool of self-discovery and expression, in your own life and in the lives of others. What I hope you discover is how clarity of expression can transform and empower lives, the power of art to enhance experience.

This section of CRW 3310 is a UCF sanctioned service-learning (field work) class. Students will spend a minimum of fifteen hours over the course of the semester on a Field Work Project (FWP). This project will address a need in our community, support our course objectives, involve a connection between the campus and the world around it, challenge students to be civically engaged, and involve structured student reflection. We'll spend time reflecting on our FWP experience discussions and structured reflection. While there is a 15 hour minimum for service to pass the course (roughly 1 hour per week), your FWP efforts will be the core of much of the learning in the course. Therefore your "grade" for your FWP will come from the tangible class-related projects that come out of it rather than simply from completion of the hour minimum.

Your grade for your Field Work Project will be based on

- evidence of planned coaching activities at your site

- attendance and being committed to your community site group

- evidence of learning the elements of craft in order to convey them to others

- participation in your FWP group

- your Field Work Notebook (insight, self-reflection, mechanics, growth as a writer and a mentor)

Attendance at your FR Site:
If you do not complete your 15 hours of Field Research/Service your grade will be affected:

- 12–14 hours: your final grade for the course will be lowered 1 full letter grade

- 10–11 hours: your final grade for the course will be lowered 2 full letter grades

- Fewer than 10: you will fail this course

What, specifically, will you be required to do?
You will take poetry into the community. You will select a community partner "site," where you will go once a week for 1–1.5 hours. What you do with poetry on site will depend a great deal on the population you

choose to work with. If you work with the elderly, you may read to them, you may let them read to you, or you may listen to their memories and translate them into poems. If you work with children, you may also read to them, have them read to you, or you may show them how to write some poems. Your job is to see what happens when people are exposed to poetry.

Tentative Schedule
FWN is the acronym I'm using for Field Work Notebook. You will find a FWN with your name on it in the Discussion blog on Blackboard.

Monday, January 12, 2009

- Begin thinking about where you'd like to conduct your Field Work.
- Take the UCF Service-learning Survey. Via Course Mail, send me proof of you taken it.
- Reading Response 1: Complete Assignment 1, and then post your response to the poetry as a reply to Reading Response 1 in Discussions.

Friday, January 17, 2009

- FWN 1: Post in your FWN where you plan to conduct your Field Work
- Read Assignment 2 about Contemporary Poetry. Read in *Poet's Companion* pp. 19–38 & 85–103 & 195–198
- In Discussions post a reply to the questions about the poems on Week 2 Assignments

Tuesday, January 20, 2009

- FWN 2
  - What do you expect to discover at your Field Work site? What do you think the attitudes will be of the people you work with?
  - You should have completed all applications, background checks, etc. so that you can begin your Field Work by 2/4. You are responsible for getting this done ASAP. Post an update in your FWN.

Friday, January 23, 2009

- Reading Assignment 3

Friday, January 30, 2009

- FWN 3: Why did you choose the site you chose--I know you HAD to choose something, so don't say that it was an assignment and you had to pick something--I want you to analyze yourself, analyze your choice. You could have chosen a nursing home or a school or a homeless shelter.

1   So what is it about the place you chose that has meaning for you?

2   Read the essay by David Hassler, a writer who teaches service-learning at Kent State and volunteers for Writer-in-the-Schools. Why did he choose to do this?

● Reading Response 4

● Poem 1 Due

Tuesday, February 3, 2009

● Must begin Field Work by this date

● **Workshop ONE.** Round 1: I will post Poem 1 for Workshop

Friday, February 6, 2009

● FWN 4 Describe your reaction to your first visit at your Field Work site.

● Reading Response 5

● Post narrative critiques to each of the poems posted 2/3

Tuesday, February 10, 2009

● Respond to what others have said about the poems that were posted on 2/6

● **Workshop ONE.** Round 2 : I will post 6 more poems

Friday, February 13, 2009

● FWN 5

  ● Post an update on your Field Work—what are you doing there, what do you hope to do, etc.

  ● Describe a time when you experienced the thrill of language and/ or poetry.

  ● Read the section "The Need for Poetry" in Dana Gioia's essay "Can Poetry Matter?" (www.danagioia.net/essays/ecpm.htm, 2013) and respond however you wish.

● Post narrative **CRITIQUES** to each of the poems posted (see Workshop Protocols for expectations).

Tuesday, February 17, 2009

- Respond to what others have said about the poems for Workshop One Round 2.

- **Workshop ONE.** Round 3 I will post remainder of poems.

Friday, February 20, 2009

- FWN 6: Discuss the elements of craft that you and your groupmates have used at your site to teach the participants about voice.

- Post narrative **CRITIQUES** to each of the poems posted 2/17 (see Workshop Protocols for expectations).

Tuesday, February 24, 2009

- Respond to what others have said about the poems.

Friday, February 27, 2009

- Poem 2 due to me
  - FWN 7: Go to these sites:

    National Service Learning: www.servicelearning.org

    Florida Campus Compact: www.floridacompact.org

    National Campus Compact: www.compact.org

    The Literary Arts Partnership at UCF: english.cah.ucf.edu/outreach

    Imagining America: www.imaginingamerica.org

    Browse through the syllabi at the National Campus Compact website: www.compact.org/syllabi/syllabi-index.php

  - Tell me something you discovered about Field Work (Service-learning) from these sites that you didn't know.

  - Civic education is part of your education. Higher education, in my mind, should not be only about you gaining knowledge in a discipline, but should show you how to put that knowledge to work in the world. What I want to know is what other types of Field Work projects would be appropriate for students in a poetry writing workshop? For example, when I teach creative nonfiction, students are free to choose ANY service project as long as it meets a need in the community. Then we use that experience to write personal essays and/or literary journalism pieces. But in poetry, it's a little different, and all I could come up with for Field Work projects has been for students to read poetry to people and/or to provide poetry writing opportunities to people who wouldn't ordinarily get those experiences.

- Remember that in order to be considered a "service-learning" project, the project must meet a need in the community AND it must teach something about the content of the course. So tell me your ideas. What else could students of poetry do that would connect with course objectives in a poetry workshop? In your response, please refer to at least one syllabus from the national campus compact site.

Tuesday, March 3, 2009

- **Workshop TWO.** Round 1 : I will post 6 poems for workshop.
- Workshop TWO begins

Friday, March 6, 2009

- FWN 8: Post something one of the participants has written from your site. Discuss how this piece of writing makes effective use of the element of craft that was taught during that session.
- Post narrative **CRITIQUES** to each of the poems posted 3/3 (see Workshop Protocols for expectations).
- **Workshop TWO.** Round 2: I will post 6 more poems.

SPRING BREAK

Tuesday, March 17, 2009

- Respond to what others have said about the poems posted on 3/3.

Friday, March 20, 2009

- Poem 3 due to me.
- FWN 9 The Annual Service-learning Showcase gives undergraduate students the opportunity to present a professional poster displaying their service learning experiences. This showcase also provides the UCF community an opportunity to hear and understand your service-learning projects as well as obtain a greater understanding of what service-learning is. The Student Government Association (SGA) will be awarding scholarships to the four best presentations.

The Showcase will be held on Thursday, April 16 from 12:30–4:00 p.m. in the Student Union Pegasus Ballroom.

The attached completed application is due by Friday, March 20 to Ms. Amy Zeh, Director of Service-learning at UCF (Ferrell Commons, room 203).

Email this to her and copy me on your email

- Post narrative **CRITIQUES** to each of the poems posted 3/6 (see Workshop Protocols for expectations).
- **Workshop TWO.** Round 3: I will post 6 poems.

Tuesday, March 24, 2009

- DISCUSSIONS: Respond to what others have said about the poems posted on 3/6.
- Workshop THREE Round 1: I posts 6 poems.

Friday, March 27, 2009

- FWN 10: Based on your Field Work, what is the purpose of poetry? How relevant is poetry to you and the world at large? What types of people would benefit the most from writing and reading poetry?
- Post narrative **CRITIQUES** to each of the poems posted 3/24.

Tuesday, April 1, 2009

- Respond to what others have said about the poems posted on 3/24.
- Workshop THREE. Round 2: 6 more poems.

Friday, April 4, 2009

- FWN 11: On www.poets.org, find a poem that is a "poem of witness"—a poem that conveys something relatable to the participants at your site.
- Post narrative **CRITIQUES** to each of the poems posted 3/31 (see Workshop Protocols for expectations).

Tuesday, April 7, 2009

- LAST DAY TO SUBMIT POEMS 4 & 5 to me for feedback.
- Respond to what others have said about the poems posted on 3/31.
- Workshop THREE Round 3: 6 more poems.

Friday, April 11, 2009

- FWN 12: Locate and post links or attachments of 3 poems that would be appropriate to use at your site as models for a specific element of craft.

- Post narrative **CRITIQUES** to each of the poems posted 4/7.

Thursday, April 16, 2009

- ATTEND UCF STUDENT SERVICE-LEARNING SHOWCASE.

Tuesday, April 21, 2009

- Respond to what others have said about the poems posted on 4/7.

Friday, April 25, 2009

- FWN 13: Look back at the post you made for FWN 1, and respond to your assumptions about your site, about the people at your site, and about you.

Friday, May 1, 2009

- PORTFOLIO DUE.

*   *   *

Syllabus sample 3

Dr. Allen Gee
ENGLISH 4950, Early College
Fall 2010, Spring 2011

Course Information: English 4950–02, CRN: 81118 (Fridays, 9:00am–11:45am, Arts & Sciences 315). 3 credits per semester.

Faculty: Dr. Allen Gee; Ashley Emmert, second year graduate teaching fellow; and Valerie Wayson, first year graduate teaching fellow.

Offices: Allen Gee, Arts & Sciences Room 3–23. Office hours are Tuesdays, 2:00–5:00, Thursdays 1:45pm–3:00pm and by appointment (it's best to make an appointment, since I meet with many students for coffee or lunch writing conferences). *Contact Information*: Phone: 445–3181; email: allen.gee@gcsu.edu.

Ashley Emmert, Arts & Sciences Room 1–53. Office hours MW 2:30–3:30 and 4:45–5:30 and by appointment. *Contact Information*: Phone: 479–883–6099, email: ake153@hotmail.com

Valerie Wayson: Arts & Sciences Room 3–49. Office hours are by appointment. *Contact Information:* Phone: 512-736-4423, email: vwayson@gmail.com

Course Description & Goals: ENGL 4950, Early College. Prerequisites: Intro to Creative Writing or permission of the instructor. This class meets weekly, on Fridays, and lasts through the fall and spring semesters. It requires a full year-long commitment. Students should not sign up for this class unless they can be certain about their presence. The rationale is that the seventh graders from Early College need to learn from dependable role models; your commitment serves to become a standard of commitment for them.

We currently teach in classrooms in Arts & Sciences and in the Kilpatrick Building.

You must be an undergraduate creative writing major to register for this class. Students must also have participated in the interview process with Dr. Gee or Ashley Emmert. For this semester, class begins with a schedule and lesson planning session. You will work with small groups of seventh graders from Early College, which is a Bill Gates funded model school at GCSU, housed in the Kilpatrick Building, with other programs from the school of education. We meet each Friday to cover lesson plans at 9 a.m. Your mentoring begins at 10 a.m. and runs until approximately 10:45 a.m. For the next hour, you'll meet with faculty and the other mentors, decompress, discuss best practices, and strategize for the following week. The semester is geared toward publication of the seventh graders' creative writing in a journal called *The Peacock's Feather*. Mentors will also work to prepare their students to give a final celebration reading which occurs in May, before graduation. While we focus on in-the-classroom development in the fall, for the spring each mentor will shift focus toward preparation. Each year we retain at least two mentors from the previous year, to help pass on teaching methods and encourage new mentors. The returning mentors can also help to serve as troubleshooters, or as backup coverage in case of long-term illness or difficulties.

Grades and Portfolios: Students will write a self-evaluation paper (10–15 pages) at the end of the semester. Students should also keep a journal of their teaching experiences as each semester progresses, and these journals can certainly serve as prompts or source materials for the final paper. Journals will be checked at the end of each semester. Rubrics, or measures, will also be provided for what should be emphasized in the evaluation papers. Mentors also begin creating their own lesson plans and schedule for their own hypothetical class. In addition, we ask that mentors research and begin to develop their own pedagogical theory. Mentors will be asked to read at least one book on pedagogy (this may require addition research) on which they will form a basis for their own pedagogy theory, detailed in a brief paper (3–6 pages) and oral report. Returning mentors will help to compile our ongoing best lessons book, which is modeled after WITS Houston's "Tried and True" series of lesson plans in addition to other responsibilities.

The overall grade is based primarily on your earnestness, devotion, effort, and teaching accomplishment, which can be seen in your students' writing. But the final grade will also reflect your attendance and the level of your participation in preparation and class discussions. Our preparation seminars depend on student commitment and consideration for the rest of the participants; you must be on time on Friday mornings, and your grade will be a reflection of your readiness. The syllabus and course schedule are always subject to change at the discretion of the instructors.

Attendance, Participation, and Late Work: Because we are working with traditionally under-served children, there are no absences allowed, except in case of serious illness, injury, or family emergencies. What typically occurs is that mentors end up not wanting anyone else to be responsible for their group. I am reasonable about absences to a point, but if a student misses too many classes and is not participating regularly, they will receive a failing grade or be withdrawn from the class and all work with Early College. Employment and vacation travel plans are not acceptable excuses. If you do miss class, be sure to arrange to turn in any work that is due that day. Enrollment in a higher level class should reflect maturity, a seriousness, and superior commitment. We don't accept late work for the final evaluative papers, unless there are extraordinary circumstances. We can all be reached by phone/voice mail, and by email.

Outside Programs: Mentors are expected to attend the final reading, which usually takes place in the A&S auditorium. The seventh graders read for their parents and friends and family. It is a celebration of reading and writing.

Schedule:

August
8/20: Orientation Day One
8/27: Orientation Day Two

September
9/3: Orientation Day Three
9/10: First Day of Teaching Color Poem
9/17: Haiku
9/24: Slam Poetry, with a visit from the performance troupe, Arts as an Agent for Change

October
10/1: Flash Fiction
10/8: Flash Fiction finishing

10/15: Field Trip Pre-Writing
10/22: Fall Break, No Class
10/29: Andalusia Field Trip (Nature Writing at Flannery O'Connor's childhood farm)

November
11/5: Revision Day
11/12: Couplets and Meter
11/19: Best Choice: undergraduate mentors select the best piece for each student to revise, and nominate best pieces from each group
11/26: Thanksgiving

December
12/3: Rehearsal Day: students read their work in an auditorium to initiate them to the idea and experience of reading aloud for an audience
12/6: Final Paper Due

January
1/15: Go over spring lesson plans/revisions with undergraduate mentors
1/21: Martin Luther King Day poems (We poems, poems that begin with "We.")
1/28: Literary Devices (metaphor, analogy, simile, reemphasize word banks)

February
2/4: Symbolism
2/11: Sonnets, Love Poems
2/18: Dialogue, perhaps leading to flash drama
2/25: Revision Day

March
3/4: Last Revision Day
3/11: Field Trip, Pre-Writing
3/18: Field Trip to Lockerly Arboretum
3/25: Spring break, no class

April
4/1: Rehearsal Planning, Early College spring break
4/8: In-class Rehearsal, reading individual best works
4/15: Early College Testing
4/22: Auditorium Rehearsal, Dr. Gee leading
4/29: Dress Rehearsal, Public Reading at 6:30p.m. in the auditorium, reception afterwards

May
5/6: Final Paper Due

Additional recourses for faculty

Forms and materials

Please see the University of Central Florida's Office of Experiential Learning's Resource Page for links to additional forms and materials that make designing and carrying out a Service-Learning/CBL project effective. www.explearning.ucf.edu/categories/For%20Faculty/Service-Learning/154_146.aspx

APPENDIX C: ADDITIONAL RESOURCES FOR TEACHERS AND STUDENTS

Websites and links to creative writing in the community projects

Some of these are listed in Chapter 7. This is not an exhaustive list, as there are hundreds of organizations around the U.S. that support writers in the community.

Nonprofit organizations and alliances

826 National
http://826national.org

826 National is a nonprofit organization that provides strategic leadership, administration, and other resources to ensure the success of its network of eight writing and tutoring centers. 826 centers offer a variety of inventive programs that provide under-resourced students, ages 6–18, with opportunities to explore their creativity and improve their writing skills.

Teachers & Writers Collaborative
http://twc.org

UrbanWord NYC
http://www.urbanwordnyc.org/

Write Around Portland
http://www.writearound.org/

Writers in the Schools Alliance
www.witsalliance.org

WITS Alliance is "a professional network of literary arts education programs and individuals." Please visit the website for links to numerous nonprofit organizations, including WITS Houston, InsideOut Literary Arts (Detroit), the Missoula Collective, Asheville WITS, Community Word NYC, and many more. Rather than list each of the alliance programs, visit the site and click on "Member Organizations."

"The vision of the WITS Alliance is that every American child will have the opportunity to work with a professional writer to develop the tools necessary for success. The Writers in the Schools Alliance (WITS Alliance) is a professional network of literary arts education programs and individuals who serve K–12 students and provide professional development for their teachers."

Write Girl
www.writegirl.org/

University Projects

Arizona State University, Young Writers' Program
http://ywp.asu.edu/about

Georgia College and State University, Allen Gee
www.gcsu.edu/creativewriting/our_writers.htm
www.gcsu.edu/creativewriting/peacecorpfellows.htm

Kent State University, Wick Poetry Center, David Hassler
www.kent.edu/wick/outreach/index.cfm

Michigan State University, Anita Skeen
http://poetry.rcah.msu.edu/

New York University, Literary Outreach Fellowships
Goldwater Hospital Writing Workshop Fellowship
http://cwp.fas.nyu.edu/object/cwp.goldwater.2.2010
Veteran's Writing Workshop Fellowship
http://cwp.fas.nyu.edu/object/cwp.veterans.2.2010
Starworks Fellowship
http://cwp.fas.nyu.edu/object/cwp.starworks.2.2010
Writers in the Public Schools Fellowship
http://cwp.fas.nyu.edu/object/cwp.writers.2.2010

Otterbein University, English Department, Terry Hermsen
www.otterbein.edu/public/Academics/Departments/English.aspx

Pennsylvania State University, Julia Kasdorf
http://english.la.psu.edu/faculty-staff/jmk28

Sarah Lawrence College, Myra Goldberg
www.slc.edu/graduate/programs/writing/courses.html

Stetson University, Mark Powell
www.stetson.edu/artsci/english/index.php

University of Arizona Poetry Center
http://poetry.arizona.edu/

University of Central Florida—The Literary Arts Partnership
http://english.cah.ucf.edu/outreach
www.writingfancy.blogspot.com

University of New Mexico, Connie Voisine
http://english.nmsu.edu/faculty/voisine.html

University of Wisconsin—Milwaukee, Center for Community and Aging
www.ageandcommunity.org/
www.timeslips.org/

NOTES AND SOURCES FOR CHAPTERS AND READINGS

Acknowledgments

Adler, Frances Payne (2002) Activism in Academia: A Social Action Writing Program. *Social Justice: Pedagogies for Social Change*, 29(4), San Francisco 136–49. Re-published in *Fire and Ink: An Anthology of Social Action Writing* (2009) Frances Payne Adler, Debra Busman, Diana Garcia (eds). Tucson, AZ: University of Arizona Press, pp. 374–86. Reprinted by permission.

Ferra, Lorraine (1989) Language and Landscape. In Dorothy Solomon (ed.) *In Inside Out* (pp. 17–23). Utah Arts Council. Reprinted by permission of the author.

Hassler, David (2002) The Prayer Wheel. *Prairie Schooner*, Vol. 76, No. 1, 96–115. Reprinted by permission of the author.

Preface

Coles, Robert. (1993) *The Call of Service: A Witness to Idealism*. Boston, MA: Houghton Mifflin.

Root, Robert L. and Steinberg, Michael. (1996) *Those Who Do, Can: Teachers Writing, Writers Teaching: A Sourcebook*. Urbana, IL: National Council of Teachers of English.

Introduction

Notes

1   National and Community Service, www.nationalservice.gov/pdf/cncs_statue_1993.pdf [accessed April 2012].

2   University of Central Florida, Orlando, FL provides resources for faculty and students across the university. Many universities with "experiential learning"

offices or similar type offices provide faculty and students with support and resources. At UCF we use the definition of service-learning at: www. explearning.ucf.edu/Overview/Options_and_Definitions/Service-Learning/ About_Service-Learning_95_270.aspx [accessed April 2012].

3   These components of service-learning (SL) are generally accepted in most programs. Learn and Serve America lists eight components of SL, but for the purposes on the CBL projects described in this book, I've compressed them into five.

Works Cited

Coles, Robert (1993) *The Call of Service: A Witness to Idealism.* Boston, MA: Houghton Mifflin.

Chapter 1

Ferra, Lorraine (1994) *Eating Bread.* Port Townsend, WA: Kuhn Spit Press.
—(2012) *What the Silence Might Say.* Townsend, WA: One-Crow-Dancing Books.
Ferra, Lorraine and Boardman, Diane (1994) *A Crow Doesn't Need a Shadow: A Guide to Writing Poetry from Nature.* Salt Lake City, UT: Peregrine Smith.
Levertov, Denise (1961) The Tulips. *The Jacob's Ladder.* New York: New Directions Books.
Rilke, Rainer Maria (1981) The Panther. *Selected Poems of Rainer Maria Rilke* (p. 139). Translated by Robert Bly. New York: Harper & Row.
Rosenblatt, Roger (2000) I Am Writing Blindly. *Time Magazine* (p. 142), 6 November, 156.19.
Whitman, Walt (1959) Song of Myself. In *Leaves of Grass* in *Complete Poetry and Selected Prose.* James E. Miller, Jr. (ed.). Boston, MA: Houghton Mifflin.
Wordsworth, William (1965) Preface to Lyrical Ballads. In *Selected Poems and Prefaces by William Wordsworth* (pp. 446–7). Jack Stillinger (ed.). Boston, MA: Houghton Mifflin.

Chapter 2

Notes

1   Campus Compact website provides numerous syllabi in different fields as examples for integrating service-learning into courses. This quote comes from Margaret Himley's syllabus at Syracuse University for a course entitled 'Citizenship, the Narrative Imagination, and Good Writing.' For more sample syllabi from Campus Compact, visit www.compatc.org > Resources > Faculty Resources > See syllabi from across disciplines and institutions.

2 Learn and Serve America is a program of the Corporation for National and Community Service. This government funded agency provides numerous resources for K–12 and higher education teachers, students, and administrators as well as individuals interested in community service. www.learnandserve.gov [accessed April 2012]

Works Cited

Anderson, Charles M. and MacCurdy, Marian M. (eds) (2000) *Writing and Healing: Toward an Informed Practice*. Urbana, IL: NCTE.

Bump, Jerome (2000) Teaching Emotional Literacy. In C. M. Anderson and M. M. MacCurdy (eds) *Writing and Healing: Toward an Informed Practice*. (pp. 313–33). Urbana, IL: NCTE.

Butin, Dan W. (2010) *Service Learning in Theory and Practice: The Future of Community Engagement in Higher Education*. New York: Palgrave Macmillan.

Dickens, Charles (n.d.) *Great Expectations*. Literature.org The Online Literature Library. http://literature.org/authors/dickens-charles/great-expectations/chapter–08.html [accessed December 2012].

DeSalvo, Louise A. (1999) *Writing as a Way of Healing: How Telling Our Stories Transforms Our Lives*. San Francisco, CA: HarperSanFransisco.

Emerson, Ralph Waldo (1957) The American Scholar. In *Selections from Ralph Waldo Emerson*. Stephne E. Whicher (ed.) (pp. 65–79). Boston, MA: Hougton Mifflin.

Fish, Stanley (2008) *Save the World on Your Own Time*. Oxford: Oxford University Press.

Foucault, Michel (1977) "What is an Author?" translation Donald F. Bouchard and Sherry Simon, in *Language, Counter-Memory, Practice*. Ithaca, NY: Cornell University Press.

Himley, Margaret (2001) Citizenship, the Narrative Imagination, and Good Writing. Syllabus. Syracuse University. Campus Compact. 1 February. www.compact.org/syllabi/writing/citizenship-the-narrative-imagination-and-good-writing/3969/ [accessed 28 December 2012].

Kasdorf, Julia (1992) *Sleeping Preacher*. Pittsburgh, PA: University of Pittsburgh.

—(1998) *Eve's Striptease*. Pittsburgh, PA: University of Pittsburgh.

—(2001) *The Body and the Book: Writing from a Mennonite Life: Essays and Poems*. Baltimore: Johns Hopkins University Press.

—(2011) *Poetry in America*. Pittsburgh, PA: University of Pittsburgh.

Kasdorf, Julia, and Michael Tyrell (2007) *Broken Land: Poems of Brooklyn*. New York: New York University Press.

Rodriguez, Richard (1982) *Hunger of Memory: The Education of Richard Rodriguez*. New York: Bantam.

What is Service-Learning (n.d.) Learn and Serve America, Corporation for National and Community Service. www.learnandserve.gov/about/service_learning/index.asp [accessed December 2012].

Whitman, Walt (1959) Song of Myself. In *Leaves of Grass* in *Complete Poetry and Selected Prose*. James E. Miller, Jr. (ed.). Boston, MA: Houghton Mifflin.

Chapter 3

Notes

1 These questions are compilations from Writers in the Schools Houston, Writers in the Schools National Alliance, and other programs around the country, including Community Word NYC, ArtsBridge America, Write Around Portland, and other community projects.

Works Cited

Campbell, Aimee (2012) Performing Poetry and Nonfiction. Teaching Plan for Creative Writing in the Community Course. University of Central Florida.

Coles, Robert (1993) *The Call of Service: A Witness to Idealism*. Boston, MA: Houghton Mifflin.

Land, Katherine (2012) Creative Writing and Film. Teaching Plan for Creative Writing in the Community Course. University of Central Florida.

Osbourne, Brittany (2008) Talk the Right Way: A Cultural Anthropological Perspective on Teaching Creative Writing to the Forgotten Youth. Final Reflection for Teaching Creative Writing Course. University of Central Florida. 10 November 2008.

Powell, Mark (2002) *Prodigals: A Novel*. Knoxville, TN: University of Tennessee.

—(2006) *Blood Kin: A Novel*. Knoxville, TN: University of Tennessee.

—(2012) *The Dark Corner: A Novel*. Knoxville, TN: University of Tennessee.

Chapter 4

Notes

1 Brittany Osbourne did her CBL project in a course entitled 'Teaching Creative Writing' during graduate school at the University of Central Florida. She had already completed a BA in Anthropology and another BA in English.

Works Cited

Anderson, Maggie, and David Hassler (eds) (1999) *Learning by Heart: Contemporary American Poetry about School*. Iowa City: University of Iowa Press.

—(2007). *After the Bell: Contemporary American Prose about School*. Iowa City: University of Iowa Press.

Ashburn, E. (2009) College Makes New Connections With Service-learning Program. *Chronicle of Higher Education*, 55(25).

Campus Compact (2012) Membership. www.compact.org/ [accessed December 2012].

Harwood, Gary, and Hassler, David (2006) *Growing Season: The Life of a Migrant Community*. Kent, OH: Kent State University Press.

Hassler, David (2005) *Red Kimono, Yellow Barn: Poems*. Brownsville, OR: Cloudbank.

—(2013) *May 4th Voices: Kent State, 1970*. [S.l.]: Kent State University.

Hassler, David, and Gregor, Lynn (1998) *A Place to Grow: Voices and Images of Urban Gardeners*. Cleveland, OH: Pilgrim.

Osbourne, Brittany (2008) Talk the Right Way: A Cultural Anthropological Perspective on Teaching Creative Writing to the Forgotten Youth. Final Reflection for Teaching Creative

Woolf, Virginia (1930) *Street Haunting: A London Adventure*. San Francisco, CA: Westgate.

Chapter 5

Works Cited

Boland, Evan (2003) The Pomegranate. In Peter Schakel and Jack Ridl (eds) *250 Poems* (pp. 264–5). Boston, MA: Bedford/St. Martins.

Boo, Katherine (2013) *Behind the Beautiful Forevers: Life, Death, and Hope in a Mumbai Undercity*. Waterville, ME: Thorndike.

Brooks, Dorothy (2012) RE: With a Little Help from my Friends. Message to Anita Skeen. July 11. Email.

DeLind, Laura B., and Anita Skeen (2013) *The Unauthorized Audubon*. East Lansing, MI: Michigan State University Press.

Driscoll, David (2008) *Quote Poet Unquote: Contemporary Quotations on Poets and Poetry*. Port Townsend, WA: Copper Canyon Press.

Eggers, Dave (2009) *Zeitoun*. San Francisco, CA: McSweeney's.

Finney, Nikky (2011) *Head Off & Split: Poems*. Evanston, IL: TriQuarterly / Northwestern University Press.

Fryer, Sarah (2012) RE: With a Little Help from my Friends. Message to Anita Skeen. July 14. Email.

Harcourt Brace. Hosseini, Khaled (2003) *The Kite Runner*. New York: Riverhead.

Hayden, Robert (2003) Those Winter Sundays. In *250 Poems*. Peter Schakel and Jack Ridl (eds). Boston, MA: Bedford/St. Martin's.

Hirsch, Edward (1999) *How to Read a Poem: And Fall in love with Poetry*. New York:

Lewis, Fran (2012) RE: With a Little Help from my Friends. Message to Anita Skeen. July 11. Email.

Lopez, Steve (2010) *The Soloist*. Leicester: Charnwood.

MacLeish, Archibald (1968) Ars Poetica. In Gerald Sanders, John Nelson and M. L. Rosenthal (eds) *Chief Modern Poets of England and America* (4th edition) (pp. 333–4). New York: Macmillan.

Miller, Patricia (2012) RE: With a Little Help from my Friends. Message to Anita Skeen. July 21. Email.

Myron, Carol (2012) RE: With a Little Help from my Friends. Message to Anita Skeen. July 15. Email.

O'Driscoll, Dennis (2008) *Quote Poet Unquote: Contemporary Quotations on Poets and Poetry*. Port Townsend, WA: Copper Canyon.

Osbourne, Brittany (2008) Talk the Right Way: A Cultural Anthropological Perspective on Teaching Creative Writing to the Forgotten Youth. Final Reflection for Teaching Creative Writing course. University of Central Florida. 10 November.

Schmid, A. Allan (2012) RE: With a Little Help from my Friends. Message to Anita Skeen. July 12. Email.

Skeen, Anita (1986) *Each Hand a Map*. Tallahassee, FL: Naiad Press.

—(1992) *Portraits*. Douglass, KA: Kida Press. Limited Letterpress Edition.

—(1999) *Outside the Fold, Outside the Frame*. East Lansing, MI: Michigan State University Press.

—(2002) *The Resurrection of the Animals: Poems*. East Lansing, MI: Michigan State University Press.

—(2011) *Never the Whole Story: Poems*. East Lansing, MI: Michigan State University Press.

Skeen, Anita, and Jane Taylor (2005) *When We Say Shelter*. Maryville, TN: Night Owl Books.

Walls, Jeannette (2005) *The Glass Castle: A Memoir*. New York: Scribner.

Williams, William Carlos (1987) the red wheelbarrow. In Robert Di Yanni (ed.) *Modern American Poets: Their Voices and Visions* (p. 256). New York, NY: Random House.

Winokur, Jon (1986) *Writers on Writing*. Philadelphia, PA: Running Press.

Wright, James (1987) Lying in a Hammock at William Duffy's Farm in Pine Island Minnesota. In *Collected Poems*. Hanover, NH: Wesleyan University Press.

Chapter 6

Notes

1 *TimeSlips* can be found at: www.timeslips.org

2 For a good overview please refer to the following article at the Alzheimer's Organization's website: www.alzfdn.org/EducationandCare/storytelling.html

3 *TimeSlips* Inquiry was qualitative and grounded in narrative inquiry. Our analysis and conclusions have been validated using data triangulation; that is, examination of multiple data from many and varied sources. We followed all Human Subjects Research (including releases to use photographs and video footage), Health Insurance Portability and Accountability Act (HIPAA), and Family Educational Rights and Privacy Act (FERPA) regulations. An Internal Review Board (IRB) at the UWM approved our plan. We collected our data during 2010–12 and included the following sources: curriculum plans, course assignments, surveys, questionnaires, field notes, film footage, and student discussions. Some of these data are cited here and are characteristic samples of the entire set.

4 Designed and Taught by Dr. Basting in 2006.

5 Designed and Taught by Dr. Mello in 2007 and 2008.

6 Designed and Taught by Dr. Mello in 2005.

Works Cited

Coles, Robert (1993) *The Call of Service: A Witness to Idealism*. Boston, MA: Houghton Mifflin.

Collom, Jack, and Noethe, Sheryl (1994) *Poetry Everywhere: Teaching Poetry Writing in School and in the Community*. New York: Teachers & Writers Collaborative.

Dye, Christine (2008) How it All Began. University Central Florida. Reflection Paper. 8 December.

Foster, Tonya, and Prevallet, Kirsten (2002) *Third Mind: Creative Writing through Visual Art*. New York: Teachers & Writers Collaborative.

Gardner, H., Csikszentmihalyi, M., and Damon, W. (2001). Good work: When excellence and ethics meet. New York: Basic Books.

Gerard, Philip (2012) The Art of Creative Research. *The Writer's Chronicle*. Association of Writers and Writing Programs. October/November. 28 December. www.awpwriter.org/library/writers_chronicle_view/2258/ the_art_of_creative_research

Gutkind, Lee (2004) The 5 R's of Creative Nonfiction. *The Writer Magazine*. 1 April. www.writermag.com/en/Articles/2004/04/The%205%20Rs%20of%20 creative%20nonfiction.aspx.

Williams, W. C. (1951). *Autobiography*. New York: New Directions.

—(1973) An Interview with William Carlos Williams. Interview by Emily M. Wallace. *The Massachusetts Review*, 14(1). JSTOR [accessed December 2012].

Chapter 7

Notes

1 Additional information for each of the individual writers listed:

Christopher McIlroy works with Native American children in and around Tucson Arizona, is a full-time writer and educator www.mcilroywritingservices.com/home.php [accessed April 2012].

Allan Wolf, full-time poet, author, and educator in Asheville, NC, works primarily on the East Coast, K–12 www.allanwolf.com/ [accessed April 2012].

Glenis Redmond is a full-time spoken word poet, author, and educator based in Greenville South Carolina. Redmond works all over the country with all ages www.glenisredmond.com/ [accessed April 2012].

Michael Beadle full-time poet, author, and educator based in Canton, North Carolina. Mostly works in the Raleigh with K–12 www.michaelbeadle.com/ [accessed April 2012].

Mick Fedullo has taught poetry and other writing forms to Native students since 1979, first in Arizona, later with Northwest and Plains tribes, in Canada and even Alaska. His students have read at the Library of Congress.

Marge Pellegrino margepellegrino.com/ [accessed April 2012].

Sherwin Bitsui www.bitsui.com/ [accessed April 2012].

Works Cited

Adler, Frances Payne (1993a) Raising the Tents. *Raising the Tents.* Corvallis, OR: Calyx Books.

—(1993b) Matriot. In *A Matriot's Dream: Health Care for All* http://matriot.org San Diego and Monterey, CA.

—(1995) Multicultural Students: Bearing Witness, Willing Power. Fairfax, VA: *AWP Chronicle.* October/Novemeber. 9–10.

—(2001) The Voices Are Coming Up. In *Cracking the Earth: A 25th Anniversary Anthology.* Corvallis, OR: Calyx Books.

—(2003) *The Making of a Matriot: Poetry and Prose, 1991–2003.* Los Angeles, CA: Red Hen.

Adler, Frances Payne (2002) Activism in Academia: A Social Action Writing Program. *Social Justice: Pedagogies for Social Change*, 29(4), 136–49. Re-published in *Fire and Ink: An Anthology of Social Action Writing (2009)* Frances Payne Adler, Debra Busman, Diana Garcia. Tucson (eds), AZ: University of Arizona Press, pp. 374–86. Reprinted by permission

Anzaldua. Gloria (1987) Speaking in Tongues. In *Borderlands, La Fronteras: The New Mestiza* (p.73). San Francisco, CA: Spinsters/Aunt Lute.

Birch, Willie (1990) Knowing Our History, Teaching Our Culture. In *Re-Imaging America: The Arts of Social Change* (pp. 137–43). Philadelphia, PA: New Society Publishers.

Bliss, Julie (1998) Ashes to Life and Choctaw: Stories of My Heritage Told for the First Time. Capstone Institute for Human Communication, California State University, Monterey Bay, Seaside, CA.

Gates, Henry Louis (1991) Introduction: On Bearing Witness. *Bearing Witness: Selections from African American Autobiography in the Twentieth Century* (p. 4). New York: Pantheon.

Hass, Robert (1997) An Interview with Robert Hass. *Mother Jones, 22,* 18–22.

Lorca, Federico Garcia (1973) Theory and Function of the *Duende.* In Donald Allen and Warren Tallman (eds), *The Poetics of the New American Poetry* (pp. 91–103). New York: Grove Press.

Lorde, Audre (1984a) The Transformation of Silence into Language and Action. *Sister Outsider* (pp. 40–4). Freedom, CA: Crossing Press.

—(1984b) Poetry Is No Luxury. In *Sister Outsider* (pp. 36–39). Freedom, CA: Crossing Press.

—(1984c) An Interview: Audre Lorde and Adrienne Rich. *Sister Outsider* (pp. 81–109). Freedom, CA: Crossing Press.

MacPherson, Sandra (1986) Secrets: Beginning to Write Them Out. *Field,* (Spring) Oberlin, Ohio: Oberlin College, 19–35.

McDaniel, Judith (1987) Sanctuary. In *Sanctuary: A Journey* (pp. 123–48). Ithaca, NY: Firebrand.

Miyoshi, Maseo (1989) Editorial Note. *Critical Inquiry,* (Autumn), 200–3. Chicago: University of Chicago Press.

Morrison, Toni (1993) PBS radio interview after winning the Nobel Prize in Literature.

Olsen, Tillie (1978) One out of Twelve Writers Who Are Women in Our Century. *Silences* (pp. 22–46). New York: Delta/Seymour Lawrence.

Rich, Adrienne (1978) When We Dead Awaken: Writing as Revision. *On Lies, Secrets, and Silence, Selected Prose 1966–1978.* New York: W. W. Norton.

—(1984a) In the Wake of Home. In *Fact of a Doorframe: Poems Selected and New 1950–1984, (p. 323).* New York: W. W. Norton.

—(1984b) North American Time. In *Fact of a Doorframe: Poems Selected and New 1950–1984* (p.325). New York: W. W. Norton.

Rilke, Rainer Maria (1934) *Letters to a Young Poet.* New York: W. W. Norton.

Rukeyser, Muriel (1987) *The Collected Poems.* New York: McGraw-Hill.

Rueter Dawkins, Jessica (2008) Creative is Power. Reflection Paper. University Central Florida. 24 November.

Silvas, Erin (1998) Were You There. In *Education as Emancipation: Women on Welfare Speak Out* (pp. 20–1). Seaside/Monterey, CA: Creative Writing and Social Action Program, California State University, Monterey Bay, and EOPS/CARE Program, Monterey Peninsula College.

Smith, Page (1990) *Killing the Spirit: Higher Education in America.* New York: Viking. 56–57

Weisel, Elie (1987) In Judith McDaniel's' *Sanctuary: A Journey.* Ithaca, NY: Firebrand.

Chapter 8

Notes

1 The lines from Nikki Giovanni's poem "Boxes" are used by permission of the author and may be found in *Cotton Candy on a Rainy Day* (1978).

2 See "Aces in the Deck: Four Principles for Assessing and Strengthening Student Poems," by Terry Hermsen & Stephen Morrow (2008) and Chapters 1–5 in *Poetry of Place: Helping Students Write Their Worlds* (NCTE, 2009)

Works Cited

Abramson, Seth (2012) A Brief History of the Creative Writing MFA (Part I). *The Suburban Ecstasies.* 9 July 2012. Web. 28 December 2012.

Adams, Kathryn (2001) *A Group of Their Own: College Writing Courses and American Women Writers 1880–1940.* Albany, NY: State University, New York Press.

Association for Writers and Writing Programs (2012) Guidelines and Hallmarks of Quality. www.awpwriter.org [accessed December 2012].

Emerson, Ralph Waldo (2009) The American Scholar. *Emerson Central.* Jone Johnson Lewis. [accessed December 2012].

Frost, Robert, and Lathem, Edward Connery (1969) Stopping by Woods on a Snowy Evening. In *The Poetry of Robert Frost* (p. 224). New York: Holt, Rinehart and Winston.

Giovanni, Nikki (1978) Boxes. In *Cotton Candy on a Rainy Day* (pp. 34–35). New York: William Morrow.

Hermsen, Terry (2008) The River's Daughter: Poems. *Huron, OH: Bottom Dog.*

—(2009) *Poetry of Place: Helping Students Write their Works.* Urbana, IL: National Council of Teachers of English.

Hermsen, Terry and Morrow, Stephen (2008) Aces in the Deck: Four Principles for Assessing and Strengthening Student Poems. In *Teaching Artist Journal,* 6(1), 20–34 and Chapters 1–5 in *Poetry of Place: Helping Students Write Their Worlds (*NCTE, 2009*)*

Hugo, Richard (1979) *The Triggering Town.* New York: W. W. Norton.

Harper, Graeme (2010) *On Creative Writing.* New Writing Viewpoints, Series Ed. Graeme Harper. Bristol: Multilingual Matters.

McGurl, Mark (2009) *The Program Era: Postwar Fiction and the Rise of Creative Writing.* Cambridge, MA: Harvard University Press.

Myers, D.G. (2006) *The Elephants Teach: Creative Writing Since 1880* (pp. 46–7). Chicago, IL: University of Chicago Press,

Oliver, Mary (1983) In Blackwater Woods. In *American Primitive: Poems* (pp. 82–3). Boston, MA: Little Brown.

—(1992) Sleeping in the Forest. *New and Selected Poems* (p. 181). Boston, MA: Beacon.

Wheelwright, Philip Ellis (1962) *Metaphor & Reality.* Bloomington, IN: Indiana University Press.

Williams, William Carlos (1966) This is Just to Say. In *The Collected Earlier Poems of William Carlos Williams* (p. 354). New York: New Directions.

Wright, James (1990) Lying in a Hammock at William Duffy's Farm in Pine Island, Minnesota. In *Above the River: The Complete Poems* (p. 122). New York: Farrar, Straus and Giroux.

Yeats, W. B. (1956) The Second Coming. *The collected Poems of W. B. Yeats* (p. 184). New York: Macmillan.

Chapter 9

Works Cited

Baikie, K. A., and Wilhelm, K. (2005) Emotional and Physical Health Benefits of Expressive Writing. *Advances in Psychiatric Treatment,* 11(5), 338–46.

Burriesci, Matt (2008) NEA Report Shows that Steer Decline in American Reading Skills Will Have Significant Long-term Negative Effects on Society. *The*

Writer's Chronicle, February. http://elink.awpwriter.org/m/awpChron/articles/mburriesci01.lasso [accessed April 2013].

Carver, Raymond (1983) Where I'm Calling From. *Cathedral: Stories* (pp. 127–46). In New York.

Esterling, B. A., L'Abate, L., Murray, E. J., and Pennebaker, J. W. (1999) Empirical Foundations for Writing in Prevention and Psychotherapy: Mental and Physical Health Outcomes. *Clinical Psychology Review*, 19(1), 79–96.

Fershtman, Eric Structured Reflection #8. Online Discussion Post. University Central Florida. 26 October 2012.

Galt, Margot (2006) *The Circuit Writer: Writing with Schools and Communities*. New York: The Teachers and Writers Collaborative.

Golden, Jane (2011) Art ignites change. Sunshine Arts Fall Fundraiser, Philadelphia, PA, November www.facebook.com/notes/sunshine-arts/mural-arts-jane-golden-says-art-ignites-change/199453716745902 [accessed October 2012].

—(2012) Personal interview, June, 26.

Hall, Anne-Marie (2009) Director, Writing Program, Department of English, University of Arizona. Email interview, 23 June.

Healy, Steve (2009) The Rise of Creative Writing & the New Value of Creativity. *The Writer's Chronicle*, February.www.awpwriter.org/library/writers_chronicle_view/2444 [accessed April 2013].

Hudson, Matt (2010) The Unlikely Writer: An Argument for Teaching in Prison. *AWP Job List*, March/April. http://elink.awpwriter.org/m/awpJobs/articles/mar2010.lasso [accessed March 2010].

Jordan, June (1995) *June Jordan's Poetry for the People: A Revolutionary Blueprint*. Lauren Muller (ed.) and the Poetry for the People Blueprint Collective. New York: Routledge.

Marzano, Robert J., Pickering, Debra, and Pollock, Jane E. (2001) *Classroom Instruction That Works: Research-based Strategies for Increasing Student Achievement*. Alexandria, VA: Association for Supervision and Curriculum Development.

McCue, Frances (2007) The Arts and Civic Space: An Experiment in Community Education. *Teachers College Record*, 109(3), 590–602.

Mohatt, Nathaniel V. et al. (under review) A community's response to suicide through public arts participation: Stakeholder perspectives from the *Finding the Light Within* project and mural, manuscript.

McIlroy, Christopher (1994) *All My Relations: Stories*. Athens, GA: University of Georgia Press.

—(2011) *Here I Am a Writer*. Crawfordville, FL: Kitsune Books.

National Endowment for the Arts (2007) National Endowment for the Arts Announces New Reading Study. Report 47. www.nea.gov/news/news07/trnr.html [accessed October 2012].

Pennebaker, J. W., and Chung, C. K. (2011) Expressivewriting and its Links to Mental and Physical Health. In H. S. Friedman (ed.), *Oxford Handbook of Health Psychology* (pp. 417–37). New York: Oxford University Press.

Rabuck, Donna (2009) Assistant Director, Writing Skills Improvement Program, University of Arizona. Personal interview 23 June.

Rappaport, J. (1981) In Praise of Paradox: A Social Policy of Empowerment over Prevention. *American Journal of Community Psychology,* 9(1), 1–25.

Ravitch, Diane (2012) How, and How Not, to Improve the Schools. In Pasi Sahlberg (ed.) *Review of Finnish Lessons: What Can the World Learn from Educational Change in Finland?* and *A Chance to Make History: What Works and What Doesn't in Providing an Excellent Education for All,* New York *Review of Books,* 59(5), 17–19.

Robinson, M. (2000) Writing Well: Health and the Power to Make Images. *Medical Humanities,* 26(2), 79–84.

Ross, Jesse Jay (2010) Personal interview, May 6.

Sahlbert, Pasi (2007) Education Policies for Raising Student Learning: The Finnish Approach. *Journal of Education Policy,* 22(2), 147–71.

Scarry, E. (1998) On Beauty and Being Just. *The Tanner Lectures on Human Values.* http://tannerlectures.utah.edu/lectures/atoz.html#s [accessed March 2009].

Sindt, Chris (2010) Personal interview, April 20.

Talarico, Ross, Thien-bao Phi, and Douglas Unger (2010) No More Lip Service: Three Successful Community Literary Programs. *The Association of Writers and Writing Programs 2010 Annual Conference and Bookfair,* April 10.

Thaxton, Terry Ann (2010) Personal interview, May 10.

Trickett, E. J., and Espino, S. L. R. (2004) Collaboration and Social Inquiry: Multiple Meanings of a Construct and Its Role in Creating Useful and Valid Knowledge. *American Journal of Community Psychology,* 34(1), 1–69.

Van Winckel, Nance (1997) Writers in the Community & Community in the Writers. *Writer's Chronicle,* October/November. http://elink.awpwriter.org/m/awpChron/articles/nancevanwinckel01.lasso [accessed April 2013].

Wallerstein, N. B., and Duran, B. (2006) Using Community-based Participatory Research to Address Health Disparities. *Health Promotion Practice,* 7(3), 312–23.

Winston, J. (2006) Beauty, Goodness and Education: The Arts Beyond Utility. *Journal of Moral Education,* 35(3), 285–300.

Wiseman, Angela (2007) Poetic Connections: 'Creating Metaphorical Spaces' in a Language Arts Classroom. *Language Arts,* 85(1), 43–51.

Chapter 10

Works Cited

Goodman, Nelson (1978) *Ways of Worldmaking.* Hassocks: Harvester Press.

Osbourne, Brittany Talk the Right Way: A Cultural Anthropological Perspective on Teaching Creative Writing to the Forgotten Youth. Final Reflection for Teaching Creative Writing course. University of Central Florida. 10 November 2008. Print.

Sanabria, Samantha. (2012) Reflection. The Literary Arts Partnership Internship at Orange County Academy. University of Central Florida. 2 December.

Chapter 11

Notes

1 An alternative version of this essay was presented by the author at AWP
Chicago, 14 February 2009.

Works Cited

Anderson, C. M., and MacCurdy, M. M. (eds). (2000) *Writing and Healing:
Toward an Informed Pedagogy*. Champaign-Urbana, IL: NCTE.
Blackhawk, Terry (1999) *Body & Field: Poems*. East Lansing, MI: Michigan State
University Press.
—(2002) "Ekphrastic Poetry: Entering and Giving Voice to Works of Art." *Third
Mind: Creative Writing through Visual Art*. Tonya Foster and Kristin Prevallet.
New York, NY: Teaching & Writers Collaborative. 1–13.
—(2007) *The Dropped Hand*. Grosse Pointe Farms, MI: Marick.
—(2012) *The Light Between: Poems*. Detroit, MI: Wayne State University
Press.
Britzman, Deborah (1998) *Lost Subjects, Contested Objects: Toward a
Psychoanalytic Inquiry of learning*. Albany, NY: SUNY.
College Board (2013) Video Transcript: How Important is your College
Major? https://bigfuture.collegeboard.org/get-started/video-transcription/
how-important-is-your-college-major [accessed April 2013].
Ellsworth, E. (2005) *Places of Learning: Media, Architecture, Pedagogy*. New
York: Routledge.
Foster, Tonya, and Kristin Prevallet (eds). (2002) *Third Mind: Creative Writing
through Visual Art*. New York: Teachers & Writers Collaborative.
Franco, Betsy (2000) *You Hear Me?: Poems and Writing by Teenage Boys*.
Cambridge, MA: Candlewick Press.
Gallagher, Tess (1976) Perspectives in White. In *Instructions to the Double:
[poems]* (p. 77). Port Townsend, WA: Graywolf.
Greene, M. (1995) *Releasing the Imagination: Essays on Education, the Arts, and
Social Change*. New York: Jossey-Bass.
hooks, bell (1994) *Teaching to Transgress: Education as the Practice of Freedom*.
New York: Routledge.
Koch, Kenneth (1970) *Wishes, Lies and Dreams: Teaching Children to Write
Poetry*. New York: Chelsea House.
MacCurdy M. M. (2000) From Trauma to Writing: A Theoretical Model for
Practical Use. In C. M. Anderson and M. M. MacCurdy (eds) *Writing and
Healing: Toward an Informed Pedagogy* (pp. 158–200). Champaign-Urbana,
IL: NCTE.
Marsh, Reginald (1951) *Savoy Ballroom*. Detroit Institute of Arts, USA / The
Bridgeman Art Library. Painting.
O'Connor, Flannery (1969) *Mystery and Manners: Occasional Prose*. Sally
Fitzgerald and Robert Fitzgerald (eds). New York: Farrar, Straus & Giroux.

Freud, Sigmund (1963) The Problem of Anxiety. New York: Psychoanalytic Quarterly Press.

—(1968) *Delusion and Dream, and Other Essays*. Philip Rief (ed.). Boston, MA: Beacon.

—(1990) The Relation of the Poet to Day Dreaming. In James M. Thompson (ed.) *Twentieth Century Theories of Art* (pp. 124–31), Ottawa: Carleton University Press.

UCF (n.d.) 2012–2013 SLSS Scholarship & Recognition Awards Criteria. www.explearning.ucf.edu/categories/For%20Students/Service-Learning/159_143.aspx [accessed April 2013].

Winnicott, D. W. (1986) Transitional Objects and Transitional Phenomena: A Study of the First Not-me {possession. In Peter Buckley (ed.) *Essential Papers on Object Relations* (pp. 254–71). New York: New York University Press.

Chapter 12

Works Cited

Astin, Alexander W., Vogelgesand, Lori J., Ikeda, Elaine K. and Yee, Jennifer A. (2000) *How Service Learning Affects Students*. Los Angeles: Higher Education Research Institute. http://gseis.ucla.edu/heri/PDFs/rhowas.pdf [accessed April 2013].

Books of Hope (2010) My Class Cares. 28 July. http://booksofhope.org/ [accessed April 2013].

Card, Orson Scott (1991) *Ender's Game*. New York: Tor.

Cohen, Lindsay (2008) Reflection. University of Central Florida. Creative Writing in Community course.

Collom, Jack and Noethe, Sheryl (eds) *Poetry Everywhere: Teaching Poetry Writing in School and in the Community*. New York: Teachers and Writers Collaborative.

Grunder, Sarah (2009) Letter (reflection) to the author. 14 May.

Hunter, Lindsay (2009) Re: (no subject). Email to the author. 26 June.

Kluger, Jeffrey (2007) What Makes Us Moral. *Time*. www.time.com/time/specials/2007/article/0,28804,1685055_1685076_1686619,00.html [accessed April 2012].

Koch, Kenneth (1970) *Wishes, Lies and Dreams: Teaching Children to Write Poetry*. New York: Chelsea House.

—(1973) *Rose, Where Did You Get That Red? Teaching Great Poetry to Children*. New York: Random House.

—(1996) Teaching Great Poetry to Children. In *The Art of Poetry: Poets, Parodies, Interviews, Essays, and Other Work*. Ann Arbor, MI: University of Michigan.

Miller, Derek (2007) Reflection. University of Central Florida. Poetry Writing Workshop.

Miller, Meghan (2010) Letter (reflection) to the author. 30 April.

Perlstein, Linda (2007) *Tested: One American School Struggles to Make the Grade*. New York: Henry Holt.

Rezende, Trisha (2009) Email to the author. 10 October.

Rifkin, Jeremy (2010) 'The Empathic Civilization': Rethinking Human Nature in the Biosphere Era. *Huffington Post.* 28 July. www.huffingtonpost.com/jeremy-rifkin/the-empathic-civilization_b_416589.html [accessed April 2012].

Rzicznek, F. Daniel (2006) *Cloud Tablets.* Kent, OH: Kent State University Press.

—(2007) *Neck of the World.* Logan, UT: Utah State University Press.

—*(2009) Divination Machine.* West Lafayette, IN: Free Verse Editions/Parlor Press.

—(2011) *Vine River Hermitage.* San Diego, CA: Cooper Dillon Books.

—(2010) *The Rose Metal Press Field Guide to Prose Poetry: Contemporary Poets in Discussion with Practice.* Brookline, MA: Rose Metal Press.

Simic, Charles (1986) *Unending Blues: Poems.* San Diego, CA: Harcourt Brace Jovanovich.

—(1994) Stone. In Jack Collom and Sheryl Noethe (eds) *Poetry Everywhere: Teaching Poetry Writing in School and in the Community.* New York: Teachers and Writers Collaborative.

Slack, Gordy (2007) I feel your pain. *Salon.* www.salon.com/news/feature/2007/11/05/mirror_neurons [accessed April 2012].

Thakhar, Abha (2010) Personal interview. 20 March.

The Morality Quiz (2007) *Time.* 4 January. www.time-blog.com/graphics_script/2007/moralityquiz/ [accessed April 2012].

Ward, Shaun Reflection. (2 December 2008) University of Central Florida.

Appendix A

Works Cited

Behn, Robin and Twichell, Chase (1992) *The Practice of Poetry: Writing Exercises from Poets Who Teach.* New York: HarperPerennial.

Bernays, Anne and Painter, Painter (1990) *What If?: Writing Exercises for Fiction Writers.* New York: HarperCollins.

Burroway, Janet (2007) *Imaginative Writing: The Elements of Craft.* New York: Pearson/Longman.

Collins, Billy (1999) Nostalgia. In *Questions about Angels: Poems* (pp. 90–1). Pittsburgh, PA: University of Pittsburgh.

Didion, Joan (1976) Why I Write. *New York Times Book Review* [New York] 5 December.

—(2005) *The Year of Magical Thinking.* New York: A. A. Knopf.

Dybek, Stuart (1990) Blight. *The Coast of Chicago.* New York: Knopf.

Ferra, Lorraine (1994) *A Crow Doesn't Need a Shadow: A Guide to Writing Poetry From Nature.* Layton, UT: Gibbs Smith.

Johnson, Denis (1992a) *Jesus' Son: Stories.* New York: Farrar, Straus, and Giroux.

—(1992b) Car Crash While Hitchhiking. In *Jesus' Son: Stories.* New York: Farrar, Straus, and Giroux, 1992.

Koch, Kenneth (1990) *Rose, Where Did You Get That Red?: Teaching Great Poetry to Children.* Urbana, IL: Vintage.

—(1999) *Wishes, Lies, and Dreams: Teaching Children to Write Poetry.* New York: Harper Perennial.

Levine, Philip (1968) Animals Are Passing from Our Lives. In *Not This Pig: Poems* (p. 79). Middletown, CT: Wesleyan University Press.

Oliver, Mary (1994) *A Poetry Handbook.* San Diego, CA: Harcourt Brace.

O'Malley, Austin (1915) *Keystones of Thought.* New York: Devin-Adair.

Orwell, George (n.d.) Why I Write. In *The Complete Works of George Orwell.* George Orwell.org, www.george-orwell.org/Why_I_Write/0.html [accessed November 2012].

Saunders, George (1996) The Wavemaker Falters. In *CivilWarLand in Bad Decline: Stories and a Novella* (p.43). New York: Random House, 1996.

Appendix B

Works Cited

Addonizio, Kim and Laux, Dorianne (1997) *The Poet's Companion: A Guide to the Pleasures of Writing Poetry.* New York: W. W. Norton.

Anderson, Charles and MacCurdy, Marian (eds) (2000) *Writing & Healing.* Urbana, IL: NCTE.

Galt, Margot Fortunato (2006) *The Circuit Writer: Writing with Schools and Communities.* New York: Teachers & Writers Collaborative.

Gioia, Dana (2009) Can Poetry Matter? www.danagioia.net/essays/ecpm.htm [accessed April 2013].

Jordan, June (1995) *June Jordan's Poetry for the People: A Revolutionary Blueprint.* Lauren Muller (ed.). New York: Routledge.

McCormick, Jennifer (2004) *Writing in the Asylum: Student Poets in City Schools.* New York: Teacher's College.

Swope, Sam (2004) *I am a Pencil: A Teacher, His Kids, and Their World of Stories.* New York: Holt.

INDEX

"A Red Wheelbarrow, a Hammock, and a Pomegranate: Why So Much Does Depend Upon Poetry" 90–100
"Activism in Academia: A Social Action Writing Program" 127–39
Adler, Frances Payne 5, 126, 127–39
Alcivar, Silvi 4, 18–28, 38, 126
"Assessment Wicket, The: How Can We Judge the Value of Writers Teaching in the Schools?" 145–64
assisted living facilities 1, 9, 18–28, 34, 48, 72, 106–15, 233
Association of Writers and Writing Programs 36, 122, 124, 131, 143, 170, 276
Australian Society of Authors 124

Basting, Anne 9, 106–15
"Becoming an Ocean: Teaching Poetry in Nursing Homes" 18–28
"Birth of an American Scholar" 43–6
Blackhawk, Terry 4, 209–15

Chatterjee, Lisa 5, 167, 191–4
"Children We Leave Behind, The" 191–4
"Citizens of Words: Service–Learning in Creative Writing Education" 170–6
Coles, Robert xiii, 4, 37, 52, 102, 228
community partners 3, 9–11, 33–5, 48, 51, 53, 70–2, 86, 174, 189, 190, 204, 270
community-based learning xi, 1–4, 8–11, 29–34

Ferra, Lorraine 4, 12–18

Fiedler, Heather 5, 9, 43–6
funding 1, 36, 42, 58–9, 70, 87, 124, 132, 138, 230, 276

Gee, Allen 4–5, 57–65, 70, 125 284–7, 290
Gilman, Sharlene (S.E.) 5, 38, 215–23

Hassler, David 4, 70, 72–84, 125, 231
Hermsen, Terry 4, 30, 144–64, 291
"How Service-Learning Cultivates Empathy and Social Responsibility" 234–40

immersion and research 8, 70, 103–6

jails, working with 38, 54–7

Kasdorf, Julia 4, 35–43, 70, 125, 273–6, 291
"Keeping it Real: Creative Writing Under the Shadow of Standardized Testing" 177–85

"Language and Landscape" 12–18
"Lawtey Workshop, The" 53–7
Learn and Serve America 29–30, 294, 295
"Linking the Creative Writing Program With the Community" 57–65

McIlroy, Christopher 4, 30, 126, 176–85, 299
Mello, Robin 5, 106–15
Mohatt, Nathaniel 5, 30, 169–76

National Association of Writers in Education (NAWE), Great Britain 124 nonprofit organizations xi, 1, 2, 4, 31, 47, 69, 124–5, 167, 207, 209–15, 289–90

Office of Experiential Learning, University of Central Florida 9, 203–5, 207, 270, 288
O'Neil, Carly Gates 5, 234–40
outreach and the university 206–7

Parsons, Scott 5, 194–201
"Poetry From the Inside Out" 209–15
"Poetry-in-the-World: Where Service Learning Goes Beyond the Classroom" 229–34
Powell, Mark 5, 53–7, 291
"Prayer Wheel, The" 73–84
publication of CBL projects 205–6
publication of participants' writing 56, 176, 188–90, 211, 214, 226, 231–2

Reagler, Robin 4, 116–22, 125
reflection prompts, structured 11–12, 34, 52–3, 71–2, 89–90, 105–6, 126–7, 143–4, 168–9, 191, 208, 228–9
responses from college students about CBL projects 41, 51, 68, 88–9, 104–5, 123, 165–6, 188, 225–6, 227–8, 239, 240
Rzicznek, F. Daniel 5, 229–34

schools, working with 58–65, 73–84, 116–22, 145–64, 177–85, 192–4, 195–201, 209–15, 229–34, 234–40
service-learning xii–xiii, 2–3, 29–46, 69–71, 102, 111, 114, 170–6, 203–7, 229–34, 234–40
shelters, working with 87–8, 165–6, 216–23
Skeen, Anita 4, 90–100, 125, 290
structured reflection prompts 11–12, 34, 52–3, 71–2, 89–90, 105–6, 126–7, 143–4, 168–9, 191, 208, 228–9
student responses to CBL project 41, 51, 68, 88–9, 104–5, 123,

165–6, 188, 225–6, 227–8, 239, 240
" 'Sublime, the Unsettling, and the Exuberant, The': Changing Students' Attitudes Toward Aging through TimeSlips Creative Storytelling" 106–15

Teachers & Writers Collaborative, xi, 121, 122, 272, 289
teaching artists, individual 4–5, 101, 119–21, 125–6, 167, 299–300
"Teaching, or How to Fall in Love" 116–22

"What is an Author Off-Campus? The Writer in the Community and the Corporate University" 35–43
Whitman, Walt 14, 45
"Who is the Self that Performs? Teaching and Learning Creative Identities and Creative Writing at a Youth Shelter" 215–23
Williams, William Carlos 92, 102, 104–5, 145–6
Wordsworth, William 8
working with assisted living facilities 1, 9, 18–28, 34, 48, 72, 106–15, 233
working with community partners 3, 9–11, 33–5, 48, 51, 53, 70–2, 86, 174, 189, 190, 204, 270
working with jails 38, 54–7
working with schools 58–65, 73–84, 116–22, 145–64, 177–85, 192–4, 195–201, 209–15, 229–34, 234–40
working with shelters 87–8, 165–6, 216–23
"Writing Out of Grief" 195–201
writing residency, defined 2–9
writings by participants 13, 15, 16, 17, 17–18, 20, 22, 23, 26, 28, 45, 64, 76, 79, 81, 82, 82–3, 93–4, 94–5, 96, 97–8, 99, 122, 137–8, 148, 152–3, 153–4, 155, 160, 161–2, 177, 178, 181–2, 182–3, 184–5, 211, 212–13, 214–15, 218